9/24 aw

The Unbearable
Whiteness of Being

The Unbearable Whiteness of Being

Farmers' Voices from Zimbabwe

Rory Pilossof

Published in Zimbabwe
by
Weaver Press
PO Box A1922
Avondale, Harare
Zimbabwe
www.weaverpresszimbabwe.com

Published in South Africa
by
UCT Press
an imprint of Juta and Co. Ltd
1st Floor, Sundare Building
21 Dreyer Street, Claremont
7708 South Africa
www.uctpress.co.za

Cover: Danes Design, Harare
Cover photo: David Brazier
Typeset by forzalibro designs
Printed by Academic Press, Cape Town

ISBN 978-1-77922-169-8 (Zimbabwe)
ISBN 978-1-92409-997-6 (South Africa)

Contents

Acknowledgements

The research, writing and completion of this book has been aided by a community of people and institutions to whom a great deal of gratitude is extended. By far the largest proportion of that thanks is reserved for Professor Ian Phimister. It is no overstatement to say that without his support, guidance and counsel, which have been ever-present right from my undergraduate years at the University of Cape Town, I would not have had the opportunity to undertake the research necessary to produce this book.

The generous financial support of several institutions has made this book possible. Firstly, I am hugely grateful to the Overseas Research Studentship, and the University of Sheffield Studentship. I also received grants from the Beit Trust Emergency Support Fund, the Royal Historical Society Research Funding and The Petrie Watson Exhibition.

Justice for Agriculture generously allowed me access to their interview archive. The Commercial Farmers' Union of Zimbabwe were also helpful in allowing me to consult their collection of *The Farmer* magazine. Furthermore, thanks must go the Research and Advocacy Unit who gave me the opportunity to explore the stories of white farmers in Zimbabwe. In Oxford, the Rhodes House Library provided invaluable access to other records and secondary sources. Chapter 2 draws on an article first published in the *Journal of Developing Societies* (26: 71-97, March 2010).

My thanks are also extended to all the farmers I interviewed and talked to in the process of my research. Many spoke of personal traumas and events that were difficult to relate, and their courage is exemplary.

Many others have helped me through the last three years. Special mention must go to Gary Rivett, who provided not only much needed intellectual stimulation, but ready and welcome relief from my research. He has contributed in so many ways to the creation and completion of this book and I thank him dearly for his companionship. I must also thank Miles Larmer, Mike Rook, Felicity Wood, Ben Purcell Gilpin, Alois Mlambo, Tony Reeler, Simon de Swardt, Jonathan Saha, Rachel Johnson, Charles Laurie and Andrew Iliff for their help and assistance. Weaver Press, and Murray McCartney in particular, have been a pleasure to work with and their input and attention to detail has vastly improved the book before you.

I also want to thank my family, Ray and Jayne Pilossof and Shane Samten Drime "Billy-the-Lionsblood" Pilossof, for humouring me through this process. And Boo, for all the sacrifices and trying to understand.

Lastly, I would like to thank Lance van Sittert, without whose inspiration and mentorship this journey would never have taken place.

List of Acronyms

CCJPZ	Catholic Commission for Justice and Peace in Zimbabwe
CFU	Commercial Farmers' Union of Zimbabwe
CIO	Central Intelligence Organisation
COHRE	Centre on Housing Rights and Evictions
CZC	Crisis in Zimbabwe Collation
ESAP	Economic Structural Adjustment Programme
EU	European Union
GAPWUZ	General Agricultural and Plantation Workers' Union of Zimbabwe
ICG	International Crisis Group
IMF	International Monetary Fund
IPFP	Inception Phase Framework Plan
JAG	Justice for Agriculture
MDC	Movement for Democratic Change
MFP Trust	Modern Farming Publications Trust
MFU	Matabeleland Farmers' Union
NCA	National Constitutional Assembly
NCC	National Constitutional Commission
NLHA	Native Land Husbandry Act
RAU	Research and Advocacy Unit
RF	Rhodesian Front
RNFU	Rhodesian National Farmers' Union
RTA	Rhodesian Tobacco Association
SI6	Statutory Instrument 6
TRC	Truth and Reconciliation Commission
UDI	Unilateral Declaration of Independence
UNDP	United Nations Development Programme
WB	World Bank
ZANLA	Zimbabwe National Liberation Army
ZANU	Zimbabwe African National Union
ZANU-PF	Zimbabwe African National Union –Patriotic Front
ZAPU	Zimbabwe African People's Union
ZCTU	Zimbabwe Congress of Trade Unions
ZIPRA	Zimbabwe People's Revolutionary Army
ZJRI	Zimbabwe Joint Resettlement Initiative
ZNLWVA	Zimbabwe National Liberation War Veterans' Association
ZTA	Zimbabwe Tobacco Assocation

List of Tables and Map

List of Appendices

A Note on Currency

Throughout this book I have used the original currencies quoted in sources and documents referenced. Before independence these were generally Pounds Sterling (£) and Rhodesian Dollars (R$). After independence the currency was converted to Zimbabwean Dollars (Z$). For ease of comparison I have supplied a US$ equivalent, using contemporary conversion rates.

Foreword

One of the most difficult challenges confronting post-colonial socie-ties in southern Africa which had a resident white population is how to redress the inequalities of inherited land ownership and distribution. Consequently, the governments of Zimbabwe, Namibia and post-apart-heid South Africa have to confront challenges of how to resolve the land question in a situation where the black majority demands redress of colo-nial inequalities and a more equitable racial distribution of land.

With respect to Zimbabwe, in particular, much has been written on the land question by a wide range of scholars including Robin Palmer, Henry Moyana, Sam Moyo, Jocelyn Alexander and Ian Phimister. Such studies have focused, *inter alia,* on the history of colonial land aliena-tion, the racialisation of land under various colonial laws, including the Land Apportionment Act of 1931 and the Native Land Husbandry Act (NLHA) of 1951, the role of African land grievances in fuelling the armed liberation struggle of the 1960s and 1970s, the Lancaster House Constitution's role in the immediate post-colonial land reform process and the general inability of the post-colonial government to fully address the land question by the end of the twentieth century. The farm invasions from 2000 onwards and the political, social and economic impact of the chaotic fast-track land redistribution exercise have also been subjected to scholarly analysis. Until now, therefore, analyses have focused mainly on how colonial land policies have impacted on the African population, and the African people's responses. What has been conspicuously absent is the voice of white farmers themselves, presenting their perceptions of the history of the country and the land question and their views on either the necessity, desirability or the modalities of land redistribution. In fact, until now, there has been no serious study of how white farmers articulated their perceptions of their role in and attitudes to these and other national matters. This is rather surprising given the fact that white farmers have always been at the centre of the controversies surrounding the land question in Zimbabwe.

As a keen student of Zimbabwean history and an occasional contributor to scholarly debates on the country's recent past, I am particularly excited by the publication of Rory Pilossof's book. It breaks new ground and makes an invaluable contribution to scholarship on Zimbabwe in general and studies of Zimbabwe's agrarian history in particular. It provides the important missing piece to the puzzle of the history of the land question by examining how white farmers' perceptions and representations reflect their attitudes to land, land reforms and the country's history, while also providing insights into the 'role white farmers themselves have had in the events that have unfolded'. It is vital for this voice to be heard, for as the author rightly observes, there can be no full understanding of or solution to the country's land problem without an appreciation of the role white farmers have played and what their perceptions have been.

Pilossof captures the 'voices' of this critical segment of the community extremely well. Always grounded in the social, economic and political realities of the group under study and the country at large, *The Unbearable Whiteness of Being* traces and analyses the 'ebb and flow of white farming discourses' from the 1970s to 2004 and demonstrates that, while there were many and sometimes competing views on these and other issues and while white farmers did not always speak with one voice, there was, nevertheless, 'a coherent language employed to talk about events and experiences in Zimbabwe and Rhodesia'; a language that suggests a distinct sense of identity and view of the country and makes for a more sophisticated understanding of the white farmer's role in its unfolding history.

This book is essential reading for anyone interested in understanding not only the complexity of the Zimbabwean land question but also how identities and notions of citizenship are shaped, contested and deployed in a post-colonial setting. Although Pilossof focuses on Zimbabwe, he speaks to a much wider readership than those interested in this country alone. His findings and insights are relevant to southern Africa as a whole, particularly to those countries where the racialisation of land in the colonial or apartheid period has raised similar challenges after the political transition. There too, an understanding of the white discourses on land and related issues may be crucial in appreciating the dynamics at work and in the quest to find a solution to the vexed land question.

A.S. Mlambo
Professor of History
University of Pretoria
South Africa

Map of Zimbabwe

Introduction
Why the Voices of White Farmers?

If Karenin had been a person instead of a dog, he would surely have long since said to Tereza, 'Look, I'm sick and tired of carrying that roll around in my mouth every day. Can't you come up with something different?' And therein lies the whole of man's plight. Human time does not turn in a circle; it runs ahead in a straight line. That is why man cannot be happy: happiness is the longing for repetition.

Yes, happiness is the longing for repetition, Tereza said to herself.
– Milan Kundera.[1]

'We call them gooks'.
– Farmer 3.[2]

In 2006, after having been out of the country for a while, I returned to Zimbabwe and took up employment with the Research and Advocacy Unit (RAU), who assisted various organisations and civic bodies with research they were undertaking in Zimbabwe. The first (and last) project I was contracted to assist with was interviewing white farmers about their experiences since 2000 with the commercial farming lobby group, Justice for Agriculture (JAG). That project sought to document the abuses suffered by (white) commercial farmers and the losses they had incurred as a result of the state-sponsored land occupations that began after the Constitutional Referendum in February 2000. It was while working on this project that I became interested in the history and evolution of the white farming community in Zimbabwe. Working alongside and conducting interviews with evicted white farmers gave me direct and unadulterated insights into what they had undergone, as well as first-hand experience of their responses to what had transpired.

Alongside the very visible emotional and psychological scars of the land occupations and evictions, many of the farmers I interviewed related their experiences in what I initially found to be remarkable ways.[3] They described the people who moved onto their farms, and the events that followed, in language and terminology reminiscent of the Liberation War, which had ended over 20 years earlier. As the epigraph to this introduction attests, the use of such words as 'gook', 'terr' and *mujiba* were commonplace, all highly loaded and negative terms that came into prominence within the white farming community during the war. ('Terr' is/was shorthand for terrorist; 'gook' was adopted to describe black guerrillas after US veterans who had served in Vietnam joined the Rhodesian forces as mercenaries; and *mujiba* was the Shona word for young boys who acted as informants and messengers for the guerrilla forces.)

Such language and reaction made me question why this response was so widespread, and the ease with which the discourse of the Liberation War was so easily resuscitated. One of the farmers I interviewed mentioned that his son had recently completed a thesis on white farmers and their interactions with the state. This was Angus Selby's 'Commercial Farmers and the State: Interest Group Politics and Land Reform in Zimbabwe'.[4] He lent me his copy, which, because of its broad historical overview of white farmers, proved invaluable reading. However, about language and discourse of white farmers after 2000, Selby had very little to say. His only comment was, 'Like ZANU-PF's reversion to liberation war rhetoric many older farmers resorted to terminology from that era, referring to invaders as "gooks" and younger invaders as "*mujibas*"'.[5] No explanation was given as to why this was the case. This book is an attempt to provide answers to the clear and obvious echoes of past discourses in the white farming community. It seeks to explore the voice (or voices) of white farmers in Zimbabwe in order to establish a deeper understanding of their attitudes not only towards events of the very recent past (2000 and after), but also of the longer trajectory of Zimbabwe (and Rhodesia's) history.

Throughout Zimbabwe's tortured past, land has been one of the categorical focal points for control, mobilisation, resistance and nation building, evidenced in both its colonial and post-colonial manifestations. As a result, the country's white farmers, on and around whom so much of the countryside's formative legislation and development has hinged, have not only received a great deal of attention from politicians, writers, journalists and intellectuals, but have also played a dynamic role in cataloguing and representing their own affairs. The dramatic events in Zimbabwe's countryside since 2000 once again brought Zimbabwe's white farmers into the spotlight. The wholesale destruction of the white farming community by forces aligned to the incumbent ZANU-PF, made white farmers headline news within Zimbabwe, across the region and around the world. Countless articles, reports, opinion pieces and letters flowed forth from the world's media and print machines, all of which have created an immense archive on white farmers and the tribulations they have undergone as a result of the controversial fast-track land reforms.

Despite the volume of this attention, there has been a remarkable lack of critical engagement with the 'voices' of white farmers, and how they have framed the events that have transpired. The descriptions, explanations and narration of events as supplied by evicted white farmers have typically been appropriated and reproduced with no investigation into the problems and language of these narratives. As a result, white farmers have been predominantly framed as innocent victims of the violent actions sanctioned by Mugabe and his ZANU-PF since 2000. The troubled history of commercial farming in Rhodesia and Zimbabwe, and the role of white farmers and landowners, have been overshadowed by the nature, scale and speed of the fast-track land reforms.

Taking stock of the complicated history and place of white farmers in Zimbabwe/Rhodesia neither negates nor belittles their experiences. The trauma they have been through is well documented and bears such a graphic and horrific representation that only the most obtuse would try to deny its significance. What I am suggesting is that the way white farmers have talked, and continue to talk, about the land reforms and their evictions, demands a great deal of scrutiny because it contains much more than a mere description of confusing and chaotic events. The language and description used so often has a very real and deep connection to pre-independence tropes of land, belonging and race. In addition, much of the evidence used to justify place and history, relies on highly problematic readings of the past. An investigation of this discourse not only offers insights into the white farming community's stances on the land, land reforms and the country's history, but also offers the opportunity to examine the role white farmers themselves have had in the events that have unfolded – a process that is crucial if the 'land issue' is ever to be resolved, legally or otherwise, in Zimbabwe.

It must be acknowledged that a singular and cohesive white rural identity (or voice) does not exist. As Anthony Chennells has commented, 'In Zimbabwe, where a short twenty-four years has reduced an arrogant and politically all-powerful white elite to an anxious and embattled minority,

3

the idea of a stable white-colonial identity is untenable.'[6] This is not just because of rural/urban divides, or generational differences in the white populations. Rather, the complex nature of the country's white population, fused with the post-colonial reshaping of national, economic and social spheres means that within the white population there exists (and has existed) a wide range of beliefs and ideas, informed by a number of circumstances. More recently, with specific focus on the country's white farmers, Selby has made similar remarks. He argued that the 'white farmers, as a community, as an interest group, and as an economic sector, were always divided by their backgrounds, their geographical regions, their land uses and crop types. They were also divided by evolving planes of difference, such as affluence, political ideologies and farm structures'.[7] Thus any stereotypical portrayal of them conforming to a single identity is bound to be fraught with inaccuracies. Both Chennells and Selby have demonstrated the importance of disaggregating the white farming community so as to avoid treating them as a homogenous, monolithic whole.

Despite the complex and disparate nature of processes of 'identification', and the divisions in the white farming community, there *are* continuities and points of connection in the way experience has been related and talked about.[8] The interviews and interactions I had with farmers while at JAG confirmed this, as do so many of the reactions by white farmers to the fast-track land reforms recorded elsewhere. What this book will illustrate is that this convergence of discourse and opinion has been true for the white farming community throughout the history of Zimbabwe/Rhodesia, and has been more evident in recent times of trauma and violence. In order to highlight these convergences, the three events focused on are the Liberation War; the years of violence in Matabeleland and the Midlands in the 1980s, or Gukurahundi; and the land occupations after 2000. Following the evolution of white farming discourse and identity since around 1970 offers the opportunity to garner a deeper understanding of how white farmers and their representative bodies have engaged with the country and the political changes that have taken place, all of which serves to supply the necessary depth and understanding to fully appreciate the reactions white farmers have had to events since 2000. In addition, it helps explain why some of the events in the rural landscape unfolded the way they did. Understanding white farming interactions with government, politics, land reforms and land occupations helps illuminate the impact white farmers and their organisations have had on 'the land question' in Zimbabwe.

A range of sources are used to give insight into white farming voice: *The Farmer* magazine; autobiographies written by white farmers; and oral testimonies of white farmers. Read together, these provide a means to trace and track the changes (and continuities) in the discourses employed. It must be noted immediately that there is a strong Mashonaland bias to these sources. *The Farmer* was run and produced out of the Commercial Farmers' Union of Zimbabwe (CFU) offices in Harare and all of the autobiographies looked at have been written by white farmers from the Mashonaland Provinces (West, Central and East) and one from Masvingo Province. The JAG collection of oral testimonies largely represent the experiences of white farmers from Mashonaland, Masvingo, Manicaland and the Midlands. JAG, whose central offices are in Harare, had hoped to carry out interviews with white farmers from Matabeleland but the difficult political situation and research climate, plus the lack of funding, prevented this from taking place. Where possible, efforts have been made to include the voices of white farmers from Matabeleland. However, it must be remembered that the vast majority of white farmers operated in the Mashonaland provinces. Table 1.1 (overleaf) shows the numbers of registered commercial farms by the administrative provinces of the CFU in the year 2000. (For administration purposes, the CFU divided the province of Mashonaland West into two units as it was too large otherwise.)

Only 13 per cent of commercial farms were in Matabeleland and over 60 per cent were in the Mashonaland Provinces. While this is not an excuse for ignoring the voice of white farmers from Matabeleland, it does reveal that this sector of the community was relatively small and would probably not dramatically alter the presentation of voice laid out here.

It must also be acknowledged that the sources and records I have used, despite their bias and inadequacies, are ones that were available to me at the time I began this project. Undertaking academic research in Zimbabwe is not without its challenges, particularly when it concerns such a sensitive topic. The political climate was extremely tense in Zimbabwe when I started my doctoral research and this had a negative impact on the availability of material. The most notable example was that the CFU denied me access to their archives, which I suspect was largely due to the political undercurrents at the time. The only documentation they gave

Table 1.1 The Number of Registered Commercial Farms by CFU Administrative Province in 2000[9]

CFU Administrative Province	Total number of Farms in Province	Percentage of Farms in the Country
Mashonaland East	1064	19.5
Mashonaland Central	871	16
Mashonaland West (South)	428	7.9
Mashonaland West (North)	975	17.9
Masvingo	350	6.4
Midlands	426	7.8
Manicaland	555	10.2
Matabeleland	719	13.2
Other (Harare, Bulawayo)	58	1.1
TOTAL	**5446**	**100**

me access to was their collection of *The Farmer* magazine. Compounding this problem of sensitivity was the reality that so many of the other public archives in Zimbabwe (such as the National Archives of Zimbabwe and the Central Statistics Office) were in such disrepair and disorder that doing any detailed research was inconceivable.[10]

In order to do this project I had to rely on resources that were either outside of these archives (such as *The Farmer* magazine, the autobiographies of white farmers and sources in South Africa and the United Kingdom) or ones that were created and collected by other organisations (such as the interviews by JAG). Each of the sources I have chosen to use has its own distinct character and ties into different traditions or practices specific to that particular mode of voice. This has fundamentally informed how this book is constructed. I have devoted a chapter (or two in the case of *The Farmer*) to each of my key sources, in the hope this will show how influential that particular expression of voice was, how it relates to the other voices examined, and how they have developed in conjunction with each other. As such, each chapter adds another layer to the analysis of white farming voice and its development and evolution.

Since each chapter and form of voice it carries needs such detailed discussion, the book does not follow a chronological order. Rather each chapter discusses a theme and relates it to the discussions that have already been introduced.

While the book is primarily focused on the voices and experiences of white farmers in Zimbabwe, the findings and conclusions have wider historiographical and conceptual implications. Firstly, this study adds significantly to growing historical understandings of the complexities involved in the transitions from colonial to independent societies in Africa, and in doing so expands on Frederick Cooper's observations about the 'ambiguities of independence', and Brian Raftopoulos and Alois Mlambo's explorations of 'becoming' a nation.[11] With its focus on the end of the colonial project and the post-colonial experience, the book is primarily concerned with the survival tactics of disempowered elites or the remnants of empire. Many of the assessments of their decisions and actions may thus be useful to those who study similar moments and transitions in other settings.

The construction of identities is another area where the arguments presented in the following chapters connect to wider scholarship. The sources used, in particular *The Farmer* magazine and the memoirs of white farmers, reveal a great deal about how the process of identification played out in Zimbabwe. The readings and methods employed here can easily be transposed to other settings. This book also connects to the developing field of diaspora studies. In exploring how those affected by dislocation have reacted, and the manner in which they have narrated these experiences, this study offers insights and understandings that could be useful to research in other areas and disciplines. It also provides a valuable contribution to the historiography of what is commonly referred to as the 'crisis in Zimbabwe', which is widely considered to have begun in the late 1990s.

Lastly, this work challenges the confining categorisations of what 'African' history is, and who it can speak for. Over a decade ago, Ann Stoler and Frederick Cooper implored researchers to 'take apart the shifts and tensions within colonial projects with the same precision devoted to analysing the actions of those who were made their objects'.[12] These same arguments must apply to post-colonial societies in Africa, and the experience of those white communities that are remnants or 'orphans' of empire. This book is an attempt to do just that, and, in doing so, offers the possibility of developing a richer and deeper historiography on Zimbabwe, as well as a range of tools and approaches that will benefit historical research in southern Africa and further afield.

The layout of the book is as follows:

Chapters One and Two provide the historical background of white farmers in Zimbabwe. They cover the development of the farming community, the establishment of its representative bodies and the changing agricultural activities of white farmers pre- and post-independence. These chapters supply the material context of white farmers that grounds the discussions of voice and discourse that follow.

The story and history of land (and its ownership and control) that I lay out in Chapters One and Two is necessarily my own understanding of how this complicated and contentious issue has played out over the last 120 years. What I present is a concise version of a topic that is riddled with heated debates, points of conflict and divergent readings of the past. The version I put forward is probably not one that most white farmers would agree with. Other versions of the history of land and farming, such as those of ZANU-PF, or communal black farmers, or black farm workers, have different emphases. It is not possible for me to cater for all of these visions of history in this entire book, let alone this first two chapters. Since this book is about white farmers' visions of the land and the politics surrounding it, I have attempted to supply information that can be used to critique and engage with that vision, and not dismiss and disprove it. I hope that it grounds the discussions of white farming voices that follow, as well as supplying some of the fundamental aspects of the material context.

Chapter Three is primarily concerned with the political interactions and involvements of the farming community and the CFU. It uses *The Farmer* magazine to explore what I have termed the 'affirmative parochialism' of the white farming community, and how this has informed their discourses of 'apoliticism'. Both of these terms are discussed and outlined in this chapter and are then used throughout the book. It is important to note that both the ideas of 'affirmative parochialism' and the discourse of 'apoliticism' are recurrent throughout the book and are not only expressed in *The Farmer*. The chapter discusses the importance of *The Farmer* magazine to the community and how it sought to speak to and for white farmers. It uses a detailed and long-term reading of *The*

Farmer to illustrate how it changed over time and how it, the CFU, and the farming community at large, all reacted to changes in the political climate during the period under investigation (c. 1970–2004).

Chapter Four looks more closely at how *The Farmer* discussed and represented episodes of violence and conflict. It introduces the concept of a 'discursive threshold', a helpful way of conceptualising the way significant events result in shifts of discourse. Two key discursive thresholds are identified, 1980 and 2000, and the chapter shows how these fundamentally altered expressions of voice in the white farming community. These changes in voice and discourse do not necessarily mean that it is always a 'new' discourse that emerges. The discursive threshold of 2000, for instance, shows a resuscitation of discourses prevalent in the 1970s, which had disappeared from public expression in the 1980s and 1990s. Crucial to this chapter is understanding how the representations and narrations of victimhood and violence changed from the Liberation War to the land occupations after 2000 and what these changes reveal about the shifts in attitude of white farmers and their representative bodies. This has further implications on how the affirmative parochialism of white farmers manifests itself after these discursive thresholds.

Chapter Five then examines how the discursive threshold of 2000 influenced the autobiographies of white farmers written thereafter, and how these reflect much of the language and terms of reference used in *The Farmer*. It also shows that, while the decision made by white farmers to write about their experiences is based on an attempt to tell the 'real' or 'true' story of the land occupations, their production is not the result of an established literary tradition or practice within the community. Since so many of the books examined are self-published, or published by some form of vanity press, they offer an insight into an 'authentic' form of white farming voice.

Chapter Six seeks to illustrate how many of the discourses found in *The Farmer* and the autobiographies find expression in the oral accounts of white farmers who have been evicted from their farms since 2000. It uses the JAG collection of interviews and shows that despite the differences and divisions between farmers, there is a remarkable cohesion of discourse, narration of experience and understanding of what transpired in Zimbabwe's rural landscape after 2000. What the chapter ultimately reveals is that within the white farming community, beyond the hierarchy of the CFU, common understandings present themselves, giving a clear indication of how white farmers defined themselves and those around them, and also how they have 'imagined' the post-colonial experience.

Notes

1 Kundera, 1986, p. 298.
2 Farmer 3 was interviewed by me as part of a project run by the organisation Justice for Agriculture (JAG). This project, the interviews conducted and how these are used in this book are explained in more detail in Chapter Five. Interview with Farmer 3, 2 March, 2007, Harare.
3 Despite being evicted from their farms and denied the opportunity to farm, most ex-farmers continue to identify themselves as white farmers. As this is how they typically label themselves, regardless of whether they still farm or not, I will use this term throughout the book.
4 Selby, 2006, p. 300.
5 Ibid., p. 300.
6 Chennells, 2005, p. 135.
7 Selby, p. 10.
8 I have used the term 'identification' instead of 'identity' in accordance with Frederick Cooper and Rogers Brubaker's understanding of it. Their eloquent and convincing critique of the term 'identity' reveals its shortcomings as a term of analysis. For Cooper and Brubaker, 'identification lacks the reifying connotations of identity. It invites us to specify the agents that do the identifying. And it does not presuppose that such identifying (even by powerful agents, such as the state) will necessarily result in the internal sameness, the distinctiveness, the bound groupness that political entrepreneurs may seek to achieve. Identification – of oneself and of others – is intrinsic to social life; identity in the strong sense is not'. Cooper and Brubaker, 2005, p. 71.
9 Centre on Housing Rights and Evictions (COHRE) Africa Programme, 2000, Annex 3, pp. 73-5.
10 For more on this, see Eppel, 2009.
11 Cooper, 2008; Raftopoulos and Mlambo, 2009.
12 Stoler and Cooper, 1997, p. 20.

1

White Farmers & their Representatives in Zimbabwe, 1890–2000

Introduction

To say the fast-track land reform programme initiated by the Zimbabwean government in 2000 has had a dramatic effect on the country's political, economic and social landscape since goes beyond stating the obvious. The devastating effects of these reforms and the manner in which they have been carried out has produced a surfeit of literature, from journalistic accounts to personal revelations of experiences during the reform process and, ultimately, to numerous academic studies that have sought to grapple with the questions and issues it generated. However, in order to fully grasp the complexities of the current crisis it is imperative to have a firm understanding of its history. To a greater or lesser degree, nearly all of the published reflections on 'the land question' after 2000 could benefit from a deeper, more nuanced perception of its history and construction.[1] This is not to proclaim that the origins of the present crisis were inevitable and inescapable outcomes of the events of the last 100 years. It is in fact the opposite. A firm grasp of the historical construction of the crisis shows not only that it represented a significant break with the past, but that the justifications for the actions of the protagonists are based on highly particular readings of the past.

   Much of the new scholarship focuses on the white farmers themselves and explores the wholesale destruction of their community utilising a particular reading of Zimbabwean history. This chapter benefits greatly from the detail in much of this work, but seeks to add a longer and more complicated overview of the history of white farmers in Zimbabwe in order to contextualise events after 2000. Part of this story lies in tracing the land question in Zimbabwe and how it has been constructed since the arrival of the Pioneer Column in 1890. However, a much greater proportion of the chapter will be devoted to the history of white farmers and their representative bodies and how these interacted with the state since that time. In doing so it draws on the most recent literature on the topic, which has vastly improved scholarship on the story of white farmers in Zimbabwe. In particular, see Angus Selby's thesis, 'Commercial Farmers and the State: Interest Group Politics and Land Reform in Zimbabwe'.[2] However, a caveat must be applied to Selby's work. His access to the CFU archives was seemingly unlimited and his thesis contains a wealth of facts and information from this organisation, particularly comments from council meetings. Unfortunately his analysis and use of that material is not as rigorous as his source extraction. In this regard, Selby's thesis has been used more as a primary source for the information it has gathered from CFU archives that was unavailable to me during my research. However, as will be illustrated, there remain a number of gaps that still need more research. The central aim of this chapter is to provide the background and framework necessary to underpin the analysis in the subsequent chapters. The differing units of study and sources used, for example *The Farmer* magazine (Chapters Three and Four), the autobiographies and memoirs written by white farmers (Chapter Five) and the interviews with evicted farmers (Chapter Six), need to be placed in the material context of their production, and this chapter will provide a means for doing so. There will be a continual discussion between the sources used and the social and economic contexts in which they were produced, and this overview will help establish the essentials of that before the specifics are analysed in each chapter.

1890–1953: From Conquest to Federation

While the history of land in Zimbabwe has received considered attention from scholars, the history of white farmers has, by and large, only been the subject of limited specific analysis. Seminal works on the early processes of European domination, such as those by Giovanni Arrighi, Robin Palmer and Ian Phimister, clearly illustrate the processes by which European power and control became entrenched.[3] These works spurred investigations into Zimbabwe's history that sought to garner a deeper understanding of land and control of it.[4] However, the story of white farmers has been subsumed into that of the process of land alienation and there has been very little direct investigation into the composition of this community. For the period from 1890 to 1980 there are two exceptions.[5] The first is Richard Hodder-Williams' *White Farmers in Rhodesia, 1890–1965*.[6] Unfortunately this work fails to live up to its expansive title and is a classic example of micro-narrative masquerading as national history. The book is primarily concerned with the history of white farmers in one small farming area just south-east of Harare in the district of Marandellas (now Marondera). The second is John Alistair McKenzie's doctoral thesis 'Commercial Farmers in the Governmental System of Colonial Zimbabwe, 1963–1980'.[7] While both of these works do a great deal to illuminate the history of white farmers, the primary focus of both is how this group interacted with the state. The farming communities and issues of their organisation, division and mobilisation are mentioned in passing but never explored in any detail.

In contrast, the personal experiences of white farmers have often been related in various forms of life-writing. From the beginning of Rhodesia's occupation, settlers wrote and published tales of their encounters.[8] Many provide detailed insights into their experiences, the communities they were part of and the black populations around them. There were numerous farming guides written too, which offered advice on how to farm and, most importantly, 'handle the native'.[9] Chapter Five discusses some of this work which has, to date, been largely ignored by academic analysts. There is scope for more work on these writings and stories, including regional comparisons. Attempts have recently been made to do this, in works of fiction that engage with land questions in southern Africa.[10] A regional study of life-writing works such as those by settler farmers would complement these scholarly pursuits.

The settlers who came to farm in Rhodesia certainly faced a tough task. Conditions were unforgiving and unfamiliar, and far from being the dominant group, white settler farmers faced competition from black farmers keen to exploit the opportunities of the new markets created by colonialism.[11] Neville Jones wrote that, 'in those days ... no farmers grew grain, it being cheaper to trade the country's requirements from the natives'.[12] Cecil Rhodes had hoped that Rhodesia would contain gold deposits to rival those of the Rand in South Africa. This ambition was reflected in the hopes of practically all the initial pioneers and settlers who were much more concerned with mining wealth than agricultural production. As the British South Africa Company director James Rochfort Maguire stated, 'when cattle and gold are in competition for men's

Table 1.2 Number of Farms and Acreage Cultivated in Rhodesia, 1904–1922

Year	Number of Farms	Total Acreage Cultivated
1904	545	33,000
1911	1470	132,000
1914	2040	183,000
1917	2222	229,000
1920	2395	237,000
1922	2337	267,000

attention, nobody thinks of cattle'.[13] According to McKenzie, by 1899 over 15 million acres of land had been alienated, but fewer than 250 of the settlers were farmers.[14]

As a result, agriculture was largely ignored until it became obvious that there would be no second Rand. In 1908 the country's first 'white agricultural policy' was formulated, aimed at attracting European settlers to take up farming in the colony by providing credit and loan facilities. White farming numbers doubled from just over 1,000 in 1907, to 2,000 in 1911. In turn, as McKenzie pointed out, this new focus on agriculture had the effect of 'strengthen[ing] the influence of the farmer interest groups', as its unions and representatives started to find cohesion of voice and representation. The first Farmers' Association had been established in 1892, and the Rhodesian Agricultural Union was formed in 1904. However, until the implementation of the first agricultural policy in 1908, the Rhodesian Agricultural Union only represented nine local farming associations. After 1908 the associations in Matabeleland joined the union after securing equal voting rights. By 1918 the Rhodesian Agricultural Union represented over 1,200 farmers and had 46 affiliated associations.[15] In 1928 the Rhodesian Tobacco Association (RTA) was formed as a commodity association within the union, but enjoyed a great deal of independence, which it used to open its own channels of communication with government.[16] White farmers were establishing themselves as a permanent feature of the countryside. Table 1.2 illustrates the growth of white agriculture from 1904–22.

McKenzie demonstrates through a number of examples, including the push for Responsible Government and the processes of land alienation and division, that the farmers had become a powerful lobby in the colony.[18] Farmers were increasingly represented in government and the Rhodesian Agricultural Union continued to extend its influence. Under Responsible Government (1923–1965) the white farming sector fared far better than African farmers did. This was in part due to the Land Apportionment Act of 1931. By 1925 it is estimated that some 2,500 white farmers occupied just over 30 million acres. The Land Apportionment Act cemented and increased the size of the European land holdings to 49 million acres, about 50 per cent of the country.[19] In addition, numerous other pieces of legislation such as the Maize Control Act of 1931 (Amended 1934) deliberately limited African access to agricultural markets.[20]

White farmers nevertheless continued to face difficulties in establishing agriculture as a successful and commercially viable enterprise. By 1942, Hodder-Williams notes that in the Marandellas district a quarter of farmers earned less than £191 (US$764) per year, while half earned less than £425 (US$1,700) and three-quarters less than £876 (US$3,504).[21] However, while farming fortunes may not have increased dramatically during the interwar years, Hodder-Williams explains why this period was so crucial to the wealth that the sector would generate after the Second World War:

> The significance of the years between the 1918 Armistice and the start of the great post-1946 economic boom in Southern Rhodesia has often been understated. There may have been no dramatic events such as the granting of Responsible Government or the establishment of the Central Africa Federation ... but the cumulative impact of legislation, agricultural practices, and enhanced security of livelihood for the whites in fact provided a framework for economic and social relations which the post-war years merely embellished and strengthened.[22]

In 1942 the Rhodesian Agricultural Union and the Matabeleland Farmers' Union (MFU) merged to form the Rhodesian National Farmers' Union (RNFU).[23] The outbreak of World War Two, and the expenses this entailed for the colony, forced the farming representatives of Mashonaland and Matabeleland to forge a partnership, despite regional divisions. A joint proposal from the Rhodesian Agricultural Union and the MFU saw the formation of the RNFU as a single body to interact with the state and champion farming needs.[24] Crucially, the union was supported by the government, which passed the Farmers' Licensing Bill (1942), requiring every farmer to take out an annual licence payable to the union. This guaranteed it members and supplied the financial means for the union to operate and expand to become the sole representative body for white farmers.[25]

At its formation, the RNFU's organisational structure was built upon layers of local farmer representation. At the lowest level were district farmers' associations. These put candidates forward to provincial farmers' unions, which in turn fed into regional associations. The regional representatives, plus those from commodity associations (tobacco, grain, cattle and dairy), would then report directly to RNFU leadership and would constitute the council.[26] The RNFU's 'overlapping representation of regional sectors and commodity associations ensured that the central council could articulate and reconcile a variety of farming interests as well as communicate central policies back to these constituents'.[27] As McKenzie notes, the relationship with the state was not based on government control, but was more a partnership in agricultural administration.[28] At this time white farmer numbers had reached over 3,000, and the agricultural boom after the Second World War, largely driven by successes in tobacco, pushed the number to over 6,000, the highest it would reach in the country's history.[29] During this period immigration to Rhodesia was dominated by people of British origin, either travelling directly from the UK, or other parts of the Empire. Large numbers of British-born immigrants also arrived from South Africa, encouraged by a Rhodesian government keen to attract immigrants of 'good stock', with necessary skills and financial means.[30]

It was only after the Second World War that white farmers experienced an extended period of profitability. Tobacco was the major driving force behind this. There had been brief tobacco booms in the past, namely in 1913-14 and in the late 1920s; however Rhodesian farmers had overreached themselves at those times and the markets had collapsed. This time, however, a long-term market was secured in Britain.[31] Overall agricultural output increased from £5.3 million (US$21.2 million) in 1941, to £24.4 million (US$67 million) in 1951 and to £64 million (US$176 million) by the Unilateral Declaration of Independence (UDI) in 1965.[32] Output of flue-cured tobacco increased from 15,000 tonnes in 1940 to 105,000 tonnes in 1965.[33]

White farmers commonly attribute their success to the hard work and aspirations of the individual farmers involved, but as Hodder-Williams has pointed out such simplistic assessments fail to take into account the level of state intervention that allowed white farmers to succeed:

> The instinctive ideology of the vast majority of farmers, on whom the Government lavished so much of their attention and resources, was non-interventionist; the ideal Southern Rhodesian was the independent farmer, the owner and developer of a private estate competing in a free capitalist market. The reality was something very different. Weakness in face of uncertain markets, fierce competition, buyers outside their control, and often hostile natural forces at home, meant that survival depended upon legislative measures which … generally created conditions in which white settlers were most likely to survive.[34]

As white farming numbers increased, so the union grew and its position was strengthened. Soon it was legitimately able to promote itself as an organisation that spoke to and for white commercial farmers. This was supported by its healthy publishing division which not only produced the weekly farming magazine, the *Rhodesian Farmer*, but also various periodicals, reports and textbooks. By the 1970s, the union claimed that it was 'officially … recognised as the organisation representing all non-African farmers' interests'. A guide to the union produced in 1977 stressed that the RNFU was designed to 'provide lines of communications within the union at all its levels and also between Rhodesia's farmers and Government and Statutory boards as well as with other organisations connected with the agricultural industry'. The guide also mapped out the membership structure of the RNFU, which it argued showed that the 'farmer's voice is effectively heard at the highest possible level and that it is heard as one voice'.[35]

The RNFU promoted itself as an organisation that carried the voice of white farmers and was continually promoting their interests in its dialogue with government and the state. The RNFU stressed that it was always sensitive to the needs and concerns of ordinary farmers. Of course, its creation did not automatically negate divisions within the community, but it did provide a platform for those concerns to be aired and discussed. The Union also maintained that it was an 'apolitical' organisation, established to defend and promote the concerns of white farmers, but not to engage in party politics. This discourse of 'apoliticism' is discussed further in Chapter Three; suffice it to say here that while 'apoliticism' was continually stressed throughout the union's history, the dividing lines between farming interests and national politics often became blurred, particularly with the emergence of the Rhodesian Front (RF) and declaration of UDI.

1953–1980: From Federation to Independence

The establishment of the Federation of Rhodesia and Nyasaland in 1953 had little effect on the white farmers of Southern Rhodesia. Moves were put in place to 'modernise' African agriculture with the introduction of the controversial Native Land Husbandry Act (NLHA), but such developments, while hugely invasive for black peasant farmers, had little impact on white commercial agriculture.[36] Ultimately, Federation failed to achieve the one thing many whites hoped for: secure independence for Southern Rhodesia under conditions acceptable to the territory's white population.[37] By the end of the 1950s, Sir Edgar Whitehead's United Federal Party alienated white opinion by proclaiming racial partnership and planning for an African majority in parliament by the end of the 1970s. These liberal reforms were overwhelmingly rejected in the 1962 general election in which the RF won a landslide among the white electorate. Farming support was crucial to this victory and white farmers formed a large proportion of the party's members. Eighteen of the 50 RF candidates were involved in agriculture.[38] Amongst them was Winston Field, a successful tobacco farmer and an ex-president of the RTA, who became the country's new Prime Minister.[39] His successor after the RF's shift to the right, Ian Smith, was also a farming man.[40]

The Federation collapsed in 1963 and the issue of independence remained unresolved. A mood of confidence developed among the white population, engendered by the RF. For McKenzie there was a 'natural affinity' between white farmers and the RF.[41] J.R. Humphrey, former director of the RNFU, expressed the farming community's feeling that 'we can do it alone'.[42] In contrast to this confidence, the successful tobacco sector was beginning to stagnate, demonstrating the economy's worrying reliance on tobacco exports. Even before the disruptions of UDI, market forces were hardening against Rhodesian tobacco, but the crop and its producers still had a massive influence on national affairs. As a result of its importance and position, the RTA had pulled away from the RNFU and remained largely autonomous. Tobacco's economic importance gave the RTA much greater financial power than the union and it enjoyed a position of 'considerable power in the administrative system which had been established for the tobacco industry'.[43] Indeed, the RTA's position in the union was ambiguous. While it was established under the Rhodesian Agricultural Union and was entitled to membership in the RNFU, it was not always clear how it valued the partnership. Symptomatically, it did not provide council minutes to the union till after 1965.[44]

The friction between the two largest representative bodies created anxieties for the farming community and the state. However, McKenzie noted a more serious threat to the farmers' united voice. Regional differences were making themselves more obvious and threatened to destroy the RNFU.[45] As a result, there were growing demands from beef, maize and dairy producers to establish their own commodity associations along the lines of the RTA. Many farmers were dismayed with the system of representation in which small-scale or minor producers had equal voting power to those for whom that commodity was their sole activity. Many in the RNFU fiercely resisted the proposals, claiming that allowing such associations would lead to the break-up of the union and thus undermine the unified representation of the farming fraternity. Discussions were postponed for a year but in the 1970s these commodity associations were adopted as formal structures within the RNFU.[46]

These tensions were fundamentally linked to regional differences. Many in Matabeleland were dissatisfied with the low level of development in the region and felt that government was biased towards investment in Mashonaland. These faultlines were deepened by overarching concerns about agriculture's future under the RF government. With the RF's movement to the right and the replacement of Field with Smith, there were fears within farming circles that the party was more concerned with electioneering and popular politics than economics and stability. There is no more pertinent example than the declaration of UDI itself. According to Flower, the leaders of the five major industries (mining, farming, tobacco, commerce and banking) were all consulted and all advised against UDI, considering the impact that trade embargoes and economic isolation would have.[47] However, the RF refused to listen and, carried by the wave of white nationalist fervour, proclaimed its Unilateral Declaration of Independence on 11 November 1965.

The effects were immediate and dramatic. Britain, Rhodesia's largest trading partner, immediately banned the purchase of tobacco and sugar, which represented 71 per cent of exports in terms of value. In December, it extended its restriction to all minerals and foodstuffs. At the beginning of 1966, it imposed a total embargo on Rhodesian trade, making the purchase of any of its products a violation of British law. The United Nations imposed an oil embargo in April 1966, followed by mandatory sanctions at the end of May 1968.[48] Tobacco was hit particularly hard by these trade restrictions. Annual export earnings from the crop fell from R$75 million (US$105 million) a year to R$30 million (US$42 million).[49] Understandably, there was a great deal of hostility towards the RF government from tobacco growers, many of whom lobbied hard to protect the industry and stave off an unlawful movement towards independence. The other agricultural sectors were also severely affected as markets evaporated and trade restrictions resulted in increased production costs as well as input shortages. Overall, average farm profitability fell by half from 1965 to 1968.[50]

Realising the importance of keeping farmers onside and on the land forced the RF into costly measures to ensure their survival. Throughout the UDI period white farmers each received an average of R$8,000 (US$12,000) in subsidies per year, while black peasant farmers only received 60 Rhodesian cents (US$0.9).[51] From 1965 to 1974 the government spent R$147 million (US$220 million) on the white farming sector, over R$100 million (US$150 million) of which went on price support for tobacco growers.[52] However, UDI did force farmers to diversify. Cattle and maize became obvious targets for white farmers seeking to find alternative ways to profit from their land.[53] As Selby illustrates, white farmers 'increased their share of marketed food production from 30 per cent in 1960 to 75 per cent in 1978'.[54] Black agriculture, which up to this point had produced most of the country's food needs, was systematically undermined through a series of legislative measures and the vast subsidy of white agriculture. Spending on African agriculture fell from 2.8 per cent of total government spending from 1966–69 to 1.2 per cent in 1975–76. To exacerbate this, the 6,000 white farmers in operation in 1977 had access to '100 times more credit than an estimated 600,000' black peasant farmers.[55] Until this point, white farmers were not overly concerned with 'feeding the country' – a claim that has often been deployed by farmers after 2000 as a defence of their land holdings and rights to land.[56] As this evidence shows, food production was a very recent development for the majority of white farmers and one that was always undertaken as an economic activity, rather than a patriotic one.

While there were certainly apprehensions in the farming community about the effects of UDI, the tide of white nationalism maintained the RF's support in farming circles. This was clearly reflected in the union's literature at the time. Smith was lauded as a natural leader in the *Rhodesian Farmer*, and no alternatives to the RF's chosen path were ever discussed.[57] However, while both the RNFU and the RTA often campaigned in support of the RF and Smith, they were still separate agents from government and expressed this agency in ways that diverged from the 'national interests' as set out by the RF leadership. Nevertheless, the declaration of UDI, and the RF's subsequent control of the state and the economy, limited farmer dissent and their ability to 'determine an independent course'.[58]

Meanwhile, the nationalist movements of the Zimbabwe African National Union (ZANU) and the Zimbabwe African People's Union (ZAPU), and their respective military wings, the Zimbabwe National Liberation Army (ZANLA) and the Zimbabwe People's Revolutionary Army (ZIPRA), had, after being banned in the early 1960s, started to step up their armed campaign against settler rule. During the first ten years of UDI this campaign was largely underwhelming:

> Divided, dispersed, imprisoned, exiled, penetrated by police informers and closely monitored by the Special Branch, the nationalist parties were unable to mount any campaign or incursion impressive enough to dent the whites' confident assumption of total control and enduring superiority.[59]

The Rhodesian security forces initially had an adequate measure of the nationalist insurgents. Even when the guerrilla campaign began a new concerted effort in 1972 there was no immediate sense of alarm in white society, or amongst the white farmers.[60] While the attack on Altena Farm in Centenary at the end of December 1972 has since come to symbolise a new phase in the Liberation War, it was only after 1975 that white casualties and farming deaths really began to impact on the community. With Mozambique gaining its independence in 1975, the whole eastern border of Rhodesia was opened up to guerrilla incursion, which allowed the nationalist forces much more freedom to operate. It was no coincidence that 1975 marked the 'first occasion for a full-scale debate by farmers of the impact and threat of war'. At the RNFU's annual congress serious questions were raised about the 'security situation' and it was stressed that 'profitable White farming was indispensible to the economy as a whole'.[61]

However, the 'security situation', as the war was euphemistically referred to in farming circles, continued to deteriorate. Before 1975, northern farming areas such as Tengwe, Karoi, Guruve, Centenary, Shamva and Mt Darwin had witnessed the most farming casualties.[62] After 1976 the eastern districts came under increasing attack, with Chipinga, Melsetter and Gazaland the worst affected. More than 50 farmers were killed between 1976 and 1978 in this region. Of 105 functional farms in Melsetter in 1976, only eight were still in operation after 1978.[63] By 1977 it was believed that 30 per cent of the eastern districts' 1,090 farms were vacant.[64] The security threat of these vacant farms was often lamented in farming circles and criticisms were often levelled at the 'townie farmer' who, it was insisted, put the entire district at risk in running his farm by remote control. This reflected the divisions between farmers in badly affected areas and those in more secure ones, as well as between rural and urban white communities. These tensions reached fever pitch as the war intensified and by 1976, as Peter Godwin and Ian Hancock argued, 'the escalation of war generated and intensified divisions which the illusion of greater solidarity could not conceal'.[65]

However, the RNFU continued to present the farming community as wholly united during the war. In 1979 it published *The Farmer at War*,[66] a lopsided account of the community during the 1970s that attempted to uphold the image of the farmers as a 'resourceful, courageous and united community'.[67] As the foreword, written by the then President of the RNFU, Denis Norman, stated:

> This [book] is a salute to our farmers .... It is a story of heroism and tragedy, of dedicated determination and tenacity in the face of an unprecedented onslaught on the land .... Their moral and physical courage is being sorely tried and tested over and again .... There is no doubting the willpower of the farming community.[68]

While proclaiming to speak for 'white and black' farmers, the book unwittingly shows how hollow this attempt was in its conclusion. It reproduced a list of all the members of the RNFU and their families who had been killed up to that point in the Liberation War. All of the people listed were white. What the book does show is that the white farmers believed they were innocent victims of the conflict. *The Farmer at War* made a conscious effort to portray farmers as merely defending themselves and their homes. They were not aggressors, nor were they responsible for the problems affecting the country and rural black populations. Their endeavours to keep farming were allegedly for the good of the nation, or love of the country, and not for personal or financial gain.

During the war nearly 300 farmers and members of their families lost their lives.[69] According to Selby, this was more than half of the white civilian deaths during the entire war.[70] But the effects of the war were highly uneven geographically. The RNFU itself commented in 1977 that the 'big league' of commercial farmers, the ten per cent who produced 60 per cent of output, were located in the central regions and were thus relatively unscathed by the war.[71] Vacant farms posed a major problem to the RF government, which, right from the inception of UDI, had sought to ensure continued white occupation of the countryside. In order to stem the flow of farmers off the land, the government set up several schemes to establish better defences on farms and financially assist farmers in their war efforts. Measures included the Victims of Terrorism Compensation Act in 1973, which reimbursed white farmers for 90 per cent of the value of losses suffered as a result of 'terrorist action'.[72] The RNFU became responsible for administering farm security patrols with Police Reservists, thereby fostering closer links to state. In 1973, the RNFU and the Ministry of Internal Affairs began implementing the Agric Alert radio scheme, which was to become a central feature of farming security measures in Zimbabwe right up to 2000 and beyond.[73] Finally, in July 1974 the government announced an aid scheme to reimburse farmers for the installation of security measures on their farms in designated areas. As the war progressed the number of designated areas increased and the government promised R$3,000 (US$5,100) per farm and R$1,000 (US$1,700) per homestead for security improvements.[74] Jim Barker, a white farmer from Karoi, recounts many episodes of the Terrorist Relief Victims Fund paying for livestock killed in attacks, or stolen. He also flew surveillance missions for the Rhodesian forces with his own airplane during the war and commented on how lucrative this was. This is another example of how keen the RF government was to keep white farmers on the land and in operation.[75]

While these measures may have benefitted some farmers, the RF's military strategies failed to stem the tide of guerrilla insurgents. Farmers continued to come under attack and ambush.[76] The hopes of a swift and peaceful solution faded as it became clear the Liberation War was becoming exactly that: a fierce struggle by black nationalist movements to remove the white settlers from power.[77] In addition, farming was becoming more and more challenging. Many farmers were unable to make their farms financially viable, as increasing input costs and disabling shortages ate into any potential profits. According to Riddell, in 1975–76, 60 per cent of commercial farms were not profitable enough to pay any income tax. He also suggested that the smaller farms could only survive because of government assistance.[78] Many in the farming hierarchy realised that steps needed to be taken to secure a future if and when white settler rule ended. To this effect, John Strong, RNFU President, and Sandy Fricks, ex-RTA President, met the Zambian President Kenneth Kaunda in Lusaka, proclaiming that the farming community was 'prepared for majority rule and would work with the black government'.[79] While these advances caused consternation in the farming community, it was a clear sign that the leadership was thinking about how to manage the future and secure its survival under majority rule. During this highly charged transition period, farmers were active members in a number of political movements. Both to the right and left of the RF, political parties were formed with key representation from white farmers.[80] Some farmers even supported the guerrilla fighters in their areas. Often this was done opportunistically in order to ensure safety from attack, but for some, such as Garfield Todd and Guy Clutton-Brock, 'support for the nationalist forces was a matter of conviction'.[81]

By the late 1970s, it was clear that, just like other industries and businesses, white farmers were keen on any form of peace, as long as it allowed them to continue their agricultural enterprises. Many realised that black rule was inevitable. In this context, farmers were much happier to support Bishop Abel Muzorewa or ZAPU's Joshua Nkomo, both of whom were much less antagonistic to white farming interests than the leadership of ZANU. The RNFU put its weight behind the 'majority' elections of 1979, which saw the election of Muzorewa as the national leader of the country, which was renamed Zimbabwe–Rhodesia.[82] These elections were roundly criticised for not including the leadership of ZANU and ZAPU and Muzorewa was seen as nothing more than a puppet of the RF.[83] Indeed the 'peace' did not last and it was clear a more inclusive settlement was needed. Later that year, international and regional diplomatic pressures forced Britain to find a lasting solution to the Rhodesian conflict. By the end of the decade Zambia and Mozambique had also grown weary of the war in which the death toll of their own populations was rising, as were the economic costs.[84] The leaders of these countries forced the ZAPU and ZANU leadership (ostensibly united under the Patriotic Front banner) to attend, and ultimately accept, the negotiated settlement of the Lancaster House conference.[85] The RF and Smith had few alternatives but to attend the conference too and were forced to accept that black majority rule was now inevitable. Despite a great deal of political wrangling and grandstanding (and no small amount of coercion), a deal was finally brokered, a constitution agreed upon and new elections were to be held the following year, with all parties participating.

The RNFU, renamed the Commercial Farmers' Union at this stage (after independence it was renamed the Commercial Farmers' Union of Zimbabwe), had sent a delegation to the talks and managed to secure a fundamental piece of legislation that was to prove crucial to the future of white farmers in the country. This was the market-based 'willing buyer, willing seller' clause to land reform, which was enshrined in the Lancaster Constitution.[86] By this legislation the new government could only acquire land from owners who were willing to sell at the market price and no compulsory acquisition could take place.[87] The leaders of ZANU and ZAPU were forced to accept these clauses under pressure from both the British government and the African leaders they relied upon to support their liberation campaigns in exile. The legislation secured the immediate futures of white farmers, yet it remained to be seen if the winners of the elections to be held in 1980 would respect the agreements made at Lancaster House and how events would play out after power was handed over.

1980–2000: From Independence to Jambanja

After independence in 1980 white farmers received very little coverage, academic or otherwise. As Jocelyn Alexander explained, the 'spaces and the occupants of white farms fell outside the remit of nationalist historiography'.[88] This meant that not only was the story of white farmers under-researched, but so was that of farm labourers and their families.[89] White farmers themselves played their part in fostering this silence, as they retreated from almost all forms of public engagement and preferred to participate only in their isolated communities (see Chapter Three).[90]

But the events since 2000 have refocused attention on to white farmers and have resulted in a steady flow of literature that seeks to ask more searching and pertinent questions of this community than much of the overly sympathetic journalist coverage has done (see Chapters Three, Four and Five).[91] Part of this process has been an attempt to better understand the experiences of farmers from independence to 2000. During this period, relations between the government and the white farmers underwent numerous changes, as did the economic activities farmers undertook.

Mugabe's victory in the 1980 elections caused immediate and widespread concern in the farming community. His vehement assertions during the Liberation War that not 'one of the white exploiters [would be] allowed to keep a single acre of their land' had lodged themselves in the collective memory of white farmers.[92] The swift change in this rhetoric and the ostensible reconciliation between whites and blacks that took place immediately after independence has been well documented.[93] Fundamental to the process of reconciliation was a sense that white farmers were vital to the country's economic survival and food security. According to Palmer:

> at the time of independence ... the white commercial farmers were producing some 90 per cent of the country's marketed food requirements. At this precise and important moment in time, they seemed crucial to Zimbabwe's economic survival.[94]

Mugabe reacted to this situation in practical terms by seeking to placate the fears of the white farming community. The threats of mass appropriation of white-owned land were abandoned and Mugabe set about securing a partnership between government and white farmers (See Chapter Three for more on the political manoeuvres at this time). This proved successful, as large numbers of white farmers decided to stay and continue farming in Zimbabwe. With the war over, economic restrictions lifted and the support of the government, white farmers could now focus on making farming a lucrative venture again.

The settlement negotiated at Lancaster House had forced the new government to compromise many of its ambitions. Its agreement to respect title deeds of white landowners meant that it could not carry out the immediate and extensive land seizures it had envisioned. Land reform, then, in and of itself, no longer carried the threat of mass expropriation of land. Farmers, comforted by the security this afforded them, began to reinvest in farming. In turn, agricultural incomes began to soar. In 1980 major crop sales from commercial farms amounted to Z$350 million (US$580 million). By 1985 this figure had risen to Z$850 million (US$765 million) and by the end of the decade it stood at Z$1,650 million (US$1,155 million).[95]

A boom in peasant agriculture matched the reinvigoration of the white farming sector, at least for the first half of the 1980s. Initially, Mugabe and ZANU-PF were adamant that a comprehensive land redistribution campaign would begin as soon as possible. There were significant land pressure problems at independence that had been created and compounded by 'the disruptive and dislocating legacies' of the Land Apportionment Act (1931), the Land Husbandry Act (1951) and the Land Tenure Act (1969).[96] While the government's capacity to address these pressures was limited by the Lancaster House Constitution, immediately after the war there was a great deal of land available to the government for resettlement in the form of land abandoned during the fighting. According to Selby, about 500 farms were acquired this way.[97] In addition, some white farmers were unwilling to remain in Zimbabwe under a black government, and many of their farms were acquired for resettlement.[98]

This early process of resettlement, combined with Zimbabwe's peasant agricultural reform, was hailed as a miracle, and as a role model for the region.[99] Small-scale and peasant production of maize increased from 41,000 tonnes in 1980/81 to 480,000 tonnes in 1985/86. The value of these outputs rose from Z$3.6 million (US$6 million) to almost Z$86 million (US$77.4 million). Cotton and burley tobacco also witnessed significant increases.[100] However, these impressive returns soon faltered, as realities about the tenuous position of peasant farmers, the highly uneven nature of the resettlement schemes and the lack of a political will to follow through with reform promises became apparent. By the end of the decade:

> a total of 52,000 families, or some 416,000 people, had been resettled, which is 32 per cent of the notional 162,000-family target. By the same time a total of 2,713,725 hectares had been bought for resettlement, representing about 16 per cent of the area owned by the white commercial farmers at independence. In 1980, 6,000 white farmers had owned 42 per cent of the country. By October 1989 the number of commercial farmers (no longer exclusively white) was 4,319, and they now owned 29 per cent of the land.[101]

In 1989, commercial farmers still owned 11.7 million hectares, and the land reform process had stalled.[102] Alexander has noted that 'the government's reluctance to press for further land redistribution was also influenced by the political weight of the CFU ... and the accumulation of land by the ruling elite'.[103] By 1990 it was estimated that there were about 500 black commercial farmers, many of whom were connected to the ruling elite.[104] The government itself outlined four main reasons for the retardation of the land reform process: political conflict in Matabeleland, world recession and drought, scarcity and price of land and lack of trained staff.[105] Alexander criticised these reasons:

> These factors cannot, however, fully explain the slowdown in resettlement: recession-inspired cuts in the resettlement programme were far deeper than those in other redistributive programmes; while land did become scarce, the government failed to purchase much of the land that was on offer, even when it met its criteria for resettlement; the shortage of trained staff was in part a self-imposed constraint which reflected the government's unwillingness to adopt less elaborate methods of redistributing land, notably the option of extending the resource base of communal areas under local control.[106]

While land reforms were slowing, those white farmers who remained were expanding their production and profit. By 1990, 30 per cent fewer farmers were producing 20 per cent more output on almost 20 per cent less land.[107] White farmers were beginning to reap the benefits of Mugabe's appeasement policies. Government support for farmers even dictated their solutions for the widespread 'squatter' problems that had affected much of the country's rural areas in the early 1980s.[108] Immediately after independence there were numerous examples of spontaneous population movements onto abandoned and private land. While government was initially sympathetic to these groups, Alexander has shown that this attitude soon changed. Concerned with protecting the foreign currency earnings of the commercial farms, the government sent stern messages to squatters that their actions would no longer be tolerated. Minister of Lands Moven Mahachi described the squatters as 'undisciplined and criminal elements [who] intended to frustrate the agricultural industry and resettlement process'.[109] In the late 1980s Mashonaland West and Manicaland Provinces had squatter populations of over 35,000 people.[110] In 1985 Squatter Control Committees were established to manage squatters at the district level and often dealt with occupiers in ruthless fashion.[111] By the end of the decade, squatter movements onto private and commercial land had largely been suppressed, but during the 1990s there were many similar occupations of communal and state land.[112]

These actions by the government illustrated their resolve to protect white commercial farmers as foreign currency earners. It also resulted in farmers becoming ever more confident in their position and their importance to the country. However, 1990 proved to be a watershed in farmer/government relations and marked a decisive shift in the approach by both to issues of land and its control. The working partnership that had developed in the 1980s quickly eroded and was replaced by antagonisms on both sides. Individuals from both camps who had worked hard to foster communications between them were replaced by people who were much more confrontational. This put massive strain on the working partnership.[113] In addition, 1990 saw the expiration of the Lancaster House Constitution. This meant that the government could now introduce much broader compulsory acquisition laws. Under the Land Acquisition Act of 1985 the government had the right to 'acquire any land on a 'willing seller, willing buyer' basis, but only *under-utilised* land, which was required for resettlement or other public purposes, could be acquired compulsorily'.[114] The National Land Policy introduced in 1990, which promised to acquire an additional 5 million hectares for 110,000 families,[115] addressed this clause directly and enforced a number of crucial changes in the functioning of land acquisition:

> In 1990 section 16 of the Constitution was amended (i) to enable the government to acquire any land (i.e. including utilised land) for resettlement purposes, (ii) to require 'fair' compensation to be paid 'within a reasonable time' and (iii) to abolish the right to remit compensation out of the country.[116]

As Coldham explained, 'The Land Acquisition Act was subsequently passed [in 1992] in order to create a statutory basis for the National Land Policy'.[117] It replaced the Land Acquisition Act of 1985 and, while many of the provisions and clauses remained the same, it was the clauses relating to designation and compensation that proved the most contentious. With regard to designation, the Act stated that it intended to only 'acquire land that [was] not fully utilised, that [was] owned by absentees or that [was] held for speculative purposes'.[118] Despite these stipulations, the fact that government now had the power to designate any land for acquisition deeply concerned farmers. To compound this, the Act, whilst stating that compensation for land had to be fair and be paid in a timely fashion, removed the requirements for compensation to be paid in foreign currency or externally. Fifty per cent of the payment had to be paid at the time of acquisition, and then 'at least one-half of the remainder must be paid within two years of that time and the balance within five years of that time'.[119] Moyo felt that the 1992 legislation could have achieved 'massive redistribution'.[120] However, the Act did not replace the 'willing buyer, willing seller' mode of land reform. Rather, it was designed to run alongside this market-driven policy. Ultimately, the combination of the two approaches meant that nearly all attempts at compulsory acquisitions could be contested in court. From 1993 to 1995 the gazetting of over 130 farms for compulsory acquisition was challenged in the courts and acquisition orders overturned.[121]

A major factor fuelling the calls for more radical land reform was the government's declining popularity. Numerous social, economic and political pressures began to erode ZANU-PF's political stranglehold over the country. In response, the government used the land issue as an electioneering tool.[122] White farmers were already targets of resentment because of their wealth, while the vast majority of the population were starting to feel the effects of economic stagnation. Mugabe and ZANU-PF seized upon this and opportunistically blamed farmers for the lack of progress in land reform and rural development. Calls for land redistribution and reform still carried popular appeal, and the government sought to exploit that.[123] The rural areas provided ZANU-PF with its biggest support base and were subject to increasing population pressures. It was also these populations that were most conscious of the wealth and security of the white farming communities.

By this stage, farmers were not only more confident as a group than they had been in 1980, they were also much more secure financially. Agricultural profits had soared over the first decade of independence and new ventures such as wildlife and horticulture provided alternative ways of earning valuable foreign currency. Many farmers benefited from the Economic Structural Adjustment Programme (ESAP), introduced in 1990.[124] Designed to resolve the economic woes caused by excessive state borrowing and a balance-of-payments crisis, a key tenet of ESAP was market liberalisation. This allowed white farmers access to hitherto restricted yet lucrative export markets. In fact, a range of incentives, such as favourable tax policies, were created to encourage exports. There were three key sectors in which white farmers decisively developed exports: horticulture, cut-flower production and wildlife-oriented enterprises. Expansion of these resulted in both the Horticultural Producers Association and the Wildlife Producers Association becoming new commodity boards under the CFU.[125] Farmers moved away from producing land-hungry but less lucrative crops such as grains. This was reflected in the land use figures. In 1980, 270,000 hectares were under grain crop cultivation. This fell to a low of 154,000 in 1992, before recovering to 190,000 in 1999.[126] This represented a 30 per cent reduction from 1980 to 1999. It is clear that during the first two decades of independence, the products that farmers had diversified into during UDI became less appealing and cash crops, such as tobacco and flowers, became more popular. This was also reflected in changing land usage. In 1970 commercial farmers devoted over 278,000 hectares to grain crops, and only 149,000 to industrial crops. In 1980 the ratio was 270,000 to 227,000, respectively, and by 1999 the areas devoted to each were almost equal at 194,000 and 197,000.[127]

Wildlife ventures also began to use much of the underutilised and vacant land on commercial farms. According to Moyo, in the 1990s:

> less than 5 per cent of the Communal Area farmers were engaged in wildlife and related land uses. Altogether, by 1996 close to 30 per cent of the entire LSCF [Large-Scale Commercial Farms] (about 1,500 of the farms) had become engaged in one or more of the new land uses, albeit in combination with older cropping enterprises'.[128]

By tapping into these wildlife and tourism markets, farmers were 'creating the illusion that full productive use of their lands was becoming the norm by ... using prime lands for wildlife and tourism enterprises'.[129] These activities and types of land uses began to attract a great deal of negative press from government. As land reform debates in the early 1990s began to radicalise, the issue of wildlife on farms became more and more divisive. In 1992 a member of parliament was quoted as saying:

> We need to keep a close eye on the commercial farmers ... they are playing yoyo with the nation ... the white farmers realised that ploughing and all that was hazardous ... they discovered new types of farming ... they discovered that there is a safari business where you spend very little, all you have to do is construct a tall wire, to provide water fountains from farm to farm, the rest should look after itself ... most commercial farmers do not have farms, only gardens. They hardly do any farming on those farms.[130]

Even the new Minister of Lands and Agriculture, Witness Mangwende, was on record saying that 'right now [in the early 1990s, white farmers] are busy stocking most of their underutilised land with wildlife'.[131] The increased wealth of this sector jarred with the experience of the country's poor and working class populations, rural and urban. By 1990 the initial promise of Zimbabwe's success had faded and the realities of the country's struggling economy began to make themselves evident. As Muzondidya has pointed out, 'from the late 1980s onwards, Zimbabwe's positive record abroad could no longer mask the growing social problems and contradictions at home'.[132]

The actions of the CFU and the farming hierarchy compounded these assumptions, as they did not participate in any public discussion of the land question. They continually promoted the idea that land was an issue separate from everyday politics and debate, and should be resolved only at the highest levels of government. The CFU president John Brown summarised the situation perfectly in 1990. When asked if he was to attend a University of Zimbabwe conference on land issues, he replied:

> I am not going to the conference. We think it's daft and highly undesirable that the university should be the forum where a public debate on an issue as vital to Zimbabwe as land is held. I live land and discuss it with the presidents of the other two farmers' unions, the Minister of Agriculture and the President; those are the places where I discuss agricultural land and we have a very common attitude. We don't negotiate in public.[133]

Such actions and attitudes only reinforced widespread perceptions of white farmers as arrogant and aloof.[134]

While ESAP offered many farmers new opportunities, it severely affected government spending on social services and infrastructure. The economic plight of the vast majority of the population deteriorated as jobs were cut and incomes fell.[135] Selby noted that:

> The white community's visible affluence and continued social isolation, which amplified during structural adjustment, provided a target and a catalyst for anti-white sentiment. An independent consultant identified the racial exclusiveness of the CFU as their biggest weakness and greatest threat. Racism among some whites was still prevalent and mounting scepticism among farmers towards government was often explained through condescending cultural perspectives. Some farmers maintained conservative attitudes with racial undertones.[136]

By 1997 hardly any further progress had been made on the land issue.

From 1990 to 1997 the commercial farming sector's land holdings were reduced by less than 150,000 hectares, barely two per cent.[137] This was despite the fact that government had the first option to buy all land that went on the open market.[138] White farmers had successfully challenged nearly all attempts at compulsory acquisition and continued to be viewed by large swathes of the population as a wealthy and isolated elite that was profiting enormously from its land holdings. For Selby, farmers were guilty of highly selective engagement with events around them and suffered from 'illusions of indispensability'. In addition, their 'scepticism over government's ability to proceed with reform, and a focus on the opportunities of ESAP all contributed to a collective myopia'.[139]

During the 1980s, race had not played a part in the government's public discourse on land, but during the 'second decade of independence, in a context of economic decline and state contraction, the very visible continued economic clout of whites became a target, and one that was all too easy to hit'.[140] ZANU-PF was undergoing its own internal changes at this time, resulting in more radical and impatient elements of the party coming to the fore. They were frustrated with the lack of progress on land issues, and Selby writes of the 'waning influence of technocrats', as moderate elements of the party were eclipsed by extremists who wanted more radical steps to be taken in land reform and allocation.[141] This was compounded by Mugabe's concessions to the war veterans in 1997.

These concessions came after war veterans, led by their new and unpredictable leader Chenjerai Hunzvi, criticised and besieged Mugabe at his party offices. Mugabe subsequently promised to pay veterans a lump sum of Z$50,000 each (US$4,500) and monthly pensions of Z$2,000 (US$180). These concessions marked a new partnership between the government and the war veterans, and one which was to cement itself after 2000 as part of ZANU-PF's dogged and violent campaign to retain power.[142] However, it must be remembered that throughout Zimbabwe's post-colonial history:

> the political dynamics between war veterans and the ruling party have been remarkably consistent. Their relationship has been characterised by collaboration, conflict and accommodation. Veterans and the party have used each other to pursue their different, though often overlapping, objectives.[143]

Events in 1997 signalled a new phase in this relationship, one that would have serious implications for the land question and the fast-track land reforms in the new millennium, as more extreme elements of the party began to exert their influence.[144]

In late November 1997, the government unexpectedly gazetted 1,471 farms for compulsory acquisition.[145] There was an immediate outcry from the farming community and the CFU desperately sought assurances and concessions from government over the list. Although asked by Minister of Agriculture Kumbirai Kangai not to take the acquisition orders to court, white farmers challenged the list *en masse*. By 1998, 640 (40 per cent) of farms had been delisted by the government as they did not conform to the listing guidelines. Of the 800 plus farms that remained on the list, the vast majority were struck off by the courts under challenges from white farmers who were supported by the CFU. In fact a central fund was established by the CFU to pay for legal challenges.[146] A total of 1,300 challenges were lodged by landowners, and only 109 of the 1,471 farms were obtained by the government.[147]

While farmers and the CFU continually maintained that they were in support of land reform and understood the need for land redistribution, their reactions to the government's attempts at reforms were consistent and predictable. Throughout the 1990s, compulsory acquisitions had been challenged through the legal system, leaving the government frustrated and its more radical elements disillusioned. Kangai lamented in 2003 that:

> [the farmers] were simply against any type of land redistribution. Why did they go to court, why did they oppose things like land tax? Why did they not offer land? This allowed impatient members of the party to say 'look, see ... your route is not working ... these whites are just opposed to everything, even when you try to include them'.[148]

The reactions to the land proposals and acquisition orders from 1980 and the listings of the 1,471 farms in 1997 all confirm this. Yet the 1997 listings and the fallout over them marked a key change in land debates and government action. For Moyo:

> 1997 marked the threshold of land reform strategy in Zimbabwe, given that it raised the question of whether the ruling party and its government could muster serious political resolve to challenge the legacy of settler land and property rights as enshrined in existing legislation and the 'rule of law'. Was land redistribution being conclusively tackled or was it political rhetoric, in response to intra-Zanu PF political and succession conflicts?[149]

From this point on, the government began to use increasing force to back its political rhetoric on the land issue. While the listings of 1997 resulted in limited land transfers, they raised 'expectation as well as suspicions among the land hungry'.[150] Occupations took place in central, southern and northern parts of the country with white farms the most common targets.[151] Moyo believed that government played a significant part in organising these squatter movements 'in order to put pressure on the donors and the CFU at the 1998 Donors Conference'.[152]

Held in October 1998, the International Donors Conference on Land Reform and Resettlement was hastily organised. Twenty donor countries, plus the World Bank (WB), the United Nations Development Programme (UNDP), the International Monetary Fund (IMF) and the European Union (EU), met the government and the CFU to discuss a way forward. The Inception Phase Framework Plan (IPFP) was agreed. Proposals put forward by 'Team Zimbabwe', a CFU initiative that brought together farming leaders, researchers and government-connected technocrats, were accepted.[153] These proposals had identified 118 farms (113,000 hectares) for purchase and resettlement, which would be monitored and then expanded upon. However, immediately after the conference the government issued acquisition lists for a further 845 farms, violating the IPFP. This both dismayed farmers and served to further alienate the ruling party from international agencies, which were already sceptical about the government's approach to land reform and governance. It also demonstrated ZANU-PF's capacity for offering promises and appeasements, and then immediately reneging on those as soon as it felt it had more to gain from doing so.

Meanwhile, pressures from other sectors of the population continued to mount. The Zimbabwe Congress of Trade Unions (ZCTU) in particular was highly antagonistic towards the government and it led the process of creating a new political party, the Movement for Democratic Change (MDC). In 1997 the National Constitutional Assembly (NCA) was formed to educate people about the constitution and facilitate public debate on the drafting of the new constitution. The NCA grew in popularity, despite fierce competition from the government. ZANU-PF put forward its own constitutional consultation body, the National Constitutional Commission (NCC), which lobbied aggressively for the party's proposed changes to the constitution. The two most contentious areas of their proposal were the powers it gave to the president, and the way it held Britain financially responsible for the cost of land reforms.[154] Farmers, who were now highly disillusioned by ZANU-PF rule, 'joined more widespread popular discontent among ordinary Zimbabweans', and put a great deal of effort into mobilising a rural 'No' vote in the constitutional referendum due to be held on 12-13 February 2000.[155] Despite considerable efforts to undermine the NCA and achieve a 'Yes' vote, ZANU-PF suffered a dramatic defeat in the referendum. The draft constitution was rejected by 55 per cent of the voters and ZANU-PF were caught in the embarrassing situation of having to backtrack in the face of popular defeat. The defeat marked a fundamental shift in Zimbabwean politics that had been building since the mid-1990s; and in response to these new political currents ZANU-PF unleashed a wave of violence and repression. It changed the rules of engagement and the start of the new millennium witnessed a new era of political, social and economic violence that accelerated Zimbabwe's slide into crisis.

Conclusion

The history of white farming in Zimbabwe has been a long and complicated one, as this chapter has illustrated. From 1890 to 2000, the fortunes of this community have waxed and waned in accordance with the economic, social and political contexts of the country's history. Consequently, the relationship of the white farming community with the country's political leadership has continually been renegotiated and re-established, depending on the prevailing political climate. Federation, UDI, the Liberation War, Independence and the many changes after that point have all played a role in complicating and altering the constitution of the white farming community. This chapter has also illustrated that even after independence, the interaction between the white farmers and Mugabe's government underwent a series of shifts and alterations before 2000. At the turn of the millennium, nothing about their relationship was decided or set in stone. The developments after 2000 had a clear evolution, but were not dictated by the success of ZANU-PF at the independence elections of 1980. The next chapter focuses on events from 2000 to 2004 and the dramatic effect these had on the white farming community and their representative body, the CFU.

Notes

1 It is fully recognised here that there are a multiplicity of questions about land and its historic construction in Zimbabwe. For the sake of convenience, the term 'the land question' shall be used throughout this book to represent all of those questions. It is hoped that through the course of the book the reader will be able to identify the themes and topics contained in 'the land question', and the literature surrounding them. The quotation marks will be dropped hereafter.

2 Selby, 2006. Also, see Suzuki, 2005; Raby, 2000; McCallum, 2006. This chapter will also rely heavily on McKenzie's 1989 thesis on commercial farmers in Zimbabwe. McKenzie, 1989.

3 Arrighi, 1967; Palmer, 1977; Phimister, 1988. Also, see Palmer and Parsons, 1977; Moyana, 1984; Yudelman, 1964; Arrighi, 1970; Weinrich, 1975; Pollack, 1975.

4 For an insight into this literature, see Alexander, 2007. For more on the literature covering events after 2000, see Pilossof, 2008b.

5 Phimister's *Economic and Social History of Zimbabwe*, whilst containing a great deal of information on the roots of white agriculture and the people involved, is a much broader look at class formation and white interests across the country. Phimister, 1988.

6 Hodder-Williams, 1983.

7 McKenzie, 1989.

8 For a sample of some of this literature, see Truepeney, 1965; Boggie, 1938, 1959 and 1966; Arnolds, 1980; Sommerville, 1976; Richards, 1975; Townsend, n.d.; Robertson, 1935.

9 Also see many of the farming guides that were produced for new farmers. For example, Metcalf, 1971; Tracey, 1953.

10 For an example in research that employs this methodology, see Graham, 2009.

11 Phimister, 1988, pp. 23-6.

12 Jones, 1953, p. 116.

13 Thomas, 1997, p. 23

14 McKenzie, 1989, p. 1.

15 This paragraph based on McKenzie, 1989, pp. 2-3.

16 Clements and Harben, 1962, pp. 112-3. Also, see Davies, n.d.

17 Phimister, 1988, p. 61.

18 McKenzie, 1989, chapter one.

19 Palmer, 1977, p. 185.

20 Ibid., chapter eight. Keyter, 1978.

21 Hodder-Williams, 1983, p. 170.

22 Ibid, pp. 173-4.

23 Maize legislation and control in the 1930s, which sought to safeguard the interests of the major growers, had become a highly divisive issue between farmers in Mashonaland and the ranchers in Matabeleland who needed the maize for feed. As competing representative bodies formed, the fragmentation of the community became

wearisome for government and threatened the success of the community at large. As a result the effectiveness of the farming representative organisations to affect policy and successfully negotiate with the state was limited.

24 McKenzie points out that the state also wanted to deal with only one agricultural representative body. McKenzie, 1989, p. 10.

25 RNFU, 1977, p. 1.

26 Selby, 2006, p. 49.

27 Ibid., p. 48.

28 McKenzie, 1989, p. 11.

29 There are a number of different figures for white farmers in Rhodesia by the 1960s. Rukuni stated there were 6,255 white farmers in Rhodesia by 1955. Palmer claimed there were 5,700 in 1965, while Clark records there were 7,851 (5,477 males and 2,374 females) persons engaged as land owners or occupiers by 1965. Rukuni, 1994, p. 11; Palmer, 1977, p. 91; Clark, 1977, p. 22.

30 For much more detail on the numbers of white immigrants and their origin, see Mlambo, 2002; Kennedy, 1987.

31 Clements and Harben, 1962, pp. 135-7.

32 Palmer, 1977, p. 243.

33 Mckenzie, 1989, p. 12.

34 Hodder-Williams, 1983, p. 174.

35 RNFU, 1977, p. 1. See Appendix One for diagram of RNFU/CFU structure.

36 For more on the NLHA, see Bulman, 1975; Duggan, 1980; Drinkwater, 1989; Phimister, 1993. For a discussion of the NLHA in a wider regional context see Beinart, 1984. For a critique of Beinart, see Phimister, 1986.

37 McKenzie, 1989, p. 15.

38 Ibid., p. 16.

39 For more on Winston Field, see Cleary, 1998.

40 For more on Ian Smith, see his own autobiography: Smith, 2001. Also see a later edition published after his death: Smith, 2008. Also, see Mungazi, 1998.

41 McKenzie, 1989, p. 30.

42 J.R. Humphrey, quoted in McKenzie, 1989, p. 30.

43 Ibid., p. 70.

44 Ibid.

45 Ibid., p. 71.

46 RNFU, 1977.

47 Flower, 1987, chapter two.

48 Mtisi, Nyakudya and Barnes, 2009a, p. 127.

49 Mbanga, 1991, pp. 226-8.

50 McKenzie, 1989, p. 105.

51 Phimister, 1987, p. 52; Riddell, 1978, p. 13; Stoneman, 1981, pp. 127-50.

52 McKenzie, 1989, p. 105. While the RF government offered financial support to tobacco and other farmers to keep them solvent, it also sought to reduce dependency on tobacco and encourage diversification. See Mtisi, Nyakudya and Barnes, 2009a, p.

128.

53 See Appendix Two for figures on changes in land use on large-scale commercial farms in Zimbabwe from 1970-1999.

54 Selby, 2006, p. 69.

55 Mtsi, Nyakudya and Barnes, 2009a, p. 130. For peasant perspectives on changing agricultural fortunes over this period, see Alexander, 2006; Ranger, 1978, pp. 119-20; Ranger, 1985.

56 See Chapter Five for more on this as revealed in the memoirs of white farmers written after 2000. This is a particularly persistent trope for Catherine Buckle. Buckle, 2001; Buckle, 2002. Later in this chapter there is more discussion on the changes in land uses after 1980, where horticulture and wildlife became important aspects of commercial agriculture.

57 This is discussed further in Chapter Three.

58 Godwin and Hancock, 1993, p. 74.

59 Caute, 1983, p. 40.

60 Ibid., p. 40. This is corroborated by the lack of reporting in *The Rhodesian Farmer*. See Chapters Three and Four in particular for more analysis on why this was the case.

61 Godwin and Hancock, 1993, p. 133.

62 These areas lost more than 80 members during the war. See Trevor Grundy and Bernard Miller's, *The Farmer at War* for a list of all farmers killed in the war. The list gives details of when and where farmers were killed. Grundy and Miller, 1979, pp. 132-41.

63 Selby, 2006, p. 80.

64 *Rhodesian Farmer*, 18 November 1977, p. 7.

65 Godwin and Hancock, 1993, p. 149.

66 Grundy and Miller, 1979.

67 Selby, 2006, p. 77.

68 Grundy and Miller, 1979, p. 7.

69 Ibid., pp. 132-141.

70 Selby, 2006, p. 78.

71 *Rhodesian Farmer*, 18 November 1977, p. 3.

72 Caute, 1983, p. 99.

73 McKenzie, 1989, p. 200.

74 Ibid., pp. 212-3.

75 Barker, 2007, p. 221.

76 Some farmers assisted and made compromises with guerillas in their areas. See Mtsi, Nyakudya and Barnes, 2009a, pp. 129-30.

77 Godwin and Hancock, 1993, p. 11.

78 Riddell, 1978, p. 13. While this may have been the case, Caute shows the extraordinary lengths many white farmers went to in order not to pay any tax, and the concessions and loops available to do this. See Caute, 1983, pp. 100 and 124-6.

79 Mtsi, Nyakudya and Barnes, 2009a, p. 130.

80 For example, Allan Savory, a farmer and conservationist led the National Unifying

Force (NUF) in opposition to Smith.

81 Mtisi, Nyakudya and Barnes, 2009a, p. 130.

82 See Grundy and Miller, 1979, and the pictures on pages 102 and 104.

83 Mtisi, Nyakudya and Barnes, 2009b, pp. 163-4.

84 Ibid., p. 165.

85 For the pressures put on the Patriotic Front by Presidents Kenneth Kaunda and Samora Machel, see Sibanda, 2005, p. 218.

86 Selby, 2006, p. 104.

87 For a more detailed assessment of land and the Lancaster House agreement, see Moyo, 1995.

88 Alexander, 2007, p. 189.

89 For literature on the situation of farm labourers before 2000, see Clark, 1977; Rubert, 1998; Rutherford, 2001b.

90 This is also illustrated by the fact that between 1980 and 2000 no white farmer published a memoir or autobiography. See Chapters Three and Four for discussions on the changes in white farming discourse.

91 For a sample of this journalistic work, see Hill, 2003; Meredith, 2003; Meredith, 2007; Norman, 2004; Meldrum, 2005; Lamb, 2006.

92 Robert Mugabe interview in Dimbleby, 2000. Also, see Mugabe, 1983.

93 Sachikonye, 2005.

94 Palmer, 1990, p. 167.

95 All figures from Central Statistics Office (CSO), 2001, p. 177. Crop sales from commercial farms still represented over 87 per cent of national totals. See Appendix Three for a table showing major crop sales in Zimbabwe from 1970–1999.

96 Selby, 2006, p. 129.

97 Ibid.

98 Palmer, 1990, pp. 169-70. Palmer shows that there was a spike in land bought by the government in 1982-83, and a sharp decline after that. Over 900,000 hectares were bought in 1981–82 and 1982–83, and only 159,000 bought in 1983–84.

99 Norman, 1986.

100 Ibid., p. 15. Cotton increased from 32,000 tonnes (Z$11.7 million or US$16 million) to over 130,000 tonnes (Z$85.8 million or US$77 million), and burley tobacco from 233,000 tonnes (Z$327,000 or US$467,000) to 937,000 tonnes (Z$1.5 million or US$1.35 million).

101 Palmer, 1990, p. 169.

102 CSO, 2001, p. 157. See Appendix Four for a table of the total number and area in hectares of large commercial farms in Zimbabwe from 1970-1999.

103 Alexander, 1993, p. 195. Also, see Stoneman and Cliffe, 1989, pp. 56 and 62.

104 Sachikonye, 2005, p. 8.

105 Alexander, 1994, p. 335. Also, see Palmer, 1990, p. 170; Drinkwater, 1989, pp. 287-305.

106 Alexander, 1994, p. 335.

107 Selby, 2006, p. 178.

108 'Squatters' is placed in quotations marks to reflect that the term is a contested

one. The land occupations at this time were also contested events. Quotation marks dropped hereafter. For a white farmer's reactions to squatters on his land, see Caute, 1983, p. 444.

109   Quoted in Alexander, 2003, p. 88.

110   Alexander, 1993, p. 198. Selby notes that these numbers were corroborated in CFU Council meeting minutes at the time. Selby, 2006, p. 166.

111   Alexander points out the irony in land redistribution at the time: those who took up action as squatters benefitted largely because government wanted a quick resolution to the issue. However, those who remained in the communal lands and did not partake in land occupations were often overlooked in land redistribution. Alexander, 2003, pp. 90-2.

112   Ibid., p. 94. Also, see Hammar, 2001, pp. 550-74; Nyambara, 2001, pp. 534-49.

113   This is covered in detail in Chapter Three.

114   Emphasis in original. Simon Coldham, 1993, p. 83.

115   Alexander, 2003, p. 93.

116   Coldham, 1993, p. 83.

117   Ibid.

118   Ibid.

119   Ibid., p. 85.

120   Moyo, 2000a, p. 12.

121   Moyo, 2004, p. 18.

122   Muzondidya, 2009 pp. 190-4.

123   Sachikonye, 2005, p. 8.

124   Muzondidya, 2009, pp. 192-3.

125   Selby, 2006, p. 196. From the mid-1980s wildlife farming and management became a prominent topic in *The Farmer* magazine, illustrating how important this sector became for commercial farmers.

126   CSO, 2001, p. 158. See Appendix Two for figures on the changes in land use on large-scale commercial farms in Zimbabwe from 1970–1999.

127   Ibid. See Appendix Two.

128   Moyo, 2000, p. 163.

129   Ibid., p. 164.

130   Unnamed member of parliament quoted in Selby, 2006, p. 198.

131   Ibid., p. 216.

132   Muzondidya, 2009, p. 188.

133   John Brown quoted in Palmer, 1990, p. 181, footnote 62.

134   Another example of the CFU's aloofness was the issue of a farming union merger. There had been talk since independence of merging all the agricultural unions in Zimbabwe, but the CFU broke ranks in January 1991 when it unilaterally issued its own land policy proposal calling for safeguards on land seizure and compensation.

135   Muzondidya, 2009, pp. 188-90.

136   Selby, 2006, p. 242.

137   CSO, 2001, p. 157. In 1990 the commercial farming sector consisted of 4,992 farms covering 11,433,986 hectares. In 1997 there were 5,146 farms covering 11,291,152 hectares. The difference is 142,834 hectares. See Appendix Four for fig-

ures on the number of commercial farms in Zimbabwe from 1970–1999.

138 According to Palmer, 'If the government decided, for whatever reason, that it did not want the land, it issued a "no present interest" certificate, which was valid for a year and left the owner free to sell on the private market'. Palmer, 1990, p. 170.

139 Selby, 2006, p. 230.

140 Alexander, 2003, p. 93. Also, see Moyo, 2000b, pp. 23 and 33.

141 Selby, 2006, pp. 239-41. This term was coined by Mandivamba Rukuni in an interview with Selby.

142 Muzondidya, 2009, p. 198.

143 Kriger, 2003b, p. 105.

144 Kriger has written extensively on war veterans in Zimbabwe. For her books, see Kriger, 1992, 2003a, For articles, see Kriger, 2001, 2003c, 2003d.

145 For a full reproduction of this list, see *The Farmer*, 4 December 1997, pp. 23-75.

146 Selby, 2006, p. 239.

147 The Utete Report clamed that 1,393 objections were received, 510 of which were upheld and, 'for the remaining 883 farms Government had to go through lengthy judicial processes'. Utete, 2003, p. 15. (This report will be referred to and referenced as *The Utete Report* throughout.) Also, see Selby, 2006, p. 239; Moyo, 2004, pp. 18-19; International Crisis Group (ICG), 2004, p. 54, footnote 123.

148 Kangai quoted in Selby, 2006, p. 241.

149 Moyo, 2004, p. 19.

150 Alexander, 2004, p. 96.

151 Ibid., pp. 96-8. Alexander supplies a detailed list of areas affected and offers insights into who initiated them and who was involved. She concludes that these movements were both managed and popular. Also, see Marongwe, 2003; Rutherford and Worby, 1998; Alexander, 2006, p. 184.

152 Alexander and McGregor, 2001, p. 511, footnote 3. Also, see Moyo, 2000a, p. 11.

153 'Team Zimbabwe' consisted of CFU hierarchy and government land technocrats including Dr Robbie Mupawose, Professor Mandivamba Rukuni and Professor Sam Moyo. Selby, 2006, p. 268, footnote 699.

154 ICG, 2004, p. 71.

155 Selby, 2006, p. 275.

2

No Country for White Men

White Farmers, the Fast-Track Land Reforms and *Jambanja*, 2000–2004

How does a man decide in what order to abandon his life?
– Anton Chigurh[1]

Introduction

The increasing hostility of ZANU-PF – which was exacerbated by the rising popularity of the MDC – meant that white farming communities entered the new millennium in a cautious manner. Unsure of how the land issue would develop, many farmers became active participants in the political upheavals around them. Central to this was their lobbying for a 'No' vote against ZANU-PF's constitutional proposals in the referendum of 2000.[2] The ruling party saw this defeat as a direct affront to their continued rule and feared the repercussions it would have for the general elections due to be held later that year. ZANU-PF and Mugabe were not prepared to chance another electoral setback, and so began a campaign of violence and terror to ensure victory.[3] Much of their hostility was focused on white farmers.

In the urban areas there was a massive crackdown on the MDC and other opposition movements. In the countryside, widespread and co-ordinated land occupations began within a matter of weeks. On 24 February 2000, the first occupations were reported in Masvingo. From there:

occupations spread to Mashonaland and Manicaland in the next few weeks, and involved not just veterans but also people from communal areas, chiefs and urban residents. Mashonaland rapidly came to the fore, spurred on by the increasingly prominent and fiery Provincial Governor Border Gezi, and a number of influential veteran leaders, and thereafter this region dominated in terms of numbers of occupations and violence. Matabeleland only later entered the fray.[4]

At the forefront of these land occupations were veterans of the liberation war. Under the leadership of Chenjerai Hunzvi and Joseph Chinotimba, vice-chairman of the Zimbabwe National Liberation War Veterans' Association (ZNLWVA), veterans began occupying commercial land across the county. However, as Nelson Marongwe pointed out, it was very rare for the occupiers to consist entirely of war veterans. By his estimates, they constituted only 15-20 per cent of land occupiers and were supported by numerous other populations, such as those from communal lands, rural and urban landless, other ZANU-PF supporters and various opportunists.[5] Nevertheless, war veterans became figureheads of the movements onto white land. Many of the occupations were peaceful, but some were highly confrontational and violent. This initial period saw the beginning of what has come to be known, by both farmers and occupiers, as *jambanja*.

2000–2004: Jambanja

The word *jambanja*, apparently popularised by a chart-topping song '*Jambanja Pahotera*', about two couples caught in extra-martial affairs, became synonymous with the land occupations.[6] With no precise definition, the word was, and still is, used to encompass a range of violent and angry confrontations on the land, which varied in degree, severity and manner. The journalist Tagwirei Bango summarised the spirit of the word in the *Daily News* newspaper:

> For new words to get accepted into a language, they must reflect the mood of the time, fill in a vacuum in the standard lexicon and be accepted as an appropriate form of expression. Thus, the word *jambanja* which became part of our vocabulary in the past two years, helped people to accept their confusion with an executive order directing the police to ignore crimes classified as political. *Jambanja* means state-sponsored lawlessness. The police are not expected to intervene or arrest anyone in a jambanja scene because those taking part will have prior state blessing and approval. But, only one interest group, war veterans and ZANU(PF) supporters, is allowed to engage in a *jambanja*.[7]

From these early *jambanjas* and land occupations, there was substantial evidence that many were supported and co-ordinated by government and state officials. Jocelyn Alexander and JoAnn McGregor found that many of the war veterans occupying farms 'consistently maintained that they had received direction from the national level of their association regarding which farms to occupy'. Government officials supplied lists of farms.[8] In addition, army personnel, members of the Central Intelligence Organisation (CIO) and police were directly involved in some occupations, while local politicians and their employees were often seen assisting 'settlers' to remain on the land with food handouts and cash payments.[9] 'Settler' is a highly charged word in Zimbabwe because of its colonial legacies and was deliberately employed by ZANU-PF to describe those who moved on to white owned land as part of the fast-track land reforms. Its use by ZANU-PF and the war veterans undermined the white farmers' claims to a settler heritage and past.

Caught off guard by the scale and the speed of the land occupations, the CFU and the affected farming communities were initially at a loss as to how to react. Very quickly though, these communities revived communication systems that had been established during the Liberation War and the insecurity of the 1980s.[10] District 'reaction units' were organised in the same way as wartime 'reaction sticks'.[11] The Agric Alert radio system was revived, with evening call-ins and daily 'sit-reps', or situation reports, were delivered and recorded.[12] The CFU began producing its own sit-reps, which started in March 2000 and continued to be disseminated publicly until 2003.[13] As the communication networks of the war were reinvigorated, so too was the language associated with it: 'terrs', 'gooks' and *mujibas* became colloquial terms for describing the land occupiers in farming circles.[14] The occupations themselves became known as 'invasions', and were soon the primary concern of the white farming community.

Eric Worby has noted that 'invasion' became the standard definition for movements onto white farms, because it suited both sides: 'It should be obvious that the term "invasion" bears a heavy, if ambiguous, moral load. Both the agents and objects of the process – invaders and invaded – have found sufficient righteousness in its implications for the term to remain remarkably uncontroversial.'[15] What this shows is that the discourse adopted by the farming community was directly affected by the language and approach adopted by Mugabe and ZANU-PF. The extremely confrontational and militaristic approach adopted by the government to frame the land occupations, underpinned by their decision to label the entire movement the Third Chimurenga, fed white farming fears of violent mass movements onto commercial farm land. After the

February referendum, the land occupations gathered steady pace.

On 16 March, one month after the referendum, the CFU issued a sit-rep showing that over 600 farms had so far been invaded, with 377 currently occupied by war veterans and land occupants.[16] The next day the Supreme Court ruled that the land occupations were illegal and gave the squatters 24 hours to vacate the farms. The court order issued by Judge Paddington Garwe 'directed police to assist with the eviction of squatters and ignore any countermanding directives from President Mugabe'.[17] Mugabe gave this ruling short shrift and ordered the land occupations to continue. He said, 'We want whites to learn that the land belongs to Zimbabweans', thus giving licence for the invasions to pick up again and escalate.[18]

At the beginning of April, parliament passed into law the constitutional amendments that had been rejected in the February referendum. The law declared that:

> the former colonial power [the UK] has an obligation to pay for compensation for agricultural land compulsorily acquired for resettlement, through an adequate fund established for the purpose; and if the former colonial power fails to pay compensation through such a fund, the Government of Zimbabwe has no obligation to pay for agricultural land compulsorily acquired for resettlement.[19]

With these amendments, the government believed it had a much freer and stronger hand in pursuing land reform (however impractical it was to expect one sovereign state to act in accordance with another's Constitution). By 14 April, over 1,000 farms had been invaded, and 612 occupied.[20] Based on information gathered from the CFU, the Centre on Housing Rights and Evictions (COHRE) released a report later in 2000, summarising the land 'invasions' up to May 2000 (see Table 2.1, overleaf).[21]

By this time over 1,500 (or 28 per cent) of commercial farms had been invaded. 411 (27 per cent) of the invasions had been violent and had cost in the region of Z$430 million (US$7.2 million).[23] The verification of these figures is difficult. As Marongwe has stated:

> Statistics regarding the actual numbers of farms occupied varied according to source and time. Thus the [ZNLWVA], [the CFU], the police and the press each gave different figures on the extent of occupations. The figures from police, for example, only related to commercial farmers who had actually reported cases. Various experts have suggested that statistics could be

Table 2.1 Number of Farm 'Invasions' per Province in Zimbabwe

CFU Administrative Province[22]	Number of invasions	Percentage of farms invaded	Total number of farms in province
Mashonaland East	415	39	1,064
Mashonaland Central	331	38	871
Mashonaland West (South)	137	32	428
Mashonaland West (North)	234	24	975
Masvingo	84	24	350
Midlands	98	23	426
Manicaland	111	20	555
Matabeleland	115	16	719
TOTAL	**1,525**	**28**	**5,446**

deliberately manipulated to support particular agendas ... and so figures for total farms occupied at any given time, or for levels of violence, cannot be divorced from organisational propaganda. In addition, the informal nature of the occupations meant that the date tended anyway to be rather crude.[24]

Nevertheless, there is a general consensus that by June 2000 there were widespread land occupations across the country. With the approaching election, the occupations had increased in frequency and violence. After the referendum loss, Mugabe and ZANU-PF began to refer to the struggles over the land as the Third Chimurenga.[25] In terms of ideology, this campaign focused on the land question as the unresolved crisis of the First and Second Chimurengas.[26] Mugabe wrote later:

We knew and still know that land was the prime goal for King Lobengula as he fought the British encroachment in 1883; we knew and still know that land was the principal grievance for our heroes of the First Chimurenga, led by Nehanda and Kaguvi. We knew and still know it to be the fundamental premise of the Second Chimurenga and thus a principal definer of the succeeding new Nation and State of Zimbabwe. Indeed we know it to be the core issue and imperative of the Third Chimurenga which you and me are fighting, and for which we continue to make such enormous sacrifices.[27]

A massive propaganda operation was undertaken, with continuous and repetitive advertisements in the local press stressing the importance of the latest evolution of the struggle. The 'centrepiece' of ZANU-PF's political strategy after 2000 was their slogan: 'The land is the economy, the economy is the land.'[28] This slogan framed all of Zimbabwe's political, economic and social woes as arising from failed land reform. In addition it created the illusion that the sole solution to these problems was successful redistribution of land to 'loyal' Zimbabweans. Indeed, the occupation of farms in Masvingo in February 2000 was 'hailed as the founding moment of the "Third Chimurenga"'.[29] The whole crusade of the Third Chimurenga was steeped in the nationalist discourse of the Liberation War. Mugabe appeared dressed in army fatigues and urged his followers to declare war on those who did not support ZANU-PF.

After the referendum defeat, ZANU-PF MP Isaac Mackenzie warned whites:

> Let me assure you whites here, that once you support MDC, ZANU is not going to treat you as business people, but as politicians. Then if you are treated as politicians, it is like signing your own death warrants. The political storm will not spare you. Let you be informed that our reserve force, the war veterans, will be set on you.[30]

White farmers were the main target of this attack. The language surrounding the land reforms and ownership debates became less about land, and more about war and political affiliation.

As one MDC parliamentarian explained, 'Every time there has been pressure, the government has responded with pressure of its own, and white farmers are a soft target.'[31] For instance, in April 2000 Mugabe declared that 'until the whites transform positively and really show that they are allies who are prepared to live side by side with us, we will consider them as enemies.' Later in the year he cemented the farmers as enemies of the state: 'Let us bring home to the commercial farmers of the CFU that they have declared war against the people of Zimbabwe who have every determination to win it and will no doubt win that fight.'[32] The rhetoric of the Third Chimurenga was designed to group all those who were against the government, into 'the enemy'. As Brian Raftopoulos has commented:

> The thrust of the attacks was delivered in an anti-imperialist trope that identified internal opposition as unpatriotic 'enemies of the state', and therefore

beyond the pale of the rule of law. Furthermore the attacks sought to justify the denigration of civic and political rights as minority concerns, in the name of a selective articulation of redistributive issues around the land question.[33]

The language employed, coupled with the government's sanctioning of violence, meant that all those labelled as the opposition, or enemies of the state, were open to attack and violence without any legal protection from the state.

Much of this violence was directed at securing ZANU-PF a victory in the June 2000 general elections. While urban MDC members and affiliates were suffering from crackdowns, in the countryside many of the more vocal MDC-supporting farmers were the victims of targeted attacks. David Stevens and Alan Dunn were two of the more notable white farmers attacked and killed (on 15 April in Murehwa and 13 May in Seke respectively) because of their MDC connections.[34] Two other prominent famers persecuted for their MDC affiliations were Iain Kay and Roy Bennett, who have faced a multitude of abuses since 2000 but who escaped the fate of Stevens and Dunn. By the time of the June elections, six farmers had been killed due to violence on occupied commercial farms, and all were proclaimed to have MDC links.[35] Whether this is true in all cases is debateable, but this wave of killings had a massive effect on the morale of the farming community. In total, by July 2000, 32 people had been killed as a result of political violence in Zimbabwe since the land invasions began.[36]

The violence of the election campaign, while directly affecting many white farmers, was focused on a much larger target. The white population was so small that it had no real chance of influencing the election results. However, the labour force on commercial farms represented a huge voting block. It is estimated that in 2000 there were over 300,000 full-time farm labourers employed across the country. The total population of labourers and their families living on farms could have been nearly two million.[37] This meant that of the 4.5 million eligible voters in the country, fully a fifth resided on commercial farms. ZANU-PF feared that these voters, because of their affiliation to white farmers, would be disposed to vote for the MDC and could have acted as a decisive swing vote between the rural strongholds of ZANU-PF, and the urban centres which were predominantly MDC.[38] ZANU-PF was keen to reduce the voting ability and unity of this block and did so with the use of widespread and wholesale violence. The targeting of the farms was also a tactic in reducing financial support for the MDC, much of which was perceived to have come from white farmers.[39]

It is important to note that there were divisions within government about the processes of land reform and the land occupations. As Alexander has illustrated, some in ZANU-PF saw the land occupations as 'no more than symbolic "demonstrations" that would end once the state was empowered to act on land reform.'[40] After the March 2000 high court ruling against the land occupations, Minster of Home Affairs Dumiso Dabengwa openly declared that the land reforms were no longer necessary because the rejected constitutional clauses on land had been gazetted. He said that there was no longer any need to 'demonstrate' and that those still occupying land should be evicted. He was immediately contradicted by Mugabe and attacked by war veteran leaders. In April, Vice-President Joseph Msika iterated Dabengwa's comments, stating that the occupations should cease because the constitutional amendments rejected in the referendum had now been enacted. He too was singled out and criticised for his actions.[41] Mugabe dismissed his concerns and stated that, 'This is not a problem that can be corrected by the courts; it is a problem that must be corrected by the government and the people of Zimbabwe.'[42]

There were also divisions among the war veterans. Many war veterans fully supported the land occupations and led movements on farms, often remaining in situ to supervise the settlers after the initial occupation. However, many others denounced the occupations and the violence involved. In May 2000, a group of veterans formed the Liberators' Platform for Peace and Development. One of the organisers of this group said of the fast-track land reforms: 'True war veterans are not involved in these invasions. It is only a vocal few that are being manipulated by politicians and mainly political hooligans who are involved.'[43] Alexander and McGregor also noted that the Zimbabwe National Liberation War Collaborators' Association, which represented 'youth who had supported guerrillas during the war, were similarly critical.'[44] These groups maintained their anxieties about the land reforms and in 2004 the renamed Zimbabwe Liberators' Platform claimed that 'less than 50 genuine war veterans spearheaded the land invasions' and that by and large, war veterans were dismayed at the state of affairs in Zimbabwe because the abuses and political violence that had taken place meant that their 'sacrifices [during the Liberation War and after] were in vain.'[45]

The gathering range of forces against white farmers led many to seek help and advice from the CFU. Tensions rose and many questioned what, if anything, the CFU was doing for its members in the face of increasing insecurity. Talk of stayaways and farming stoppages was mooted but ultimately came to nothing as the CFU steadfastly stuck to its chosen path of negotiating with the government and war veterans to resolve the crisis (see Chapter Three for more on this approach by the CFU). This was despite the fact that neither the government nor the war veterans respected any of the promises they had made in the past. One obvious case in point was the volte-face on the 1998 Donors Conference. More pertinently, a CFU and Zimbabwe Tobacco Association (ZTA) delegation met with Mugabe and other high-ranking members of ZANU-PF in April 2000 to discuss the situation on the farms.[46] In particular, the meeting discussed the farmers' fears regarding the security situation after the death of David Stevens. Mugabe expressed regret at Stevens' death and concluded the meeting by saying 'we should never lose hope. The farmers must play their part in Zimbabwe, and we are sorry for those who have been affected by the current situation, as we know many are good neighbours'.[47] However, the violence continued to escalate and the main issues were left unaddressed.

Many in the farming community believed that the situation on the farms and the vitriolic rhetoric employed would resolve itself after the election. The ZTA president Richard Tate is alleged to have said, 'the sooner the elections are over and ZANU is back in power, the sooner we can get back to the business of farming'.[48] While this caused some consternation within farming circles, there seemed to be support for this belief from the farming hierarchy. However, the government continued to push for compulsory acquisition and designated 841 farms for acquisition, based on the 1997 lists.[49] The debates around land became increasingly polarised as the elections approached. In those elections, despite massive vote rigging and extreme levels of violence, the MDC won a very impressive 47 per cent of the vote, compared to ZANU-PF's 49 per cent.[50] This gave ZANU-PF 62 seats and the MDC 57. Without the subsequent allocation of 30 unelected seats, ZANU-PF would have found it impossible to govern.[51] Having secured this narrow victory, Mugabe and ZANU-PF maintained an active interest in the land occupations and reforms. As Alexander observed, for 'an important faction in the ruling party, the land occupations were not simply about making the case for land redistribution – they were also about creating the conditions for a particular kind of political campaign'.[52] Central to that campaign was identifying 'sell-outs' and traitors of the ZANU-PF nationalist agenda. The election result did not resolve this. Rather, the close election results revealed the strength of the opposition forces. There was therefore still a pressing need to ensure that these 'unpatriotic' elements were addressed and eliminated.

Almost immediately after the elections, on 15 July 2000, the government launched the Accelerated Land Reform and Resettlement Implementation Plan (or Fast Track Land Resettlement Programme).[53] Under this scheme the government planned to settle over 5 million hectares. Two basic models were to be used: A1, which was based on individual self-contained units that would focus on small-scale farming with some communal rights; and A2, which was intended for medium and large-scale commercial farming.[54] With this sponsorship from the state, land occupations continued, as did the violence. The process of *jambanja* spread and a new youth militia was established. This force became another active participant in the escalating aggression on white farms.[55]

The CFU continued to seek a legal solution to the problem. It launched legal challenges in July but these only served to attract more vitriol from Mugabe and Hunzvi.[56] Besides, legal directives and government defeats in court did nothing to slow ZANU-PF's resolve to follow through with the fast-track reforms. The government continued to gazette farms for acquisition.[57] With the situation spiralling out of control, the CFU tried several initiatives to negotiate with government. One of the most notable of these was its backing of a plan formulated by Nick Swanepoel and John Bredenkamp – farm owners with close ties to ZANU-PF – called the Zimbabwe Joint Resettlement Initiative (ZJRI), which proposed an immediate offer to government of one million hectares of land for planned and orderly resettlement, with a further four million hectares to follow over a longer period of time.[58] But this initiative failed dismally and only served to further fragment the farming community.[59]

It was clear by this stage that the settlers and occupants were not going to go away. Overt government support and a blatant disregard for the judicial rulings over the issue made it obvious that the problem was to have no easy resolution. It is this government support that clearly differentiates the land occupations after 2000 from those earlier in Zimbabwe's post-independent history. Documents circulating in war veteran committees allude to an Operation 'Give-Up-And-Leave'.[60] The document entitled 'On the white farmers and opposition', suggested that this Operation should be 'thoroughly investigated and planned so that farmers are systematically harassed and mentally tortured and their farms destabilised until they "give in" and "give up"'. The document is dated 25 July 2000, just ten days after the launch of the fast-track programme. By this Operation:

> a farmer was not simply marched off the land at gunpoint; instead, a motley gang of what is best described as lumpen-proletariat, headed by a war veteran, would begin a war of attrition against the farmer and family, with a series of lawless acts designed to make life intolerable for the inhabitants of the farm.[61]

Selby mentions this document too and comments that its existence was confirmed in discussions with an anonymous government official.[62]

After the June 2000 elections this became the general pattern of land invasions, as the CFU situation reports attest.[63] All of the autobiographies written by farmers after 2000 supply evidence of this type of situation occurring on their farms (see Chapter Six). However, episodes of extreme violence persisted. A JAG report documented the atrocities against farmers and farm workers over the period 2000 to 2005, and detailed a very high level of human rights violations on commercial farms, ranging from political intimidation to murder. From a survey sample of 147 farmers, the report calculated over 50,000 separate violations. Most concerned political intimidation or coercion, but the report also detailed over 2,000 cases of assault, 2,000 death threats, 300 hostage situations, 32 murders and 800 cases of torture. If these figures are extrapolated to the whole community, then the number of violations is indeed vast.[64] The report noted that war veterans and youth militia were the most common perpetrators, followed by ZANU-PF members; the list also included elected officials, army and air force members, and police.

The government took every opportunity to extol the successes of the fast-track land reforms. At the 44th Ordinary Session of the Central Committee of ZANU-PF, its first meeting after the June 2000 elections, Mugabe presented the results of the reforms. He claimed that by this time 2,190 properties, measuring just over 5.5 million hectares, had been gazetted and that over 127,000 families had been 'settled'.[65] However, as 2001 progressed the land situation became steadily more fragmented and difficult to comprehend. Farmland may have been gazetted, but white farmers mostly remained in place as they continued with legal challenges.[66] While gazette lists continued to be published, new invasions took place and the violence continued. By the end of November over 2,200 farms had been listed.[67] Sporadic listings continued over the next few months as the whole process became increasingly chaotic and unpredictable. However, on 29 June 2001, another list of over 2,000 farms was gazetted, and was republished in an 18-page supplement to the state-owned *Herald* newspaper.[68] In effect over 5,200 properties had now been listed, representing over 90 per cent of all commercial farmland.[69]

By this stage ZANU-PF had managed to infiltrate and subvert the judiciary. From the start of *jambanja*, the judiciary had been opposed to the government's abuses of power. In November 2000, the Supreme Court had declared the fast-track resettlements illegal and had ordered the removal of people who had been fast-tracked onto commercial land. Subsequently, High Court Judge Chidyausiku, widely known to have ZANU-PF sympathies, issued a Provisional Order to prevent the Supreme Court removing fast-tracked settlers. The Supreme Court responded on 24 November, declaring that Chidyausiku had no jurisdiction in the matter and that the original Supreme Court order stood. The government refused to comply with these orders and the persistence of the Supreme Court and its judges attracted the wrath of the ruling party. Explicit threats against the judges were often made. The Supreme Court held by their principles and in December declared that:

> the rule of law has been persistently violated in the commercial farming areas and that the people in those areas have suffered discrimination in contravention of the constitution. The Court further states that people in those areas have been denied the protection of the law and had their rights of assembly and association infringed. The Court orders the Minister of Home Affairs and the Commissioner of Police to restore the rule of law in commercial farming areas by no later than July 1st 2001.[70]

After this the pressure on independent judges intensified. In particular, the two white judges, Chief Justice Anthony Gubbay and fellow Supreme Court Justice Nick McNally, were targeted. After withstanding the threat of violence for some time, Gubbay eventually resigned in early 2001. Mugabe then took the opportunity to expand the court from five to eight seats and appointed judges known to support ZANU-PF, thus ensuring the court's support. The court duly reversed its previous decisions that had declared the fast-track reforms unconstitutional.[71] The court now became a 'pliant instrument of state power that would allow the government to curtail the organised political opposition and clamp down on criticism and dissent'.[72]

In 2001, Operation 'Give-Up-And-Leave' caused large numbers of farmers to abandon their farms for good. Compounding the effects of this Operation was a breakdown of all communication between farmers, war veterans, the state and other institutions. No one seemed to know who was in charge. Countless stories were recorded of farmers receiving assurances or instructions from war veterans or occupiers, only for these to be contradicted by the district or provincial administrator, who was then in turn criticised or overruled by representatives from the Ministry of Agriculture and Lands, or more senior war veterans. The politics of co-ordination and control of the invasions became a tangled, overlapping and intricate web that was often deliberately confused to further undermine farmers' and their representatives' efforts to manage the situation. (See Chapter Three for analysis of this in *The Farmer* magazine and Chapter Six for the discussion about it in oral interviews with evicted white farmers.)

Despite various internal and international attempts at resolution, the land issue remained unresolved and a constant focus of international and local media. The Commonwealth became increasingly concerned about the lawlessness in Zimbabwe. In March, after the 15th meeting of the Commonwealth Ministerial Action Group, a statement was issued that questioned the processes of law in the county.[73] As a result, a meeting was organised in Abuja, Nigeria, in September 2001. Present at this meeting were nine Commonwealth Foreign Ministers, under the Chairmanship of Nigeria, and representatives of the Zimbabwean government (Mugabe himself did not attend). A wide range of issues and solutions were discussed which included talks of suspending Zimbabwe from the organisation. It was ultimately agreed that there would be a return to law in Zimbabwe and a resolution of the land crisis. The written document stated:

> Land is at the core of the crisis in Zimbabwe and cannot be separated from other issues of concern to the Commonwealth, such as the rule of law, respect for human rights, democracy and the economy. A programme of land reform is, therefore, crucial to the resolution of the problem.[74]

With a land deal agreed upon, Britain promised to make a large contribution to land resettlement in Zimbabwe as long as the rule of law was re-established. Mugabe said he could not accept the agreement without consultation with his party, showing how politicised the whole land reform agenda had become.[75] The agreement was duly accepted and the international community saw the Abuja deal as a significant breakthrough. However, many commentators remained sceptical that the Abuja agreement would result in any real change in the situation. ZANU-PF's recent past record was littered with the ruins of broken promises and Abuja proved no different.

A fundamental problem of the agreement was that, on one hand, it was vague enough for the ZANU-PF government to manipulate it and claim it was a product of international support. On the other hand, its focus on the land issue implied that all the other social, political and economic crises were merely a result of failed land reform.[76] The Zimbabwe Human Rights NGO Forum summarised the agreement:

> The major thrust of the Abuja Agreement was the land issue, placing this at the 'core of the crisis in Zimbabwe'. Other aspects of the crisis, such as the breakdown in the rule of law, disregard for human rights and the absence of democratic principles were mentioned as being further 'implications' of the crisis. This wording of the Abuja Agreement resulted in Government focusing solely on the land issue and disregarding other matters of concern addressed by the Abuja Agreement. Subsequent perceptions of the crisis in Zimbabwe, particularly within Africa, have been tainted by this patently erroneous conception.[77]

As it was, the Abuja Agreement was extremely short-lived and can be understood in retrospect as an attempt by Mugabe and ZANU-PF to alleviate international pressure. No attempt was made to adhere to the agreement and, in the weeks after the meeting, more acquisition lists were published and the farm invasions continued.[78] Commonwealth observers arrived in Zimbabwe at the end of October to see if the Abuja conditions were being observed, found they were not and made it clear that no funds would be released until issues of law and order were resolved.[79] ZANU-PF's charade of appeasement had staved off Zimbabwe's immediate exclusion from the Commonwealth but the country was suspended from the organisation the following year. Mugabe subsequently withdrew Zimbabwe from the Commonwealth in 2003 when it was announced that the suspension would continue.[80]

In the run-up to the presidential elections of March 2002, political violence and intimidation once again increased. Fourteen people were killed in February as a result of political violence.[81] As a Human Rights NGO Forum report attests:

> It has been a frequent comment by human rights groups and election observer groups that gross human rights violations seem to be prevalent during election periods. The Human Rights Forum itself has issued a number of reports making such allegations, and at least one international human rights body has alleged that human rights violations are more common during elections than at other times.[82]

Events in the countryside conformed to this pattern and the CFU reports show evidence of increased violence and intimidation in this period.[83] Mugabe again 'won' a narrow victory in an election that was keenly contested by Morgan Tsvangirai and widely seen as rigged to prevent him attaining power.[84]

Tsvangirai's loss in the presidential election was a terrible blow for the farming community, who had put a great deal of faith in his victory. The enthusiasm and hope offered by this possibility was obliterated by Mugabe's victory. As a consequence, many farmers began to seek compromises with war veterans, occupiers and politicians in the form of subdivision proposals or co-existence agreements. According to Selby, the Provincial Governor of Manicaland, Oprah Muchinguri, was particularly keen to see such agreements reached. At the beginning of 2003, 400 of the 600 farmers in the province were operating on downsized or shared farms.[85] However, these agreements themselves became increasingly difficult to establish. The government tried to institutionalise the process, but the requirement to do so and the long-term significance of such co-existence agreements remained unclear.[86] As Selby correctly illustrated, these forms of 'co-existence' were severely biased against farmers, and were usually used by both sides for their own ends. For farmers, they offered a chance to buy time and organise their departure. For the occupiers, it was a chance to get a foot in the door, observe the farming process and acquire their share in the growing of a crop they would put little or no input into. Usually, farmers were evicted before or during the harvest, leaving the occupiers to reap the profits.[87]

Objections to the land occupations had been aired as soon as the movements onto commercial land started in February 2000, but by mid-2001 serious questions were being raised about who the real beneficiaries of the fast-track land reforms were. Defenders of the occupations, like Moyo, maintained that the land movement was the 'painful beginnings of a longer-term democratisation process'.[88] Moyo claimed that:

> Much of the negative fallout from the occupations movement, including its use for the short term political gain, has to be weighed more seriously against the longer term gains to the broader democratisation process, of creating space for awareness and participation in the basic social struggles hitherto dominated by formal state structures and urban civil society organisations.[89]

There was a sense and expectation that the rural peasant population would be able to capitalise on the spaces opened up by the land reforms. However, the fundamental problem with such readings of the land reforms, even if one ignores the horrific levels of violence associated with them, is the lack of evidence to support these claims. In contrast, there have been numerous allegations of political elites abusing the rights of farm workers and rural populations for their own ends. In addition, many rural populations have suffered directly as a result of the farm invasions, as farm stores, food sources and other social infrastructure such as clinics and schools have been shut down.[90]

The issue of who was getting the land was raised within ZANU-PF itself. In February and June 2002, the Ministry of Lands and Agriculture published lists of new landowners in the *Sunday Mail*. These lists were seized upon by many non-governmental organisations who then added their own findings to them. The Crisis in Zimbabwe Collation (CZC) produced its own list (incorporating only the February *Sunday Mail* listings) which it believed confirmed that a large number of government officials were in possession of commercial farmland.[91] JAG released another list, which built upon both of those published in the *Sunday Mail*. Its 72 pages listed 'VIP' landowners who had benefitted from government's manipulation of the land occupations.[92]

The fast-track programme, which officially ran from July 2000 to August 2002, was ostensibly designed to alleviate all land problems in Zimbabwe.[93] However, as Alexander has commented, 'struggles over land were far from complete'.[94] At the beginning of 2003, a confidential national audit compiled by Minister of State in Deputy President Joseph Msika's office, Flora Buka, was leaked to the press.[95] This report detailed serious irregularities with the redistribution of land, including:

> The displacement of resettled people by the party élite; élite struggles over

prime land particularly in Mashonaland West and Mashonaland Central provinces; the use of 'hired thugs' by sections of the Zanu PF leadership to press their demands; the problem of multiple ownership amongst prominent members of the ruling élite.[96]

The audit listed a number of party members who had been involved in these affairs, as well as a list of those who were multiple farm owners. These allegations constitute what Sachikonye has described as 'a competitive scramble for commercial farms by members of the ruling elite'.[97] They threatened to severely undermine any remaining legitimacy of the fast-track land reforms amongst their supporters. In response, the government commissioned a further audit in May 2003, the findings of which were to be made public in the form of the Utete Report. Mugabe also issued a directive ordering ZANU-PF officials to give up 'excess' farms.[98] In August the commission reported its findings. According to the report, 6,422 farms had been gazetted, amounting to just under 11 million hectares of land. Of these, 2,652 (4 million hectares) were allocated to A1 settlers; 127,000 families were allocated land, with over 97 per cent taking up the offer. 1,672 farms, totalling more than 2 million hectares, were allocated to A2 farmers. This was offered to over 7,000 beneficiaries, but with only a 66 per cent take-up rate.[99] In addition, the report claimed that there were 1,323 white farmers still in possession of 1,377 farms amounting to almost 1.2 million hectares (or 3 per cent of the country).[100] However, the Utete Report also included the caveat that some of its sections, 'dealing with the highly controversial issue of multiple ownership of farms by members of the elite, while discussed by the commission, were not [to be] made public'.[101] This statement confirms how sensitive, complicated and problematic the issue of farm acquisition by the party elite was.

According to the International Crisis Group (ICG), the report 'was an effort to limit the internal ZANU-PF conflicts that had erupted over land acquisition, while also trying to serve as a bridge to eventual reconciliation with the international community'.[102] It is debatable how far Mugabe and ZANU-PF were trying to reach out to the international community at this stage, but it is clear that there were attempts to reinforce the legitimacy of the fast-track reforms within the party, the war veteran organisations and the rural constituencies. However, the Utete Report was widely criticised outside the party as overly simplistic, in that it failed to address any of the controversies regarding violence and political intimidation on the land. In addition, the fate and suffering of ex-farm workers were barely addressed.

By 2004, it was estimated that about 600 white farmers either remained on their farms, or were farming by 'remote control'. The Utete figure of 1,323 was out of date and only accounted for farms that were officially designated for acquisition. Many farmers had left farms that had never been designated.[103] The CFU claimed that there were about 1,000 white owned farms still in operation, but as Selby points out, this was probably an over-estimate to retain some confidence in the sector. JAG estimated that less than 500 farmers were still farming. At the beginning of 2004, the actual figure probably stood somewhere between the two; any greater precision is impossible to determine, as many farmers who did remain on the land did all they could to remain anonymous. Farming communities across the country had been obliterated and many institutions that had been the bedrock of local social interaction no longer existed. At a national level the CFU itself had been declared 'irrelevant' by the Minister of Agriculture Joseph Made in 2003.[104] Its refusal to confront the government and stick to a policy of negotiation had undermined the CFU's integrity amongst many farmers. In response, a number of new organisations claiming to represent the true interests of farmers came into existence, further fragmenting the community.[105] The confusions about what was happening on and with the land continued to grow as the crises affecting the country at large worsened. What is clear is that by 2004 the farming community had been almost entirely destroyed by the government's fast-track land reforms and ZANU-PF's ambition to hold on to power at any cost.

Conclusion

The radical events since 2000 represent the latest episode in a story that refutes simplistic analysis based upon stereotypes and binaries. The contemporary nature of the fast-track land reforms means that a great deal of research is needed to fully understand its long-term ramifications and consequences.[106] As Phimister has noted:

> Such has been the pace and scale of the crisis that it has far outstripped the ability of most commentators either to anticipate its trajectory, or to develop an historically grounded critique of its dynamics. Virtually every book, article

or position paper produced ... has been struck by the enormity of Zimbabwe's predicament, but only a handful have been able to see beyond its immediate causes.[107]

It is hoped that these opening chapters provide some of this depth by making connections between events after 2000 and those earlier in Zimbabwe's history. The already highly politicised and complex debate on the land question in Zimbabwe has been further complicated and politicised by the controversial events since 2000. Because they have occurred within an interrelated political, economic and social crisis, the place of white farmers in Zimbabwe's past and present remains confused and contested.

The story of white farmers and their part in the land invasions has often been simplified and manipulated to fit particular narratives. From ZANU-PF propaganda to international journalism, white farmers and what they represent have been employed to support or undermine broader political projects. The chapters that follow will develop understandings of white farmers by investigating their own reactions to the political and economic changes in Zimbabwe. By analyzing their own forms of expression and writing, the book will delve behind the simplistic constructs of white farmers and seek a deeper and more nuanced representation of them and their relationship to post-colonial Zimbabwe. In doing so, it aims to build upon the work of Selby and McKenzie, who have written in detail on the history of white farmers but have omitted sources that reveal how the farmers themselves saw and understood their interactions with the state, government and country at large. The next chapter begins this process with a detailed look at one of the most influential pieces of white farming literature, *The Farmer* magazine. It explores how this magazine covered many of the events discussed in the last two chapters and the political outlook of the white farming community. It thereby taps into many of the farming discourses that are examined throughout this book and traces their development, flux and evolution.

Notes

1   McCarthy, 2007, pp. 177-8.
2   Raftopoulos, 2009, p. 210.
3   The Justice for Agriculture (JAG) Trust and the General Agricultural and Plantation Workers Union of Zimbabwe (GAPWUZ), 2008; GAPWUZ, 2010.

4 Alexander, 2006, p. 186.

5 Marongwe, 2003, pp. 179-182.

6 Chaumba, Scoones and Wolmer, 2003, p. 540.

7 *Daily News,* 27 November, 2001, quoted in Chaumba, Scoones and Wolmer, 2003, p. 540.

8 Alexander and McGregor, 2001, p. 511 and footnote 2.

9 Alexander, 2003, p. 100. Marongwe also talks about war veterans paying people to occupy land, but not where that money came from. Marongwe, 2003, p. 169.

10 Alexander, 2003, p. 99.

11 Selby, 2006, p. 300.

12 Catherine Buckle talks of the reinstitution of the Agric Alert after 2000 in her autobiography. Buckle, 2001, chapter one.

13 All CFU situation reports used to be online on the CFU's website. However, that website has been terminated and the information no longer shared publically. The CFU has a new website (www.cfuzim.org), but this no longer carries the situation reports. These reports were reproduced on the online news service, zimbabwesituation.com. The situation reports referenced here have been collected from the zimbabwesituation.com website.

14 Selby, 2006, p. 300.

15 Worby pointed out that there were alternative ways of describing the land occupations: 'Other descriptors are, however, in circulation. The Commercial Farmers Union – the main political organ of the white commercial farmers – has used the term "illegal occupier" to describe land invaders in the chronicle of events posted on its official website. [Sam] Moyo ... identifies several more terms in this morally laden lexicon, including "land grabbing", "trespassing" and, his own choice, "self-provisioning"'. Worby, 2001, p. 476, footnote 1.

16 CFU, *Situation Report,* 16 March 2000.

17 ICG, 2004, p. 75.

18 Ibid.

19 This was done on 5 April 2000. Ibid., pp. 76-7.

20 CFU, *Situation Report,* 14 April 2000. Unfortunately this was the last situation report that contained these figures. The ones that followed for the next two years were more qualitative about events. No more public lists of total numbers of farms invaded were produced.

21 Centre on Housing Rights and Evictions (COHRE) 2000, Annex 3, pp. 73-5.

22 The CFU administrative provinces are slightly different to the provincial boundaries. The large number of farms in Mashonaland West province made it too administratively problematic, so it was divided in two to make Mashonaland West (South) and Mashonaland West (North).

23 Although the COHRE report supplied figures of the costs of the land occupations, it gave no indication of how this cost was calculated and by whom. This makes these figures problematic, but does give some indication of the impact and scale of the land occupations. COHRE 2000, pp. 73-5.

24 Marongwe, 2003, p. 167.

25 Lawrence Vambe supplies this definition of *chimurenga*: 'The term *chimurenga*

comes from the name of a legendary *Shona* ancestor, *Murenga Sororenzou*. Believed to be a huge man with a head (*soro*) the size of an elephant's (*renzou*), *Murenga* was well known for his fighting spirit and prowess, and legend has it that he composed war-songs to encourage his soldiers to continue the fight against their enemies in pre-colonial Zimbabwe. In the 1970s, African freedom fighters in bases in Tanzania, Mozambique, and Zambia, and some local Zimbabwean artists struggling for Zimbabwe's independence, derived inspiration from *Murenga's* fighting spirit and composed songs in a genre that they called *chimurenga*. The word *chimurenga* refers to war or the struggle against any form of tyranny'. Vambe, 2004, p. 167.

26 Logan, 2007.

27 Emphasis in original. Mugabe, 2001, pp. 92-3. These comments were based upon remarks made by Mugabe at the 48th ordinary session of the Central Committee meeting on 21 September 2001.

28 Raftopoulos and Phimister, 2004, p. 368.

29 Alexander, 2006, p. 186.

30 Quoted in Bond and Manyana, 2002, p. 82.

31 ICG, 2004, p. 75.

32 Zimbabwe Human Rights NGO Forum, 2007, pp. 24-5.

33 Raftopoulos, 2003, p. 231.

34 Selby, 2006, p. 292. Buckle argued that Stevens was not killed 'because he was white or a farmer', rather he 'was murdered for political reasons only', because he was MDC and because he sought to expose ZANU-PF corruption. Buckle, 2002, p. 54. For similar assessments of Alan Dunn's murder, see *CNN.com*, 8 May, 2000. http://archives.cnn.com/2000/WORLD/africa/05/08/zimbabwe.01/ [accessed 20 February 2010].

35 For the murder of Martin Olds (Nyamandhlovu, 18 April 2000), see *BBC News Online*, 18 April 2000. http://news.bbc.co.uk/1/hi/world/africa/717734.stm [accessed, 20 February 2010]. For the murder of John Weeks (Seke, 14 May 2000), see *BBC News Online*, 15 May 2000. http://news.bbc.co.uk/1/hi/world/africa/748598.stm [accessed, 20 February 2010]. For the murder of Tony Oats (Zvimba North, 31 May 2000), see *BBC News Online*, 1 June 2000. http://news.bbc.co.uk/1/hi/world/africa/772544.stm [accessed, 20 February 2010]. For the murder of Willem Botha (Zvimba North, 23 May /2000), see Buckle, 2002, pp. 202-6.

36 Zimbabwe Human Rights NGO Forum, 2000.

37 GAPWUZ, 2010, p. 13. Also, see the JAG Trust and GAPWUZ, n.d.; Sachikonye, 2003.

38 Zimbabwe Human Rights NGO Forum and the JAG Trust, 2007, p. 16; the JAG Trust and GAPWUZ, 2008, pp. 13-4.

39 In particular there was an occasion where a white farmer was shown signing cheques and handing them over to the MDC. Willems, 2005, pp. 101-2.

40 Alexander, 2006, p. 186

41 Ibid., p. 196, footnote 51. Also, see Harold-Barry, 2004, p. 269.

42 ICG, 2004, p. 77

43 Alexander and McGregor, 2001, p. 514.

44 Ibid.

45 Ibid., pp. 40 and 42. At the end of March 2000, the CFU estimated that 15-20 per cent of land occupiers were war veterans. Also, see Alexander, 2003, p. 100, footnote 32.

46 The meeting held on 17 April 2000 was reported in a CFU *Situation Report*, 20 April, 2000. Those who attended the meeting were President R.G. Mugabe, Acting Minister of Lands and Agriculture Joyce Mujuru, Deputy Minister of Lands and Agriculture Olivia Muchena, CFU President Tim Henwood, ZTA President Richard Tate, CFU Director David Hasluck and Father Fidelis Mukonori.

47 CFU, *Situation Report*, 20 April, 2000.

48 Selby, 2006, p. 312.

49 ICG, 2004, p. 79.

50 Raftopoulos, 2009, p. 215.

51 Harold-Barry, 2004, p. 269. With this result ZANU-PF lost the majority needed to change the constitution. The MDC challenged 37 seats won by ZANU-PF in court.

52 Alexander, 2006, p. 186.

53 For the implementation of the Accelerated Land Reform and Resettlement Implementation Plan, see Utete, 2003.

54 Alexander, 2006, p. 187.

55 Ibid. Also, see Solidarity Peace Trust, 2003.

56 For examples, see Alexander, 2006, p. 188.

57 Buckle, 2001, pp. 235-41.

58 Compagnon, 2011, p. 175.

59 Again regional differences made themselves apparent in this initiative. For Selby, this initiative and its failure represented another rift between Matabeleland and Mashonaland farmers. Selby, 2006, pp. 309-10.

60 Personal copy of this document.

61 The JAG Trust and GAPWUZ, 2008, p. 14.

62 Selby, 2006, p. 303, and footnote 838. Also, see a report by Lamb and Bamber in the *Daily Telegraph*. *Telegraph.co.uk*, 26 August, 2001. http://www.telegraph.co.uk/news/worldnews/africaandindianocean/zimbabwe/1338605/Mugabes-secret-plan-to-evict-all-whites.html [accessed, 24 February 2010]. In this article the details of the report are accurate but it was wrongly dated. They say it was circulated in July 2001 but the date on my copy is 25 July 2000. The article is a classic case of sensationalism, extending the issue of 'eviction' to all whites and not just farmers. The article also stated that 'Farmers who resist, it [the Operation document] says, should face the "Pamire-silencing method", a reference to Chris Pamire, a businessman and former Zanu-PF supporter who fell out with Mr Mugabe and was killed in a mysterious road accident. "You know what happened to Pamire" has become a widely used threat.'

63 CFU, *Situation Reports*, June and July 2000.

64 When the survey sample of 147 is extrapolated to the full farming population, then the number of people affected could be well over one million. Whilst this is plausible, this figure may be an exaggeration. Nevertheless, such figures do indicate the prevalence of violence in Zimbabwe's countryside. Zimbabwe Human Rights NGO Forum and the JAG Trust, 2007, p. 2.

65 Mugabe, 2001, pp. 80-1.

66 The Zimbabwe Human Rights NGO Forum and the JAG Trust report noted that over 90 per cent of farmers challenged acquisition orders in courts. Zimbabwe Human Rights NGO Forum and the JAG Trust, 2007, section 3.4.

67 ICG, 2004, p. 84.

68 *The Herald*, 17 November, 2001 (23 farms listed), and 14 December, 2001 (268 farms listed).

69 Harold-Barry, 2004, p. 270.

70 Buckle, 2001, pp. 238-40.

71 ICG, 2004, pp. 89-90.

72 Legal Resources Foundation, 2002.

73 Zimbabwe Human Rights NGO Forum, 2001a, pp. 5-6. The statement was typically understood, but nevertheless committed the organisation to discuss the issue further. The statement read: 'They recalled that at their thirteenth meeting in May 2000, Ministers had expressed concerns over a number of issues in the run-up to Zimbabwe's parliamentary elections. The Ministers were concerned that problems continue, and noted especially recent reports of intimidation of the judiciary and the media. They recalled and affirmed the principles embodied in the Commonwealth Harare Declaration to which all Commonwealth members have pledged their commitment.' Also, see Zimbabwe Human Rights NGO Forum, 2003.

74 The Abuja Agreement, 6 September 2001. For the full text of the agreement, see COHRE, 2000, pp. 84-5.

75 Zimbabwe Human Rights NGO Forum, 2003.

76 Mugabe, 2001, pp. 100-1. Also, see Utete, 2003.

77 Emphasis in original. Zimbabwe Human Rights NGO Forum, 2003, p. 7. Also, see COHRE, 2000, pp. 41-2; ICG, 2004, pp. 95-6.

78 Buckle, 2002, pp. 187, 189, and 191. Buckle records that 110 farms were listed on 7 September, 23 on 17 November, and 268 on 14 December.

79 Ibid., pp. 188-9.

80 Harold-Barry, 2004, p. 272.

81 Buckle, 2002, p. 195.

82 Human Rights NGO Forum, 2006, p. 5.

83 CFU, *Situation Reports*, February and March 2002.

84 Another tool used against the farm worker population was the Citizenship Act of 2001. This stated that anyone with a parent who was not a Zimbabwean by birth, would no longer be considered a citizen of Zimbabwe, and was thus ineligible to vote. 'The government suggested that up to one-third of the farm workers should be considered foreign, despite the fact that they had lived and worked in Zimbabwe for more than one generation.' While the act disenfranchised many white voters too, there were not enough of them to sway the election, but it affected a significant number of farm workers and their families, many of whose parents had come from Mozambique, Malawi and other neighbouring countries. ICG, 2004, p. 93. In addition, see GAP-WUZ, 2010, pp. 56-63; Rutherford, 2007, pp. 105-23.

85 However, Selby also points out that the next Provincial Governor, Mike Nyambuya, was less enthusiastic about such agreements and by 2004 only 200 farmers were

still operating in such a way. The rest had presumably been evicted from their land, but Selby is not explicit on this. Selby, 2006, p. 301.

86 Through the LA3 forms government encourage white farmers to withdraw court cases and submit title deeds, which many farmers refused to do.

87 This paragraph is based on Selby, 2006, pp. 301-2. In an interesting parallel, many white farmers had made alliances with guerrilla forces during the Liberation War in order to protect themselves and continue occupying their land. White farmers also employed similar tactics after 2000 to try and secure a deal to remain on the land. See Chapters Three and Four for more connections to this and discussions of 'affirmative parochialism'.

88 Raftopoulos and Phimister, 2004, p. 371.

89 Moyo, 2001, p. 330. Also, see Yeros, 2002; Moyo and Yeros, 2005.

90 GAPWUZ, 2010, pp. 67-76.

91 Crisis in Zimbabwe Coalition, 2002, Annexure 7, pp. 103-105.

92 This list is available to download on the Zimbabwe Situation website, titled 'Allocation of Farms to Politicians etc'. http://www.zimbabwesituation.com/index.html#down [accessed, 18 June 2010].

93 Utete, 2003, p. 15.

94 Alexander, 2006, p. 192.

95 Selby, 2006, p. 317. For a copy of the report, see SW Radio Africa. http://www.swradioafrica.com/Documents/addendum.htm [accessed, 18 June 2010].

96 Raftopoulos and Phimister, 2004, p. 370.

97 Sachikonye, 2003, p. 42. Also, see Maroleng, 2004, p. 9.

98 Alexander, 2006, p. 192.

99 Utete, 2003, p. 24.

100 Ibid., p. 5.

101 Ibid., p. 2.

102 ICG, 2004, p. 109.

103 For example Catherine Buckle, a point she makes throuhout in her book. Buckle, 2001.

104 Selby, 2006, p. 280.

105 By 2005 there were five bodies representing existing or former white commercial farmers: the CFU, JAG, the Zimbabwe Tobacco Association, the Southern African Commercial Farmers' Association (which was formed by white farmers in Matabeleland to represent their interests after the land occupations in 2000) and Agric Africa (which was a established to pursue the compensation claims of white farmers). Selby, 2006, p. 313.

106 For some of these gaps in the current literature, see Pilossof, 2008a.

107 Phimister, 2005a, p. 119.

3

Discourses of Apoliticism in The Farmer

Any attempt to detach personal experience from critical practices risks leaving memories in the possession of specific groups
– Frederick Cooper[1]

Introduction

This chapter and those that follow focus on the experiences and discourses of white farmers as expressed in written and oral form. The core findings are based on a detailed reading of memoirs and autobiographies (Chapter Five), and on extensive interviews with white farmers still residing in Zimbabwe (Chapter Six). Both of these sources are located in very immediate and specific contexts. Having emerged after 2000 as a direct result of the land reforms and invasions, these texts and interviews are very much artefacts of the events that so fundamentally affected the white farming community. Though the delivery and focus of the farming voice may have changed after 2000 (as Chapters Four, Five and Six all illustrate), it built upon discourses, ways of expression, myths and beliefs held within, and promoted by, the farming community that already existed. This chapter will explore the evolution of farming voices from 1970 to 2000 and reveal how much of the language, discourse and ways of talking so evident in the farming community after 2000 were present before then, and how they have evolved since.

The Farmer magazine, which served the farming community for over 70 years until it was discontinued in 2002, at the height of the land invasions, has hitherto received remarkably little attention in discussions of white farmers in Zimbabwe and their history.[2] It is a wonderfully rich source that offers a range of insights into many important aspects of the community's history, including detailed accounts of the issues and dilemmas that have affected the farming community (such as the coming of independence and the post-2000 land reforms). The principal and express purpose of the magazine was to speak to and for the white farming community. This was a purpose that was well established under white minority rule, but one that had to adapt to the ambiguities of independence and conform to the new political paradigm.

Having to renegotiate and re-imagine their place in a newly independent, black-ruled Zimbabwe was a complicated process for a wholly white group (commercial or otherwise). The CFU and *The Farmer* had the difficult task of ensuring they still spoke to and for their white rural constituencies, while, at the same time, showing themselves willing and active participants in the new national project of 'Zimbabwe'. There are obvious parallels with the Afrikaans mainstream media in post-apartheid South Africa. Of these, Wasserman has written:

> the repositioning of Afrikaans media in the post-apartheid era has been more complicated than a crude shift from ideological nationalism to consumerism. While on one hand there was marked attempt to turn Afrikaans into a mere commodity to be sold to a niche market, this consumerist turn was precariously balanced with an attempt to position Afrikaans within a new identity politics.[3]

In a sense, *The Farmer* was doing just this. It was a direct participant in protecting and fashioning the identity of 'Zimbabwean' white farmers, but at the same time it sought to show the new black government that they, as a group, were comfortable with the new nation and would not do anything to undermine or jeopardise it. Even more pertinent to this chapter, Wasserman and Botma have commented:

> while media in post-apartheid South Africa are central participants in the continued power struggles for control of public discourse and political agendas, explicit support for political parties (as was the case under apartheid) has disappeared. Instead the media's political positioning now only becomes evident through a critical reading of their structures, routines and discourses. Such a reading brings to light the fragmentation and disproportionate distribution of symbolic capital indicative of the fractures and contestations in broader society, as well as continuing political power struggles.[4]

This type of reading is provided here, to illustrate the divisions and power struggles evident within both the white farming community and the country at large, and how the discourses *The Farmer* employed refracted and shaped such divisions.

This chapter will give a general overview of the magazine and its history. It will look at how it was run and managed and the politics of its publication in independent Zimbabwe. It will also consider the message and voice of the magazine, how this was influenced by the CFU and how it discussed crucial issues affecting the farming community. At its core, the chapter is about the political engagement of white farmers over the period under analysis (c. 1970–2002); it provides a thorough examination of their attempts to remain apolitical and shows how these were influenced by their attitude of 'affirmative parochialism' (see below for the explanation of this term).

Contextualising *The Farmer* & Media in Zimbabwe

The publication and production of this type of media has received very little attention in Africa, or globally. Studies have largely concerned themselves with the role of independent versus state controlled media, and the processes of democratisation, interspersed with random case studies on niche or alternative publications.[5] However, *The Farmer* magazine fulfils a very different function as a medium of print in an independent African nation.[6] Its primary concern was informing and speaking for the white farming community of Zimbabwe and, as a result, it had little interest in reporting on wider events that had no bearing on the community. Indeed, its constitution dictated that it was 'apolitical' and it had no direct aims in promoting a 'democratic' society, or in seeking to reach a wider audience beyond that of its already established, well defined and coherent demographic.[7] As a reforming, but far from disenfranchised, elite, white farmers, their Union and as a consequence their publications had to be reconfigured to the new political circumstances after independence. This process is illustrated remarkably well in *The Farmer*. The magazine had to walk a very sensitive political tightrope: while it sought to serve a powerful, white minority this minority resided at the forefront of the new government's ambitions to reform the countryside. It is also clear that the CFU believed that the magazine was read by important audiences outside of the farming community, and in particular government ministries and departments. Thus the magazine was also used as a lobbying tool to promote the image and importance of white farmers.[9]

Apoliticism & Affirmative Parochialism

The term 'affirmative parochialism' provides a useful way to understand the widely articulated discourse of 'apoliticism' within the white farming community.[9] In thinking about the approaches white farmers employed to deal with the state and government, I found the basic understanding of parochialism too narrow. Parochialism is usually invoked in a negative context, typically signifying the narrow, provincial or insular. However, emphasising the affirmative nature of the white farmers' parochialism stresses that it was a chosen strategy. This does not negate or preclude a negative interpretation; it also opens the space for questioning the motives of this inward-looking approach by the white farming community and its leadership which, when assessed in relation to the time of its adoption, assists in understanding why certain decisions were made and enables a more considered appraisal of such actions.[10] The CFU sought to preserve the white farming community as it was, and felt the best way to do this was to promote its isolation and focus only on those issues that affected it. They insulated themselves from events around them by claiming to be 'apolitical'.[11] (The quotation marks will henceforth be dropped from the terms apolitical and affirmative parochialism.) *The Farmer* was an active participant in this process, under the directorship of the CFU. However, this parochialism of the CFU was not consistently implemented. It not only waxed and waned from 1980 to 2002 due to changes within the farming community and hierarchy, but also responded to fluctuations in the political, social and economic climate. Nevertheless, it was a strategy the CFU reinvigorated when the land invasions started in 2000.

We are apolitical, but we do, however, support the government[12]
At the heart of this chapter is an exploration of the discourses of apoliticism employed by white farmers and their representatives. Being political meant having a political alliance and being involved in party politics; the white farming community resisted being defined as such and sought to isolate themselves as apolitical entities that merely served the national interests. As a result they set themselves apart from (and above) the political wrangling of parties and personalities. White farmers often made the distinction between 'national policies, national issues, national affairs' and party politics.[13] While they always saw themselves as having the

national interest at heart (as well as their own opinions of what national policies should be when it came to issues of land and its control and ownership), they believed that they could distinguish themselves and the land they occupied from the politics of elections, race and the land question.

However, there are a number of problems with this stance. Firstly, as Jeffrey Olick stated, 'politics is much more than who gets what, where, when, and how, because such questions often neglect both the symbolic dimensions of politics and the constitution of political interests in the first place.'[14] White farmers had very real 'political interests', particularly after independence, in that they relied on the country's government for their very existence. In the colonial period they benefited from generous subsidies, market policies and land grants; thereafter, favourable land reform policies and market practices ensured their continued existence in the countryside. Farmers claimed to be apolitical but this, in essence, meant that they supported the 'government of the day', as this was the only way to ensure their survival.

In defining themselves as apolitical they assumed a position and a citizenship (i.e. the right to be Rhodesian/Zimbabwean) that they felt was uncontested and accepted by all. However, when this was questioned and directly attacked by government in the 1990s, as Raftopoulos has shown, white farmers had to become 'political' again to proclaim their right of position.[15] This is most clearly illustrated by their early support of the MDC, which invited such a harsh backlash from government that farmers retreated yet again and sought solace in being apolitical. For Engin Fahri Isin:

> becoming political should be seen neither as wide as encompassing all ways of being (conflating being political with being social), nor as narrow as restricting it to being a citizen (conflating polity and politics). The moment the dominated, stigmatised, oppressed, marginalised, and disfranchised agents expose the arbitrary, they realise themselves as groups and constitute themselves as political.[16]

Claiming citizenship cannot be done without being political, yet doing so created severe problems for the farming community and their union.

What is clear is that there is an ebb and flow to this political engagement that is evident in *The Farmer* magazine. Although the union (and *The Farmer*) has always claimed to be apolitical, even during the years of colonial and minority rule, this discourse became more pronounced after independence with an obvious and radical withdrawal from direct political engagement by practically all white farmers. Even Denis Norman, who was president of the Rhodesian National Farmers' Union (RNFU, the CFU's predecessor) at independence and became Zimbabwe's first Minister of Agriculture, said of his time in government: 'I was apolitical and wanted to remain that way.'[17] This appears like a highly untenable position for a government minister, yet it is one that the entire white farming community accepted. They believed they could separate (their) land from politics and make such a stance serve their needs. Indeed, so effective was this withdrawal that it became a defining feature of the farming community. In 2000, John Makumbe stated, 'the white commercial farmers said in 1980 we will not participate in politics, we will farm and make money. I think they said to hell with politics, so they have not contributed politically to good governance and democracy'.[18] Without questioning whether or not white farmers' active participation could have improved governance and democracy in Zimbabwe, the reality was that farmers retreated from the political arena in the belief that this was the most likely way to ensure their survival in Mugabe's Zimbabwe. When this tactic no longer guaranteed exception from Mugabe's attempts to hold on to power, white farmers changed tack and sought to confront the government, as clearly shown by their concerted attempts to affect a 'No' vote in the constitutional referendum of February 2000. However, when this too failed, much of the white farming community, and in particular the CFU, reverted to their apolitical stance in the hope that this would enable their survival in the face of the onslaught on their land, homes and livelihoods by ZANU-PF.

The History, Content & Production of *The Farmer*

The Farmer was not the only agricultural periodical in Zimbabwe. There were two monthlies: *Tobacco News* and *Cattle World*.[19] The South African Farmers Union's magazine, the *Farmer's Weekly*, was also very popular.[20] While these publications attracted specific agricultural audiences, various aspects of *The Farmer* set it apart. Firstly, it was broad and inclusive and sought to speak to the entire farming community, rather than to particular sectors. Secondly, and more importantly, it was published – to all intents and purposes – by the CFU and therefore carried the weight of the union's history and role in Zimbabwe. One letter published in

1994 lauded *The Farmer* as 'the best thing about the CFU' and labelled it the union's 'greatest asset.'[21] Richard Winkfield, a contributor to the magazine for over 16 years concurred, suggesting that *The Farmer* was the single most important implement of the CFU to pursue its goals and communicate with its constituency.[22] Since the magazine's closure, many farmers have been wondering what the union actually does for them. In 2009, Winkfield stressed the importance of starting a new magazine: 'It is very important we put across the message of the CFU because people [think] the CFU [is] not doing anything.'[23] Indeed, there are now moves underway to resuscitate a magazine in *The Farmer*'s image.[24]

The organisation and structure of the magazine are difficult to explore in detail. Since its closure in 2002, papers relating to the administration of the magazine have been unavailable. I therefore contacted key members of *The Farmer*'s editorial board, members of its parent body the Modern Farming Publications Trust (MFP Trust) and contributors to the magazine. The most notable of these were Michael Rook, who joined the editorial team of *The Farmer* in the 1970s and went on to become General Manager of MFP Trust; Felicity Wood, who began working for *The Farmer* in 1989 and became the editor in 1991, before becoming the Editorial Director in 1997; and Richard Winkfield, a Trustee of the MFP Trust. These people provided a wealth of information on the organisation of *The Farmer*, the role of the CFU in running the magazine and how this evolved after independence. All this has been supplemented by a close and detailed reading of the magazine itself. The vast majority of archives, including the CFU's own collections, have fallen in to such disrepair they are essentially unusable; *The Farmer* is one of the few sources left that allows researchers an extended and consolidated look at the farming community.

The genealogy of *The Farmer* is itself unclear and open to interpretation. A magazine entitled *Countrylife*, edited by Lionel Noaks, was founded in 1928, and in 1993 was adopted by *The Farmer*'s editorial board as their original precursor.[25] The earlier date was added to the cover of the magazine, thereby claiming a longer history. However, the precise beginnings of the magazine are unclear. While the final edition of *The Farmer* claimed a coherent and established path back to 1928, it had not done so consistently throughout its history. In 1973 the magazine celebrated its 30th anniversary. According to the anniversary edition, in 1940 Sir Humphrey Gibbs launched *Vuka*, a publication that was adopted in 1943 by the then RNFU as the official journal of the union.[26] There was no mention of 1928, *Countrylife* or Noaks. In 1999, *The Farmer* claimed that the magazine was started by Gibbs and first edited 'on his wife's kitchen table at their Nyamandhlovu farm in 1928'.[27] If this had been the case surely Gibbs would have informed the *Rhodesian Farmer* during the 1973 thirtieth anniversary celebrations, at which he was present.

Vuka underwent several organisational and name changes before it became *The Farmer*. At the end of 1946 it was renamed *The Rhodesian Farmer*.[28] It finally became *The Farmer* in 1979 and stayed that way until its closure in 2002. By independence, *The Farmer* was a weekly magazine, and, but for a few years in the mid-1980s when financial difficulties forced the publishers to make it bi-weekly, remained so until its demise.[29] Furthermore, circulation levels were high within the farming community. At the time of independence, all farmers received a free subscription as part of their levies to the CFU. Even more importantly (and not to be taken for granted) farmers actually read the magazine. A survey carried out by a CFU restructuring committee in 1995 showed that of a sample of just over 1,000 farmers (nearly a quarter of the white farming population), 96 per cent reported that they read it regularly. As the bulk of its readership paid no separate subscription fee, *The Farmer* had to source much of its revenue from advertising; given its wide distribution to such a focused target demographic, it was a prime location for many industries to advertise in.[30]

The Farmer's central concern was to inform its constituency about how to improve their situation with better farming methods. However, due to a lack of expertise in many of the areas covered, the magazine often faced a shortfall of such material.[31] To offset this, *The Farmer* found other ways to fill its pages. With a wide range of pressing concerns affecting the white farming community before and after independence, this was not hard to do. Issues such as land reform, drought management, labour relations and rights, security and safety concerns all featured heavily. So too did the activities of the union and the farming community. Reports of agricultural shows, events, field days and meetings, such as the CFU's annual congress and the various council meetings, all found generous coverage. In addition, it had a relatively healthy letters section and regularly printed feedback from the farming community at large.

Table 3.1 Tag lines of *The Farmer*, 1942–1982

Year	Title of Magazine	Tag line[32]
1942	*Vuka*	Official organ of the Matabeleland Farmers' Union
1943	*Vuka*	Official organ of the Bulawayo Branch of the Rhodesian National Farmers' Union
1946	Changed to *Rhodesian Farmer*	Official organ of the Rhodesian National Farmers' Union (RNFU) and the Rhodesian Tobacco Association (RTA)
1954	*Rhodesian Farmer*	Farm journal of the Federation
1964	*Rhodesian Farmer*	Official journal of the RNFU and the RTA
1978	*Rhodesian Farmer*	Official journal of RNFU
1979	Changed to *The Farmer*	Official journal of CFU
1982	*The Farmer*	Tag line removed and never restored

The magazine was always closely aligned with the union, as the tag lines of the magazine indicate. Table 3.1 shows that from 1942 to 1982 the magazine, in whatever guise it was published, was clearly linked to the union in an official capacity.

However, after independence, this situation changed. The CFU, conscious of the new political dynamics, sought to distance itself from the publication. In 1982 it established the MFP Trust to run the magazine and dropped the 'Official Journal' tag line.[33] These measures were not only instigated to placate the new government, but were also cautionary, amid anxieties that the union would be 'infiltrated' by the government. Rook explained:

> As I recall, MFP Trust was set up [after] independence to safeguard the finances and editorial freedom of the CFU's magazine section in the event that the union would be forced to merge with the organisations representing black master farmers and peasant farmers.[34]

The MFP Trust was established to run the magazine 'independently' of the CFU. But as Rook pointed out, the CFU still had a large degree of influence over the magazine:

> At the beginning [of the 1980s] the CFU president automatically chaired the

Trust with other farming CFU members. Latterly [after 1990] as the union became more involved in land issues it distanced itself from the day to day running of *The Farmer* and allowed the Trust to be chaired by farmers that were not part of the CFU head office structure. However CFU still retained its influence over *The Farmer* as every serving president and CFU director were automatically appointed to the Board of Trustees.[35]

Despite this control, *The Farmer* and the CFU went to great lengths to exaggerate the autonomy of the magazine. Rook explained:

To maintain *The Farmer's* credibility and influence amongst licence holders the CFU hierarchy at times coerced *The Farmer* to go into print assuring readers that it had editorial freedom. *The Farmer* accepted that trade-off with CFU in the knowledge that such an expression of independence could and would be used to full advantage the next time it crossed the line and confronted CFU policy.[36]

The Farmer, then, was not an independent magazine with a mandate to publish what it liked. It was essentially controlled and manipulated by the CFU.

The Editors

While the CFU had established various mechanisms to manipulate and control the magazine, as important in shaping *The Farmer* were the various editors in charge. From 1966 to 2002 there were nine editors, each with their own style and approach to the magazine and each informed by the context of the time (Table 3.2, overleaf).

After UDI, white farmers became a massive burden on the state, and were the front line in the fight against the black 'terrorist' movements. Yet many farmers and the farming Union wanted to retain the image of apoliticism. Thus the following review starts from 1966, to show how the various editors of the magazine responded to these issues and how they negotiated the publication through the radical changes Zimbabwe experienced thereafter.

1966–1976: Dudley Dickin & Ed Duggan

Dickin and Duggan followed very similar patterns of editorship. Neither made their presence felt in the pages of the magazine, nor did they allow

Table 3.2 Editors of *The Farmer* Magazine, 1966–2002

Years in Office	Editor
1966–1974	Dudley Dickin[37]
1974–1976	Ed Duggan
1976–1983	Bernard Miller
1983–1990	Myfanwy van Hoffen
1990–1991	Allistair Syme
1991–1997	Felicity Wood
1997	Nicholas Holme
1997–1998	Felicity Wood/Maud Murungweni[38]
1998–1999	Charles Kabera
1999–2002	Brian Latham

the *Rhodesian Farmer* to become embroiled in the political turmoil of the time.[39] None of the fundamental crises affecting the country in general, and the white commercial farmers in particular, received significant coverage, despite the fact that UDI, the ensuing international sanctions and the intensifying Liberation War caused massive problems for the farming sector.[40] Production costs rocketed, markets became harder to access and the financial situation of many farmers became untenable. The state started a massive campaign to subsidise farmers and keep them on the land.[41] Along with these economic and financial pressures, the fight for black majority rule intensified. Various comments were made about international sanctions and the internal security situation, but very little was said about the impact of these on the farming community. As such, the *Rhodesian Farmer* reacted to UDI in much the same way as many other sectors of white Rhodesia: they ignored the problems and sought to keep their positive, if not highly myopic, outlook intact. As Godwin and Hancock have commented, belief in 'Smithy' and the RF and a wilful ignorance of the liberation movements protected much of white society from analysing their situation in any significant detail.[42]

None of the attacks on farmers by the 'terrorists' received any coverage, even those resulting in farming deaths. The first report of such violence, 'Compensation for Terrorist Victims', was published in 1973. It reported on draft legislation that proposed that the state would compensate 'victims who have suffered damage and loss as a direct result of terrorist activities.' The legislation was to 'cover loss and damage to movable property, personal possessions and household effects, the death of, or injury to, livestock, and the destruction of standing or harvested crops and death or personal injury.'[43] The presentation of this bill shows the remarkable speed of the state in putting forward measures to protect farmers and keep them on the land. By 1973 only three RNFU-registered farmers had been killed. In 1973 a further seven died, apparently from 'terrorist' activity.[44] Farmers were the front line in the war, and as such were vital to the state even if they were unproductive and costly.[45] The Victims of Terrorism Compensation Act of 1973 reimbursed white farmers for 90 percent of financial losses caused by 'terrorists'.[46]

At the same time, the RF government instigated a massive propaganda campaign to keep up the morale of the white population. The nationalist movements were portrayed as weak and poorly supported, with no chance of halting continued white rule.[47] This attitude infused itself into the *Rhodesian Farmer* and no attempt was ever made to offer an alternate assessment of the situation, despite the troubling realities the farmers were facing. This approach typified the magazine's parochial attitude and the deliberate attempt by the RNFU to align itself to those in power. However, once it became clear that the success of the black nationalists was inevitable, the RNFU started its own negotiations with them, independent of the RF, to secure its own future.

Besides these indirect indications of the escalating guerrilla campaign, direct coverage was rare in the *Rhodesian Farmer*. Rather, it focused primarily on matters of farm management and the activities of the union. As the tag line of the magazine at this time indicates ('The official organ of the RNFU and RTA'), the publication was very much aligned with the union and its politics. There were constant messages from the RNFU leadership and the magazine was clearly used as an avenue for them to communicate to their constituency. Where the national political leadership was written about, it was done in glowing terms. In November 1973, Ian Smith was hailed for his integrity, honesty and vision. According to the article, the declaration of UDI 'ranks in magnitude with the troubled Declaration issued by the United States of America almost 200 years ago'. Ian Smith himself was described as 'a dominating figure of heroic stature. A man who, like Caesar, Cromwell or Napoleon, stamped his image on his generation by the sheer force and weight of his personality'.[48] An interview with Smith was carried in the same issue. When asked if there was a lull in the security situation because the desperate 'terrorists' were 'turning against the indigenous African natives', Smith answered categorically that it was not a lull, but permanent state of affairs. He felt that the situation would continue to improve 'until terrorism [was] eliminated'.[49]

Duggan and Dickin made sure they kept the magazine devoid of political statement and very much in line with the RNFU strategy of engaging with the RF. The *Rhodesian Farmer* also presented white farmers as a very united group. But, as Selby has shown, there was much politicking behind the scenes as farming leaders argued about the best ways to handle the crises facing them.[50] These fissures were to increase over the next few years as the situation continued to deteriorate, but the *Rhodesian Farmer* gave no indication of this. After 1976 such a stance became untenable, because of the intensification of the war, and when Bernard Miller took over in that year he brought a very different style of editorship to the magazine.

1976–1983: Bernard Miller

Before arriving at the *Rhodesian Farmer*, Miller had been deputy editor of the *Financial Gazette* in Salisbury. Prior to that he worked as a journalist in the UK.[51] He was in charge of the magazine during the height of the Liberation War, when casualties amongst white farmers were at their heaviest. He also had to manoeuvre a magazine dependent on an increasingly fragmented farming union through the period of the (later) disgraced Zimbabwe–Rhodesia settlement, the eventual coming to power of ZANU-PF in 1980, and the public reconciliation of white farmers and the Mugabe government. These pressures are clearly evident in the magazine. Increasing calls for farming unity were often published alongside calls for political solutions to the ensuing crises that fully catered for the protection and survival of white farmers. The dramatic rise in the death toll plus the weakening of the RF, accompanied by the increasingly hostile rhetoric of land expropriation espoused by ZANU and ZAPU, created the discursive space for the *Rhodesian Farmer* to comment on such affairs directly.

As Miller took up the editorship, ZANU and ZAPU were stepping up their guerrilla campaigns dramatically. Up to 1976, only 20 registered members of the RNFU had been killed by guerrilla activity. In 1976, 31 were killed, followed by 52 in 1977, 115 in 1978 and over 80 in 1979.[52] Both parties, but particularly ZANU, began to articulate a much more radicalised version of their Marxist ideologies. Mugabe said in 1976, 'In Zimbabwe, none of the white exploiters will be allowed to keep a single acre of their land'.[53] As a result, farmers came under severe pressure, resulting in numerous fissures within the farming community and hierarchy.[54]

The *Rhodesian Farmer* increasingly reflected the hopes of the farming community, and began to carry longer and more expressly political editorials. Miller largely defended white farmers' right to land and the importance of their continuity for the good of the country. His editorship covered the years of negotiation and settlement, and he attempted to address this process and to advocate for the protection and continued activity of white commercial farmers. At the same time the RNFU, particularly under the leadership of John Strong, became more active in trying to secure a future for white farmers. This political engagement attracted a negative reaction from many in the farming community who castigated Strong for his position.

In a series of meetings across the country, Strong was accused of being too political.[55] Letters submitted to the *Rhodesian Farmer* expressed the same concerns, which the magazine published with the justification:

> In recent weeks Rhodesian Farmer has published letters attacking the President and Council for allegedly involving the union and its members in politics. / The letters are published in good faith because it is believed that the views of the writers are a sincere attempt to express their fears in their own forum – *Rhodesian Farmer*, which is owned by farmers, and run to serve them and their industry. / It is not the intention here to challenge these views. The Union has already done so pointing out that its initiatives are entirely non-political.[56]

The RNFU and the *Rhodesian Farmer* claimed that the issues and agendas it was pursuing were not indeed 'political', but rather 'national' concerns. Strong, when challenged about being too political responded:

> It is necessary for me to draw attention to the distinction between what are national policies, national issues, national affairs...and that of party politics. / The Union has always been involved in national affairs and national issues.

> We are constantly being called upon – within the context of protecting and promoting agriculture – to be involved in national issues. / Party politics, though is a different matter… and can never be the subject of debate within the union.[57]

Such attempts to circumvent the political implications of their actions show the knots the farming hierarchy tied itself in whilst trying to maintain its apolitical stance. Such attitudes and beliefs continued, and became even more entrenched after independence. The highly political nature of land and its ownership continually reinforced the need to claim apoliticism, even when it was impossible to do so, as it clearly was towards the end of white rule.

Security concerns were also much more prominent during this period. There were many articles on the dangers that vacant and deserted farms posed to the country and fellow farmers. In 1976, Cecil Wolhuter, Matabeleland branch president of the RNFU, warned that the vacant farms in Matabeleland were serious security risks. He also took the opportunity to castigate 'weekend' farmers, who he called 'parasites', for benefiting from the courage and determination of 'real' farmers who consistently put their lives on the line.[58] A year later the *Rhodesian Farmer* picked up on a parliamentary report by Senator Mrs E.A.J. Maclean. Miller used his editorial to evoke sentimental images of vacated land and the perils facing white farmers:

> Unoccupied farms … deserted homesteads echoing their misery across the emptiness of abandoned lands, once won from the wilds and tamed …. Fertile soils, once tilled with care, love and made productive now reverting back to bush providing protection for murderous predators.[59]

The editorial went on to explain that in some eastern districts, over 30 per cent of farms were vacant, with the situation worsening all the time. However, it was also noted that this situation was not constant across the country. Miller then pointed out that 'the major producers – the big league ten per cent – who are responsible for 60 per cent of agriculture's annual turnover of R$504 million (US$756 million) do not operate in the peripheral zones but are mostly centrally-based' and thus largely free from interference.[60] Regardless of this, it was felt that the only way to secure the defences of all farmers was to get farmers back onto the vacated land. A possible solution was 'Kibbutz-style farmer-soldiers [who] might well improve a situation that has reached grave proportions'.[61] Regardless of how these defences were to be organised, the RNFU promised, in the President's 1977 Christmas message, that farmers would 'remain the Frontier of our National effort.'[62] For an apolitical entity, this was a very strong and clear message of support for the RF and the fight against the 'terrorist' threat.

On the political front, it was clear by 1978 that the RF's position had become untenable. International pressures, plus the perceived betrayal of South Africa, meant that Smith and his government had to negotiate with black nationalist movements. It was now clear that some form of black-led government would result. In response to these developments, the RNFU had to negotiate its place in the nation and economy, and the *Rhodesian Farmer* became a key tool in stressing the importance of the farmers to the country and the need to secure their future. Miller wasted no opportunity to highlight the need for political assurances: 'Farmers have the determination and skill to survive but need political will to back them up and secure farming.'[63] There were also calls for unity in the community. At the beginning of 1978 Miller outlined in an editorial the government's plans for a new constitution and an agreement with black nationalists. He outlined the possible benefits of peace and a negotiated settlement, and balanced this assessment by suggesting that such developments 'will bring changes that some see as retrogressive'. Who that 'some' was, is not explained, but it clearly pointed to elements within the farming community who remained highly sceptical about majority rule.

Miller ended that editorial by lauding farmers: '1978 could be the most challenging year yet. Courage, faith and goodwill will be needed. And that farmers and their families possess these three attributes and will use them to our mutual benefit there should be no doubt'.[64] This description of white farmers became standard for Miller, and one he continued to deploy. Later that year he made as much as he could of the courage, bravery and backbone of the farmers. He noted, though, that all of this would count for nothing if the political will to protect and encourage farmers was not present, and he called on the Interim Government to state its position on white farmers immediately and offer assurances on land and property rights. Tellingly, he also asked for the government to assure farmers that, in the event of sale or expropriation, they would be allowed to remit their profits elsewhere.[65]

The RNFU and the *Rhodesian Farmer* were attuned to the rapid pace of political change and 1978 saw significant changes to the running of

both organisations. At its annual congress, the RNFU passed a resolution to change its name to the CFU, if the country changed its name,
as it did in 1979.[66] As Godwin and Hancock wrote, a vote was held at
the same time to change the name immediately, but failed to gain the
necessary two-thirds majority. The opposing argument was that Rhodesia 'wasn't finished yet'.[67] The Union now allowed black farmers to
apply for membership, as the congress was addressed and attended for
the first time by black ministers of state. In line with this, the *Rhodesian
Farmer* was renamed *The Farmer*.[68] The decision to become the Commercial Farmers' Union – 'Zimbabwe' and anything 'Zimbabwean' was
'black' at this time, – may have been seen as apolitical, but was a choice
that made a very clear statement of intent and identity.[69]

At the beginning of 1979, Miller wrote that no one was sure what the
year would bring, other than there would definitely be changes:

> Whether these will be hopefully for the better does not depend so much on
> Rhodesians – Black and White – but on outside Western forces which have to
> date showed a marked reluctance to accept that internally a genuine attempt
> is being made towards a transfer of power to a majority government and a
> restoration of peace.[70]

This stands in stark contrast to the ways in which Dickin and Duggan
avoided making personal statements about the future faced by white
farmers. As had been the case throughout the decade, the liberation
movements were given little credit for their role in bringing the country
to its knees. Rather, the blame for Rhodesia's demise was displaced onto
foreign powers supposedly keen to see the nation fail. The dismissal of
the highly flawed 'peace' and 'election' process in 1978–79 only added to
this sentiment. But the move to black majority rule could not be delayed
any longer. In 1980 the country held its first democratic elections and
ZANU-PF won a landslide victory.

Robert Mugabe's victory in the 1980 elections came as a shock to
much of the white establishment, not least to white farmers. An editorial
in *The Farmer* summed up the community's surprise:

> Events over the last few weeks have completely taken the proverbial wind out
> of our sails ... / The landslide election victory of Robert Mugabe and his
> ZANU(PF) shocked and dismayed most white Rhodesians who had put their
> money on the moderate Bishop Muzorewa as a 'dead cert.'[71]

Considering Mugabe's rhetoric on the land issue, such a reaction was understandable. There was a very real fear within the farming community that ZANU's success would lead to the complete destruction of white commercial agriculture. Just after independence, Denis Hills, an Englishman lecturing at the Teachers College in Gwelo (Gweru), wrote that:

> At the back of every white Rhodesian's mind is fear: fear of economic uncertainty in the new Zimbabwe, of losing jobs and property, of being outnumbered and humiliated; fear of the black man's latent frustrations and violence.[72]

This fear was palpable in *The Farmer*. The first editorial in 1980, 'Traumatic Year', attempted a review of the confusing events of 1979. Although finding some cause for optimism in recent political developments, it warned that:

> More than paper promises are required if there is to be a renewal of confidence of those whose skills and expertise are vital components to the welfare, prosperity and development of this land. / And foremost among these with the know-how are farmers whose confidence has been severely tested and who stand to lose most through the implementation of foolish political doctrine which is directly responsible for so much chaos in the Third World. / To now lose the confidence of agriculture – and in agriculture – can only spell national disaster.[73]

Such comments were an obvious defence against the doctrines espoused by the ZANU leadership, as the magazine sought to defend the position and place of white farmers. However, the farmers did not have to wait long to have many of their initial fears of land acquisition and expropriation allayed. Mugabe wasted no time in seeking to quell the concerns of whites in general, and white farmers in particular.[74] On the eve of independence he made his intentions clear: 'If yesterday you hated me, today you cannot avoid the love that binds you to me and me to you. The wrongs of the past must now stand forgiven and forgotten.'[75]

This message was delivered directly to farmers in various forms over the next few years. Firstly, Dennis Norman, then President of the CFU, was appointed Minister of Agriculture.[76] This did a great deal to bring the farmers and the government closer and fostered a degree of trust and partnership. Mugabe himself addressed the CFU's annual congress in August and further endeared himself to the farming community:

> Who doubts that our lives and the lives of seven and a half million people lie in your hands? I therefore believe that you, the farmers, hold the future of our nation in your hands. I close [this speech] with the assurance that Gov-

ernment will do all in its power to assist you in the task of building a great Zimbabwe.[77]

Having feared the worst, white farmers and the CFU welcomed such gestures and were relieved to find their position and place in the country more secure. This developing partnership resulted in a remarkable transformation of Mugabe and ZANU's image in *The Farmer*. The obvious reason for this transformation was that with the contest for power now over, the CFU and *The Farmer* aligned themselves with the winners, the new elite in charge of its fortunes. This is hardly surprising given the precarious nature of the white farmers' position, but what is striking is how far this support for the new government dictated coverage of events in *The Farmer*.

Despite government assurances, the CFU still put measures in place to protect its interests, including the establishment of the MFP Trust in 1982 to protect the publishing division of the CFU in case the unions were forced to merge.[78] However this did not mean that CFU lost control of *The Farmer*. Its ability to control the magazine was clearly evident during the editorship of Miller's successor, Myfanwy van Hoffen.

1983–1990: Myfanwy van Hoffen

Myfanwy van Hoffen had been a teacher before joining *The Farmer* as a journalist, and was promoted to editor after Miller was forced to resign in 1983.[79] By the time she took up the reins, white farmers and the state had cemented their marriage of convenience. Van Hoffen made sure she did nothing to jeopardise this relationship, despite some of the troubling events that took place during her tenure. The radical reinvention of Mugabe witnessed under Miller's editorship went unchallenged by van Hoffen. Having negotiated the arrival of black majority rule, farmers, the union and *The Farmer* were fully, and 'apolitically', aligned with the new ZANU-PF government by 1983, allowing farmers to continue their existence in much the same way as before. As a result, *The Farmer* offered no criticism of the government handling of any domestic issues over this period, whether of land reform, domestic security or opposition politics. The brand of apoliticism practised by the farmers made itself particularly felt with intriguing coverage of the land reform process and the years of violence in Matabeleland, known as Gukurahundi. In 1983, alongside the devastating drought, the most noticeable concern expressed in the pages of *The Farmer*, was about the security situation. The murderous attacks by 'dissidents' and 'bandits' on white farmers were harshly castigated, whilst at the same time the government's attempts to resolve the security situation were lauded. Gukurahundi was, at its core, about political intimidation and control, but since the victims were not white farmers, the union and the farming hierarchy took no stand against the repression. Even while farmers were being murdered – and many farmers complained that the situation was now worse than at any time during the Liberation War – the CFU and *The Farmer* refused to offer any detailed appraisals of the situation and continued to carry the ZANU-PF sanctioned line. The farmers' remarkable misreading and misrepresentation of Gukurahundi revealed the reality of 'apoliticism': they would not raise issues of a political nature with the government as long as their own interests were, on the whole, maintained.

Even when fundamental flaws started to manifest themselves in the running of the state, for example in the land reform programme, *The Farmer* refused to question the government's actions.[80] It was only towards the end of the 1980s, when farmers started to feel threatened by the imminent expiry of the Lancaster House Constitution, that questions and concerns received a public airing. The Constitution had guaranteed property rights and, with its end in sight, the CFU began highlighting the importance of commercial (white) farmers to the country. As a result, at the end of the decade and van Hoffen's editorship, cracks appeared in the white farmer/government relationship and these began to surface in *The Farmer*.

Other areas of the relationship were handled with great care. Whether the issue was of squatting, commodity prices or drought, *The Farmer* portrayed government, the CFU and the farmers as being in agreement over principles and approach. Even land reform was covered in such glowing terms that it seemed there was no conflict between farmers and government over its management, impact or importance. It was astute for the white farmers to appear to be hand in hand with government whilst the violent repression of the Matabele was under way. In 1985 the CFU president John Laurie stated at its annual congress that only 'twelve months ago many commercial farmers were in a desperate situation. The combined approach by Government, the private sector and farmers together has seen us through to this day.'[81] Laurie also reaffirmed the notion that the CFU was 'a non-political body which exists to promote and protect the interests of the commercial farmer.'[82]

To encourage a favourable assessment by government, *The Farmer* ensured that labour issues received more sympathetic coverage than they had previously done. In 1985 it carried an article on the nutrition of farm labourers. Ironically, while the headline was referred to farm labour, the article actually advised farmers how to increase productivity; it claimed that improved levels of nutrition were 'essential' to boost labour productivity, especially since wages had 'escalated by a dramatic 275 per cent over the past 5 years'. The minimum wage was Z$75 (US$67) a month at the time. The article showed that it would cost only Z$1.11 (US$0.9) a month to supply a worker with a litre of 'health-giving Nutresco Mahewu every day', an expense which would be recovered by a modest 1.47 per cent increase in worker efficiency. However, following the five-step plan outlined in the article, farmers could expect to increase their labourers' 'energy and efficiency levels by up to 10 per cent'. Nowhere in the article is there any attempt to explain why farm labourers are so malnourished and weak in the first place.[83]

In 1986, the government expressed concern about farm labour housing. *The Farmer* and the CFU responded with a strong 'Message from the President' in January: 'an enormous amount has been and is being done to improve both housing and amenities' on farms but that 'there are a few cases that are letting the side down'.[84] Laurie warned that these few were giving all farmers a bad name, that the quality of their farm workers housing was 'unacceptable' and that they sort should out their housing 'NOW'. Later in the year, at a meeting in Mvurwi, Mugabe congratulated farmers for agreeing that a plan should be implemented to improve workers' amenities. But he warned that there was still a great deal of 'social underdevelopment' on many farms that was in contradiction to the wealth of the farming sector.[85]

As well as supposedly defending the farm labourer, the magazine sought to dispel 'myths' about the wealth of farmers and protect them from callous rumours of their riches. In an editorial aptly entitled 'No Surplus Wealth in Farming Today', van Hoffen set out to contradict the impression that 'the average farmer is a wealthy man with expensive tastes'.[86] She claimed that 'this, as every farmer in every country knows, is simply untrue', and especially untrue in Zimbabwe where the only people making money out of farming were the auctioneers, as so many were being forced to sell their farms. With spiralling input costs preventing profitability, van Hoffen argued that 'every farmer, whatever the size or nature of the farm is facing the same problems these days, and largely it is the love of the land and a sense of responsibility which keeps them going'.[87] As noted earlier, such an argument connects to the often-employed defence that farmers just want to grow food for the country. During the 1980s wildlife and game farming were becoming popular and financially successful ventures. Articles such as 'Game Farming has Exciting Future', 'Game's Great Potential', 'Developing Wildlife's Poten-tial', 'Making the Most of Wildlife' and 'For Love or Money (or Both)', illustrated the potential of wildlife farming and the opportunities avail-able to commercial farmers to capitalise on it.[88] Such articles contradicted the discourse of patriotic food production.

In 1988, the signing of the Unity Accord that brought about the end of repression in Matabeleland and the destruction of ZAPU as a political threat, also offered the hope of stability to many farmers. *The Farmer* praised the government's handling of the situation and its 'mag-nanimous' decision to form the Unity government which 'has dealt a body-blow to those external forces bent on destabilisation through party dissention'.[89] *The Farmer*, and van Hoffen in her editorials, stressed the need for all to 'grasp the hand of reconciliation'.[90] She believed that 'Government has demonstrated both in word and deed that it wishes to include all Zimbabweans at all levels and values the contribution made by men of goodwill.'[91] The positive support for Mugabe and his party, present throughout the 1980s, reached fever pitch with the signing of the Unity Accord. There was obvious hope in *The Farmer* that with the troubles of Gukurahundi behind them, farmers would now be in a prime position to benefit from the expected return to stability.

However, as the decade came to a close, rather than protecting the gains they had made, white farmers and their representatives used the Unity Accord as a basis to go on the offensive and confront government. The first signs of dissent appeared in the pages of *The Farmer* in 1989. In a review of the annual general meeting of the Matabeleland branch of the CFU, Max Rosenfels, Branch President, complained that:

> since Independence, nearly four million hectares of large scale commercial farm land, or 26 per cent, have been acquired by Government on a willing seller basis. In Matabeleland, Government has purchased 900,000 hectares of land, of which only 386,000 hectares have been partially resettled. Much of this land has been mismanaged.[92]

As Selby and Palmer have shown, the end of the 1980s witnessed a deterioration in white farming/government relations.[93] There were a number of key reasons for this. Firstly the violence of the war and Gukurahundi was over, allowing farmers the political space to believe they would survive a confrontation with government. Secondly, the continued importance of commercial agriculture to the economic fortunes of the country bolstered the confidence of the farming fraternity, in turn allowing it to begin questioning government and its motivations. Thirdly, and probably most importantly, the Lancaster House Constitution was due to expire in 1990. In order to promote and publicise their importance, *The Farmer* began to lobby for continued survival of white farmers. This meant assessing the land reform programme and identifying its negative impact, which, in their literature, could be identified as having resulted from disruptions to commercial farming resulting from reform.[94]

The change in approach was not wholesale. *The Farmer* and the union still understood that battles had to be picked and, whilst they began to offer guarded criticisms of the government, they also sought to ensure that, where they could, they protected gains made by supporting ZANU-PF. For instance, at the beginning of 1990, *The Farmer* warned farmers about their public comments on the first ten years of independence:

> Many foreign journalists are in the country as we approach the tenth anniversary of our independence to write stories on that theme and, inevitably, some of them will approach commercial farmers for comment and opinion. / This is natural, since commercial farmers are a vital sector in our economy. / The comments can, and will, be nothing but favourable. [Farmers] ... should seize the chance to make their views known in a positive and optimistic way.[95]

While such a message inadvertently acknowledged that there were many unfavourable assessments of the government being articulated in the wider farming community, it also shows how conscious the magazine was in seeking to placate the political machine of ZANU-PF, and to prove that farmers and their Union were prepared to state their support for their continued rule as long as their rights and future were guaranteed.

Throughout the 1980s, *The Farmer* had remained very much the CFU's publication, carrying constant messages from the president of the CFU and outlining much of the union's policy and activity. Van Hoffen made sure that she kept the magazine in line with the discourse of apoliticism and made no attempt to enforce the independence of the magazine despite being technically allowed to do so after the forming of the MFP

Trust in 1982. In 1991, however, Felicity Wood became the editor and she made several significant changes to the running and production of the magazine, many of which pushed the boundaries of its independence from the CFU.[96]

1991–1997: Felicity Wood

Wood became the magazine's second female editor and was extremely active in seeking to reinvigorate it. Before assuming the post, she had been working with Agritex, the government extension service. Following the conservative editorship of van Hoffen, Wood hoped to revitalise the publication and increase its appeal both to farmers and valuable advertisers. As the magazine admitted in 1995, during 'the 1980s ... [it] went through a depressing period of self-censorship and appeared to encourage editorial control by the CFU'.[97] Wood's expressed aim was to 'put the farmer back into *The Farmer*'. The central element of this policy was to distance the magazine from the union and include more news and coverage of the community.[98] This was a move supported by the CFU president, Peter MacSporran, who believed that what people liked about *The Farmer* at this time was 'that they might get some truth and not just a lot of sugar coating'.[99] Direct interventions from the union were limited and the weekly messages from the CFU president were withdrawn, as it was felt that the CFU line was already covered in the weekly news roundup.[100] Wood also dispensed with regular and lengthy editorials and endeavoured to make the magazine more community focused. To this end she set up competitions, such as photograph of the year, and prizes, such as woman of the year.[101] These changes had the desired affect, making the magazine more popular and accessible than it had been during the 1980s. A letter later submitted to the magazine reacting to Wood's resignation, thanked her and stated: 'Whatever criticisms Felicity may have attracted, the farmers I've spoken to said she had done a lot of good for *The Farmer* and had revolutionised the magazine from a dull, boring monotonous weekly to something that is popular.'[102]

What really helped Wood in her designs to make *The Farmer* a more independent production was that during the early 1990s the magazine became, for the first time in its history, self-financing.[103] It stopped receiving subsidies from farmers' licensing fees via the CFU and relied solely on subscriptions and advertising revenues. As a result of these developments, *The Farmer* was forced to stop printing on glossy paper, opting instead for cheaper newsprint. Wood explained that many of the more affluent white farmers and CFU members complained and said that they could now no longer keep *The Farmer* with their other glossy farming magazines from South Africa or the UK. One farmer in particular stated that he was now forced to keep his copy of the magazine in the toilet. 'Newsprintgate', as it became dubbed by editorial staff, reveals a great deal about the identity of the magazine and the role it was supposed to play for many white farmers. It was a symbol of who and what they were. This was much more important for them than the content and affordability of the magazine.[104]

The Farmer claimed that it stopped receiving subsidies in 1992.[105] However, the financial statements of the CFU and MFP Trust reveal that the CFU only stopped contributing to the running of the magazine in 1994.[106] As proof of the magazine's increased popularity amongst both readers and advertisers, there was a significant increase in subscriptions and advertising. In 1992 the MFP Trust received just over Z$2 million (US$0.6 million) in advertising revenue, which rose to Z$6m (US$0.6 million) in 1997, the year Wood handed over editorial duties.[107] Revenue from subscriptions also increased three-fold over this period, but it was the annual profit over this period that really illustrate the success of the magazine. In 1992 it was under Z$0.5 million (US$0.08 million); by 1997 it was Z$2.7 million (US$0.27 million).[108]

Wood's approach to the political stance of the magazine was dictated by her desire to make it fundamentally a news-based publication. As the CFU line was carried in the news round-up, so too was the line of government, which at this time was becoming increasingly hostile towards white farmers. Although Wood attempted to produce a balanced publication, the magazine remained an organ of the white farming community and it still reflected this bias. Wood's tenure coincided with a very difficult time for white farmers and the CFU, and her editorials and reportage carried a great deal of comment on the issues of land reform and on character attacks on white farmers by the government. With the lapsing of the Lancaster House Constitution, the government put in motion legislation for compulsory acquisition to exist alongside the willing-buyer, willing-seller mode of land reform. This became the central concern for the CFU and farmers and, understandably, for *The Farmer*. With growing strain on the relationship between farmers and the government, *The Farmer* was allowed greater freedom to operate, as more pressing concerns absorbed CFU attentions. Wood exploited this increased liberty and pushed the boundaries of what *The Farmer* published.[109]

Wood wasted no time in expanding the coverage of *The Farmer* upon becoming editor. In December 1991 she printed an article titled 'How Others See Us'. No other article in *The Farmer* since independence had sought to elicit the opinion of wider society about white farmers. Prompted by discussions at CFU council meetings, which raised concerns about the image of large-scale commercial farmers, *The Farmer* decided to conduct an informal survey in Harare. There were several favourable responses about the good that farmers did in terms of growing food and bringing in valuable foreign currency, but these were outweighed by the negative responses, which *The Farmer* fully reproduced:

> 'The idea of a commercial farmer is appealing, it's the person in the flesh that isn't always so good' – Unemployed woman.
>
> 'They seem to be a bunch of wimps, always complaining' – Businessman.
>
> 'It is so unfortunate that we cannot do without them. … I have been angered and frustrated by their attitude to blacks' – Lawyer.
>
> 'Historically they rank amongst the country's worst employers' – Housewife.
>
> 'I don't like them, but I like what they do' – Reporter.
>
> 'They're a necessary evil' – Artist.
>
> 'They're just racially prejudiced and some couldn't care less about the plight of the poor communal peasant scraping the dry unproductive land' – Civil Servant, graduate.
>
> 'They're a bunch of ******, very racially prejudiced' – Accountant, just qualified.
>
> 'I wonder if they know how they make us feel, treating us like second-rate citizens in our own country' – Trainee bank manager.
>
> 'I don't know any' – Secretary at Agriculture House.[110]

White commercial farmers, distinctly isolated from much of society, were by the 1990s starting to generate a great deal of negative press. These feelings were not necessarily new, but found expression due to changes in the government's approach to white farmers. Their perceived wealth, contrasted with the failing economic fortunes of the country at large, was often at the root of such aggressive hostility. However, just as importantly, inferences of their attitude, apparently still infused with the racial prejudices of the country's colonial past, were key in generating much of the negative press.[111] Many of the quotes above attest to this and, during this time, similar attacks on farmers were supported, and often initiated by government, as Selby has illustrated.[112]

Such articles illustrate Wood's intention to expand the scope of *The Farmer* and address wider issues. This does not mean that she failed to remember or recognise who her readership was. Rather than alienating them from the magazine, Wood sought to expand and change the types of information to which farmers were exposed. With land reform such a central issue at the beginning of the 1990s, finding newsworthy material to fill *The Farmer*'s pages was not difficult. Government intentions towards land reform were covered, in dramatic and increasing detail.[113] To counter these developments, issues such as the failings of land reform, the perils of losing commercial (white) agriculture, and the need for 'sustainable production' measures to be implemented to keep the country, and agriculture, afloat, were constantly highlighted.[114]

The CFU responded to the government's land reform plans by issuing its own suggestions for how reforms should proceed.[115] Wood, in her first editorial of 1992, stated that the CFU's 'land reform proposals are simply based on the sustainable production of agricultural land, thereby equating rational and moral principles.'[116] Such an assessment presented the CFU's proposals as logical and devoid of political or economic considerations, as opposed to those of government, which, it was inferred were informed by short-sighted political expediency. Conveniently, the political aspects of land and land ownership were written out of the equation. It was implied that land should only be viewed in terms of production and usage and that the tortured history of land ownership should be forgotten. This sentiment, loaded with apoliticism and affirmative parochialism, was fully supported by the CFU hierarchy at the time.

Throughout 1992, the issues of land reform dominated *The Farmer*. In stark contrast to the magazine's approach of the 1980s, it was willing to openly criticise and confront government and its actions. The most striking example in 1992 was a four-page exposé of the Inyamsizi resettlement scheme 25 kilometres north of Mutoko. This had been established in 1980, on state land and 21 privately owned tobacco farms. Published in the same edition as the obituary of the President's wife, Sally Mugabe, the editorial, 'A sombre week for Zimbabweans', conflated both issues as tragedies that affected all Zimbabweans.[117] The article supplied a detailed account of the failures of the scheme and how a great infrastructure of 'dip tanks, boreholes, reservoirs and dams', plus telephone lines and 'the usual well-kept farm roads', had been apparently laid waste by mismanagement, poor farming practices and the desertion of the scheme by the intended beneficiaries.[118] The threat of widespread compulsory acquisition obviously played a role in spurring *The Farmer* into such an approach, but the CFU and *The Farmer* were confident that their position was secure and that their damning exposures of the government's failings would attract no backlash.

As the process legalising compulsory acquisition gathered pace, *The Farmer* began a staunch defence of white farmers and their achievements, as well as detailing the dangers that ill-considered and destabilising legislation could have. It claimed that the Land Acquisition Bill and the government's intentions for land reforms were no longer 'a parochial matter between farmers and Government', but 'concerned everyone in Zimbabwe.'[119] *The Farmer* again dismissed any meaningful need for land reform by asking and answering the question: 'And the spin-off gain for Government [for the proposed reforms]? Possibly little more than short term political gain.'[120] *The Farmer* also enlisted the drought of 1992: 'As the graphic effects of the drought begin to permeate the lives and futures of every single Zimbabwean man, woman and child, the idea of flawed legislation which could worsen hard-hit lives seems not just unwise but quite frankly ludicrous.'[121] The fact that the negative impact of drought was magnified by historical inequalities in land ownership was conveniently glossed over.

The gathering pace of land reform brought renewed calls for unity again within the community. Indeed, the CFU line at the time bore testament to this: 'If you designate one, you designate all.'[122] Alan Burl, the new CFU president, was much more aggressive than his predecessors in publically challenging the government. When the Land Acquisition Bill was introduced in 1990, its provision for compulsory acquisition sent shock waves through the farming community, and an emergency meeting of all CFU members was called in January 2001. It was the largest ever gathering of white commercial farmers, and caused traffic chaos in Harare. Over 4,300 farmers attended. Burl was credited with this bold move by *The Farmer*, and for his policy of bringing the land issue back into public focus.[123] Many of the leading articles on land reform in 1992 concluded with this show of concord of purpose. However, during that year, the issue was temporarily resolved. Having secured promises from government that 'efficient' farmers would be left untouched and that reform would be carried out fairly and justly, Burl said shortly after the Land Acquisition Bill was voted into law that it was 'a document we can live with'.[124] Commercial agriculture had in fact survived the 1992 legislative reforms largely intact and demonstrated the government's lack of political desire to implement hard-hitting reforms. The issue nevertheless continued to simmer and throughout the mid-1990s remained a major concern of *The Farmer*. When 70 farms were gazetted for compulsory acquisition on 30 April 1993, *The Farmer* published the entire list, as well as the shocked and disbelieving reactions of many of the farmers affected.[125] However, it soon became clear that farmers who wished to fight the designations could do so in court; the process became bogged down in legal proceedings, which often resulted in farmer victories. The fear of the reforms dissipated and coverage of the issue slowly lost much of its hyperbolic edge. By 1996, land reform and acquisition was no longer a dominant theme within the pages of *The Farmer*, though this was to change dramatically the following year with the resurfacing of the land issue and the listing of 1,471 farms for compulsory acquisition.

With so much attention on the land during the 1990s, *The Farmer* sought to show how much good the farmers were doing in the rural areas (as well as for the nation as a whole). AIDS became a pressing concern during the 1990s, and Kerry Kay, a farmer from Marondera, was instrumental in setting up a HIV/AIDS programme on farms.[126] Much to the magazine's credit, the AIDS issue received substantial coverage, even at this early stage.[127] During 1995 the rising numbers of AIDS orphans on the country's commercial farms was given extensive coverage, and gave the farming community a powerful propaganda tool for their declared commitment to the countryside.[128]

Other areas of rural life were also given attention, especially where farmers and communal populations interacted. Farm workers who were to be affected by the land reforms were sympathetically covered in a number or articles.[129] Relations between commercial farmers and those residing in the communal lands were also well covered, with many of the positive aspects exaggerated.[130] A 1993 series entitled 'Helping Hands Across the Fence' in 1993 showed how commercial farmers could help their communal neighbours and how so many had already done so with remarkable results.[131] Many of these articles were designed to illustrate how hard farming was and how possession of land and the wish to farm did not alone make such a venture successful. Nothing illustrates this better than the article, 'Even With Help, Farming is Not Easy', which detailed the tribulations of a co-operative project that, despite receiving a great deal of assistance from white farmers in the Marondera area, was struggling to make ends meet.[132]

Along with these less than subtle defences of white farmers and their role in rural communities, Wood allowed the magazine to become a forum for white farming voices. During the 1980s, 'letters from farmers, if controversial, were rejected as being unsuitable for publication'. However, Wood now opened the space for 'farmers and others ... to express their opinions on a variety of subjects throughout the magazine'.[133] Correspondence ranged from debates over land reforms to smoking in the CFU council meetings; readers often replied to each other's letters and were quite willing to submit hard-hitting or contentious letters for publication. One issue in particular that caused considerable furore was an article by Woodpecker in his regular column, 'Out on a Limb', on 17 October 1996. The article attacked Afrikaners, saying that they were 'imperialistic' racists, with a 'very patronising view of the rest of Africa – and that's when they are being polite'. Furthermore, they were 'carving up Africa' into their personal playgrounds and making a fortune in the process, at the expenses of everyone else in Africa.[134] This characterisation of Afrikaners prompted a flurry of letters, one of which read, 'If Afrikaners have no other virtues they at least have this one: they don't rush to pen and paper with derogatory statements about other ethnic groups.'[135] There was also an official response from CFU president Nick Swanepoel, stating how distasteful Woodpecker's article had been and that he would no longer be writing for the magazine. [136]

In another animated example, Mrs Wendy Lapham wrote to complain of the CFU leadership's actions during the Heroes' Day celebrations:[137]

> What extremely bad taste and insensitivity was shown by our CFU members ... when they attended the Heroes' Day celebrations. / With this action they have diminished and betrayed and dishonoured the memory of our own fallen heroes. Fifty-one years on (after the last world war) and the Germans still don't attend Cenotaph Service in London on the 11 November every year, do they? / Surely in this issue we are entitled to be partisan and loyal to our own and they, our dead, by giving up their lives deserve some sort of constant and untarnished respect and remembrance. / In an unbridled effort to show co-operation in this very one sided reconciliation part, we must be careful not to sell our own souls as well.[138]

The letter received an instant response from an ex-Selous Scout who felt that:

> Such a bigoted response is unwarranted. / Swanepoel, Hasluck and Amyot [who attended the celebrations] exemplify an age-old tradition of gracious-ness and courtesy in honouring a nation's dead. It does not detract from those fallen on the side of the vanquished in any manner whatsoever because no one wins a war except the politicians. / All dead were truly heroes, black or white on either side, because they gave up education, schooling and the comforts of society and they died for a cause which they probably did not understand. I would say those young warriors could have stood side by side building a nation and a future without a drop of blood being spilt but for the politicians. / Both black and white died on both sides. Let us remember that and hang our heads in shame.[139]

These letters display both the affirmative parochialism of white farmers, and the variety of opinions contained within their community. The first shows a clear failure to redefine past events, with no evidence of any form of reconciliation or acceptance having taken place since the end of the Liberation War. The second shows consideration for the memories and sacrifices of the dead, but in maintaining that there were no winners in the war besides 'the politicians', implies that the white farmers and the CFU hierarchy who attended the celebrations were not political agents. Such correspondence demonstrates that *The Farmer* had overcome its reservations about publishing letters that might be deemed offensive; this practice was to continue after Wood's departure, and was a central feature of the magazine until its closure.

When Wood resigned in 1997, she had radically reshaped *The Farmer*. During her six years in charge, she had made it a well-respected and popular publication once again, dramatically increasing revenues from adverting and subscriptions. In addition to the changes in publication policy, Wood had made a number of staff changes.[140] There were many more black members of staff. After her immediate successor had to resign within only a few months of assuming the job, Wood was instrumental in securing the promotion of Charles Kabera to the editorship at the end of 1998, the first and last black man to hold the post.[141] Kabera was not to last long as editor, either. In May 1999, he was murdered on a farm whilst covering a field day in Mutorashanga. The last photograph taken of him while he was still alive was used as the cover of *The Farmer*. Inside there were several articles on the events surrounding his murder, but there was never any follow-up of the case, nor was Kabera ever mentioned again in the magazine.[142] Wood recounted that hardly any of the CFU leadership attended his funeral and made the point that if he had been white, there would have been a much greater response from the CFU and the white farming community.[143] Wood became the editor again until Brian Latham was appointed at the end of 1999.

1999–2002: Brian Latham

Latham had a long association with journalism and publishing in Zimbabwe and the UK before being offered the editorship of *The Farmer*.[144] The successes of *The Farmer* in the 1990s, and freedom it had to operate, meant that Latham inherited a vibrant and active publication.[145] However, as Wood commented, he immediately set about installing himself as an old fashioned type of editor who isolated himself from his staff.[146] The start of Latham's tenure coincided with a radical shift in the political fortunes of the nation and Latham took every opportunity to link *The Farmer* to the turmoil of the time. Wood's approach was swiftly replaced by a deluge of political commentary, much of it supplied by Latham himself. Editorials returned to the magazine in dramatic fashion, often with Latham publishing two-page pieces on the political changes of the time. While these were often very popular with the farming community, they alienated and infuriated many readers.[147] They also created a great deal of tension between the magazine and the CFU, tension that ultimately led to the magazine's closure.

By 2000, the relationship between government and the CFU had taken a severe battering. The common perception is that the constitutional referendum of 2000 represented a fundamental shift. Selby has shown, however, that the relationship had been eroding throughout the 1990s, because of issues including compulsory acquisition, personality clashes and the constant and increasing demonising of white farmers by government media and press.[148] The referendum simply brought these problems to a head. The government-sponsored draft constitution contained a clause that 'obliged' Britain, as the former colonial power, to pay compensation for land taken by government.[149] The white farming community was, understandably, deeply concerned about this. Yet just as worrying for them was the rhetoric that accompanied the government's drive to push through a 'Yes' vote. Lamenting the return of 'evil', in the form of racial conflict, *The Farmer* was concerned about:

advertisements leading up to the referendum [that] openly attacked the white minority population: [such as] television ads on ZBC [which] listed all the reasons why it was finally time to 'send a clear message to the white settlers and take what is rightfully ours [the land]'.[150]

In turn, the farmers offered a strong show of force to achieve a 'No' vote. Obviously their numbers alone would not have been enough to have any dramatic impact on the result, but their labour force represented a huge potential voting block. As Selby observed:

while the NCA [National Constitutional Assembly] mobilised effectively in urban areas, farmers began to mobilise through local exercises, by urging farm-workers to reject the constitution, and by printing t-shirts and leaflets calling for a 'NO' vote.[151]

The Farmer contributed to this process. Reporting after the event, Richard Winkfield wrote in his regular column, 'Bottom Line', of how he had invited all of his permanent employees to a meeting to explain the importance of registering and voting in the referendum. Winkfield described it as less a 'political rally' (because he abhorred political exhortation), but:

more like headmaster's assembly and all I lacked was the cane ... / I told them that if the leaders of Zimbabwe continued to foster corruption at the very highest level and continued to squander hard earned money, the jobs of our workers here were going to be on the line.

Winkfield basically told all the labourers present they would have no future if they did not vote against Mugabe. Nevertheless he felt he was doing the right thing: 'We are living in enlightening times. Twenty years ago this sort of communication would have stunk of paternalism.'[152] He fails to see that method and delivery can be more important than content, and his imagery of a headmaster's assembly does him no favours.

The involvement of white farmers in the referendum represented a brief but impotent flirtation with political reawakening. The extent of their political activity after this point was quickly revised in response to ZANU-PF's backlash. Despite claiming that their involvement in the referendum was not a political action, it clearly brought the white farming community into direct conflict with political aims and objectives of Mugabe and ZANU-PF.

Mugabe, obviously shaken by this first defeat, was overtly conciliatory and promised to respect the wishes of the people. However, the practical response of the ruling party was swift and ruthless. Mugabe and other party leaders 'blamed the defeat on the white minority and ... promised retaliation in volatile political language'.[153] Almost immediately after confirmation of the result, invasions of white-owned commercial farmland started in late February 2000. The success of the NCA and the rise of the MDC as a viable opposition movement had reinvigorated much of civil society, but this genuine threat revitalised ZANU-PF's violent, authoritarian and militaristic tendencies.[154] Its vengeance was brought to bear not only against the immediate political opposition of Morgan Tsvangirai and his party, but on all those who were conveniently labelled as supporting him and his 'imperial' backers. The white farmers slotted into this paradigm with remarkable ease, in part because of their race, but also because they were seen to be supporting the MDC.[155] Mugabe's loss in the constitutional referendum has long been seen as the catalyst to the land invasions; once these started, Latham made sure *The Farmer* pulled no punches in reporting on events as and when they happened and as they saw fit. It became increasingly political, and eventually carried as much commentary on the activities of the newly formed MDC as it did on farming matters.

As *The Farmer* and the white farming community celebrated the success of the 'No' vote, a series of well coordinated land occupations started around the country. These invasions, as they were labelled by white farmers, received instant coverage in *The Farmer*. In the 2 March 2000 issue, the first post-referendum invasions were reported:

> Alleged members of the Zimbabwe National Liberation War Veterans are making yet another move to 'take back the land' in a series of seemingly well-orchestrated land invasions throughout Zimbabwe.'[156] Farms in all three Mashonaland provinces (East, Central and West), as well as the Masvingo and Manicaland provinces were 'invaded'.[157]

Henceforth, coverage of these events in *The Farmer* utilised discourse about the invasions that would be replicated by white farmers, namely that this had nothing to do with the land issue and that government was directly involved in organising the invasions.[158]

By 2 March over 70 farms had been occupied, with this number increasing by the day.[159] As it became clear that these new land occupations were on a greater scale than those that had happened intermittently throughout Zimbabwe's history, farmers, the CFU and *The Farmer* struggled to come to terms with the ramifications of what was unfolding.[160] The

CFU, unable to ignore what was happening, used *The Farmer* to speak to its constituency. *The Farmer*, however, made sure that it protected its independent image by supplying this caveat:

> This publication is not part of Zimbabwe's Commercial Farmers' Union, and does not normally give editorial space to the CFU – or to any other organisation. But this week it has, and for a very simple reason: Zimbabwe stands on the edge of chaos and it has become necessary to take sides. So within these rather slim pages, with their news of land invasions, there is also a message from the CFU's president.[161]

The Farmer was trying to stress its independence at this crucial time, but it is clear that the CFU could and did use its influence to publish messages it felt were important. This cooperation was aided by the fact that *The Farmer* was, at this early stage, obviously supportive of the CFU. A few months later, Latham came out in even stronger support for the CFU and their chosen strategy of dealing with the land invasions. In an editorial in April, *The Farmer* sought to clarify any ambiguities of alliance and affiliation; the time had come for:

> *The Farmer* to take an unusual step: telling its readership where it stands. *The Farmer* is not part of Zimbabwe's Commercial Farmers' Union. It does not belong to the union and has no affiliation with it … this is an independent magazine with no affiliation, political or otherwise, to any organisation or body. / But that said, *The Farmer*'s readership is clearly defined: large-scale farmers and rural-based businesses and industries in the region. So yes, we agree with the ethos of commercial agriculture and we believe that the CFU provides an invaluable service to the industry – and not just during a crisis.[162]

This message was constantly reinforced with calls for unity within the community, against the claims that the government was using tactics of divide and rule to fragment and weaken the strength of the white farmers.

However, the stress upon unity and a united front suggested that there were indeed divisions in the community. White farming opinion rapidly fractured as the land occupations radicalised farmers' beliefs and outlooks, and the hope of an easy or quick resolution faded.[163] Several factors increased these differences of opinion. Firstly, the number of invasions far exceeded what farmers had expected. By the end of June, the CFU reported that 1,525 farms (28 per cent of farms owned by its members) had been occupied.[164] Secondly the invasions were highly uneven pro-

cesses, differing from district to district, province to province. Thirdly, the personalities involved, such as war veterans, police and political
administrators, had a great influence on the actions on particular farms.
Overall, violence and intimidation were increasing, which further fuelled
the fears and concerns of white farmers. The murder of several farmers
heightened anxieties, and prompted some to seek more action and protection from the union.[165] *The Farmer*, still defending the CFU, replied
in its leader:

> If the CFU is not offering advice it is because there is no advice to offer ....
> What applies in the east of Zimbabwe is, invariably, at odds with what's hap-
> pening in the west. Some invaders are hostile, some deadly; but others are
> apologetic and even humorous.[166]

It was not only the lack of advice or action that caused concern within
the farming community; some farmers openly disagreed with the CFU's
decision to keep talking to the government and the war veterans to find
a solution to the occupations, especially when it seemed obvious that neither of those parties respected any promises made or agreements reached.
After the murder of Allan Dunn in May 2000, *The Farmer* defended the
CFU's decision to carry on talking 'If the CFU were to walk out of the
talks – and they still might – there is every chance that the violence will
increase tenfold, some say a hundredfold.'[167] Undoubtedly, it was very
difficult for farmers and the CFU to understand what was unfolding and
what was the best strategy for confronting the situation. The CFU char-
acteristically decided that it would be best for the farming community to
revert to its pre-referendum stance and stay out of party politics.

After the success of the 'No' vote campaign, there was initially a great
sense of unity with the farmers and other political entities. 'In Mbare
the people are laughing at this farce [the referendum] and for perhaps
the first time ever, they are sympathetic towards the nation's farmers.'[168]
However, the ensuing violence against farmers caused a rapid change in
this attitude:

> The perception (almost overwhelmingly incorrect) was that farmers had swept
> en masse to the Movement for Democratic Change. That was true until about
> a month ago. Now the perception is that the farmers have swung towards
> ZANU-PF. The MDC will cry appeasement and expediency and be not a
> little angered by this, while unionised labour will look askance at employers
> whom they believed were bastions of support on the political, if not indus-

trial, front. / Perhaps this proves what the Commercial Farmers' Union has said all along; the business of farmers is business and being apolitical has its merits.[169]

Farmers now saw themselves alone on the front lines of the battle against Mugabe and his corrupt ZANU-PF.[170] For the farmers, the land was the single origin of the crisis, and their failure to realise the many others further alienated them from much of society.[171] This message was hammered home again to farmers after the parliamentary elections in June 2000, which *The Farmer* hardly covered and made no attempt to analyse. In a response to the anger directed at the CFU from various quarters for its handling of the crisis, *The Farmer* had this to say under the tragic heading 'Out in the Cold and all Alone':

> Everyone has advice, but no one has lifted a finger to help. And that includes the MDC. / ... everyone also expects farmers, yes, through the CFU, to take on ZANU-PF single handedly. They want to watch the fight from the sidelines ... there is only one force more powerful than ZANU-PF and that's people power. And from the outset, this paper has said that ZANU-PF cannot be trusted. / ... Isolation and loneliness of a protracted struggle without friends are the likely causes of the withdrawal, nothing more. And right or wrong, the decision has been made – but can only be reversed when farmers have proper support. So far there hasn't been any sign that support will be forthcoming because whether it is apathy and nonchalance or simple cowardice we will never know, but not one has assisted commercial agriculture in any meaningful way.[172]

In the same article *The Farmer* managed to blame ZANU-PF for the farming community's isolation from domestic politics, as a part of their sinister tactic of divide and rule.

Meanwhile, *The Farmer* maintained that the farming community was unified behind the CFU leadership: 'the fact remains that organised agriculture's politics are managed by consensus – and the consensus is unequivocally in favour of the path being taken by agriculture's leaders'.[173] It also believed that there was a great deal of empathy for farmers throughout the nation: 'the overwhelming majority of Zimbabweans, be they in the communal lands or the townships, are sympathetic to the plight faced by organised agriculture'.[174] Such assertions contradicted the images of farmers 'going it alone', but evidence from within *The Farmer*'s own pages, and from without, shows that the farmers were not united, nor was there a broad consensus of sympathy for their plight.

An insight into the disunity amongst farmers is found in the letters section of *The Farmer*. In March 2000, Catherine Buckle and Nick Arkell both wrote to ask what the union was doing and why there was a deafening silence on the invasions.[175] They felt that a more decisive and aggressive stance should have been taken by the CFU and that it was not wise to continue negotiating with the government. By this time the division between the CFU's position and the editorial line of *The Farmer* was making itself clear, hence messages of complaint against the CFU's inaction found their way to print. However, an even more telling example, and a key moment in the history of *The Farmer* which fundamentally underscores the conflicts and divisions within the community, came in June 2000. The former UDI Prime Minister, Ian Smith, wrote to the magazine to criticise its editorial policies:

> I am deeply concerned that the bulk of the editorial comments in our maga-zine are directed at the political scene, and that these are in conflict with the course which Nick Swanepoel [ex-president of the CFU] and others work-ing with him are striving to secure ... for people in responsible positions of authority to provoke hostility and conflict with the powers in totalitarian control, is the height of irresponsibility, and can only further endanger our farming community. / After all, there are a number of independent newspa-pers which constantly criticise and condemn government, and they do a much better job than The Farmer. / It is a sad fact of life that our Farmer magazine ... has denigrated into a third-rate political rag. I believe the time has come for our CFU executive to disperse with this dreadful embarrassment and find a responsible replacement.[176]

This scathing letter produced a flurry of responses, in support of both *The Farmer* and of Smith. In his defence, Margaret Payne wrote to say that Smith was 'just another poor commercial farmer', and that there were 'lots and lots of people who happen to think he is a great guy and don't know that life under his government was a lot better than life under the present one'.[177] Others wrote to support *The Farmer*'s coverage and hailed it as one of the most important sources of information about what was actually happening in the rural areas. Yet others, who saw through the CFU/*Farmer* claims of independence, wrote in condemning the proximity of *The Farmer* to the CFU, accusing *The Farmer* of being as 'free thinking as the *Herald* [the state-run daily newspaper] just prior to the elections'.[178]

Whatever the pressures it was under, *The Farmer* continued its crusade to report on political events and their impact on rural affairs. In 2001 it even expanded the scope of its coverage; not only did it continue to report on the violence in increasingly graphic detail (including photos of murdered farmers), it also began to report more about the fate of displaced farm workers. The magazine produced a number of hard-hitting features on the plight of exiled farm workers and the problems they now faced.[179] This kind of coverage damaged *The Farmer*'s relationship with the CFU, which had placed its hopes on a policy of 'quiet diplomacy' with government.[180] Moments of tension are clear in the 'Leader' column, where comments about editorial freedom and the need to keep telling the story of white farmers carry much greater import when read in this context. For example, after the bombing of the *Daily News* offices in February 2001, the 'Leader' noted the reaction in the farming community. Stating that it would take a brave person to defend the bombing, the author claimed that 'increasingly, there are those who believe that brutality on Zimbabwe's farms doesn't need perhaps, we shall say, quite as much exposure as it did in the past'.[181] The implication is obvious. Those wishing to muzzle *The Farmer* would, in a sense, effectively condone what happened to the *Daily News* and the shutting down of a fellow member of the 'independent' press.

Soon, however, *The Farmer* was shut down. On 2 April 2002, with almost no warning, it published its last edition.[182] Proclaiming the 'end of an era' and that it was yet 'another victim of the Zimbabwean Crisis,' this last edition lamented the closure of a magazine that had for over 70 years served the white farming community. In his final editorial, Brian Latham expressed no regrets for its reporting of the land invasions:

> it was a story we felt had to be told. History will judge critically those who believed, for whatever reason, that there was merit in burying the truth – or even leaving the telling of the truth to other newspapers with less interest in the farming community. We were never going to pretend it wasn't happening. / Critics say we made it difficult for the Commercial Farmers' Union. Well, for us the union is its members, the people being intimidated, threatened, extorted, chased from their homes, robbed and murdered. To us, [these victims] are far more important than the people in Agriculture House [the CFU headquarters]. / We sense, but do not know, that the new paper will give less attention to the appalling plight facing farmers and farm workers.[183]

This 'new paper' never came to light.[184] It is clear from Latham's comments that there had been a great deal of pressure put on *The Farmer* to rein in its reporting. When interviewed about *The Farmer's* closure, Rook claimed that the vast majority of farmers wanted it to remain in publication.[185] He also questioned the union's claims that financial difficulties led to the magazine's closure, and revealed that he had designed a business model to keep it going. The CFU had, however, refused to consider his proposals.[186] Wood and Winkfield both pointed out that the dismissal of Latham resulted not only from the political direction of his editorship, but also because of abuses of office privilege and position.[187] Winkfield claimed that by 2002, *The Farmer* had lost much of its advertising revenue because companies and businesses did not want to be associated with the political message Latham was delivering.[188] While this may have been the case, shutting down the magazine had more to do with the control of voice and the protection of image in dealing with a dictatorial government, than it did with the eccentricities of a wayward editor.

Conclusion

It is clear that in 2002, the CFU wished to keep negotiating with ZANU-PF, and believed that *The Farmer* was a direct threat to such a policy. Its frantic attempts to control the magazine failed in part because the magazine's successes in the 1990s had given it a voice of its own that was liberated from the union; and because the last editor, Brian Latham, felt obliged to confront and report the atrocities of the land reforms. As a result the last option the CFU had was to shut the magazine down. Having given up on political involvement and having shunned any official support for the MDC, the CFU turned against dissenting voices within its own establishment in a bid to further safeguard itself.

The decision to shut down *The Farmer*, though dramatic, was a continuation of CFU policy towards the magazine rather than a fundamental shift. When one looks back to the 1980s, *The Farmer* was similarly constrained by the CFU's policies. However, the confined atrocities of Gukurahundi (and their proximity to independence) did not cause the massive fissures in the farming community as events after 2000 did because they were not directly aimed at them. The CFU's handling of the land invasions lost it the support of many farmers and of *The Farmer's* editorial board. The CFU only concerned itself with those farmers still on the land, because to pursue justice for those already evicted would mean confrontation with the government. With that number evicted growing all the time, sympathy for them and fear among the remaining farmers created anger against the CFU and its policy of 'quiet diplomacy'.

When *The Farmer* began to distance itself from the CFU's approach, the response was swift and emphatic. In keeping with its attitude of affirmative parochialism, the CFU believed that it could continue to exist outside the wider politics of events in the country. This was demonstrated throughout its dealings with the government since independence, and it expressed itself in the union's influence over the reportage and content of *The Farmer*. *The Farmer*, whilst often following the CFU line, also periodically challenged this control, but ultimately was bound to CFU directives, as events in the 1980s and after 2000 so dramatically prove. *The Farmer*'s demise is one shared by other forms of media, independent or otherwise, in Zimbabwe's repressive environment over the last decade.[189] In addition, the tactics of the CFU have been adopted by others who have come under fire from ZANU-PF. Indeed, there may be a case for arguing that the MDC, in its present guise as part of the Government of National Unity, has recently adopted a similar approach to the crisis by seeking to work within ZANU-PF's paradigms and refusing to directly confront the party.

This chapter has illustrated that studying the voices from *The Farmer* offers opportunities to explore in more detail the 'ambiguities' of independence and how these played out and evolved in the post-colonial era. It has sought to show that decisions taken and tactics employed by *The Farmer*, and by extension the CFU, were not entrenched or static, but were rather informed by changing leadership and political, social and economic contexts. As Cooper writes, 'preserving the sense of ambiguity and ambivalence is not simply a matter of academic refinement, but of recognising, in the present as much as the past, the possibility of alternative political goals and strategies'.[190] This study of *The Farmer* shows how it, as a form of media and voice, elucidated the position of a specific community, who at once symbolise a 'reforming elite' and the 'orphans of empire'.

Notes

1　Cooper, 2008, p. 195.
2　*The Farmer*, 24 August 1995, p. 26.
3　Wasserman, 2009, p. 62.

4 Wasserman and Botma, 2008, p. 4.

5 For more on the media and democracy fascination in Africa, see Hyden, Leslie and Ogundimu, 2003; Nyamnjoh, 2005; Njogu and Middleton, 2009; Tettey, 2001, pp. 5-31.

6 For insights into other forms of print media in Zimbabwe and some of the individuals involved, see Nyarota, 2006; Chuma, 2004, pp. 119-39; Melber, 2004, Zaffiro, 2002; Frederikse, 1982; Windrich, 1981.

7 Correspondence with Michael Rook, 23 and 24 April 2009. Rook was very active in trying to attract as many subscriptions as possible. By the time of the magazine's closure Rook estimated there were over 200 fee-paying subscriptions. He stated, 'I marketed *The Farmer* paid subscription service aggressively, targeting relevant organisations and individuals within the region, the rest of Africa and internationally. *The Farmer* had approximately 200 paid subscriptions at the time of it's [sic] forced closure by CFU in early 2002. Key government ministries, parastatals, embassies and relevant NGO's were identified for subscriptions, and those without budgetary provision were sent complimentary copies. And yes *The Farmer* was read by the more discerning and professional decision makers and politicians.'

8 Ibid.

9 Many thanks go to Gary Rivett for the numerous and fruitful discussions that helped bring this term to life.

10 For a similar methodological approach, see Godwin and Hancock, 1993, p. 11.

11 As the quote that opens the following section attests.

12 Quote from Mr Hammy Hamilton, Eastern Districts CFU Branch Chairman. *The Farmer*, 15 October 1987, p. 10.

13 *Rhodesian Farmer*, 9 December 1977, p. 9.

14 Olick, 2007, pp. 108-9.

15 Raftopoulos, 2003, pp. 226-36.

16 Isin, 2002, p. 276.

17 Selby, 2006, p. 73. Yet this did not stop Norman offering a great deal of support and praise for government's approach to land reform and management in his own book on peasant agriculture. Norman, 1986.

18 *The Farmer*, 23 March 2000, pp. 9 and 24.

19 Correspondence with Rook, 13 July 2009.

20 This magazine is still on sale in Zimbabwe at the present. Its coverage of the land occupations after 2000 was limited, but there were occasional articles and features on the issue. However, much of the language and discourse so obvious in *The Farmer* about place, security, land reform and black rule is also present in *Farmers Weekly*. A study and comparison of the two would reveal some interesting parallels.

21 *The Farmer*, 17 November 1994, p. 6.

22 Interview with Richard Winkfield, 1 October 2009.

23 Ibid. This sentiment was confirmed in an interview with Felicity Wood. Interview with Felicity Wood, 5 October 2009.

24 Interview with Winkfield, 1 October 2009; interview with the CFU President Deon Theron, 10 October 2009. After *The Farmer*'s closure in 2002, Winkfield started a newsletter titled *Countdown*, which was meant to fill the void *The Farmer* left. It

carried a great deal of press from the CFU on the land occupations, but was generally very farming and advertising oriented. The newsletter closed after 13 issues. Rook and Wood have both since informed me that they had been contacted by the CFU about assisting with the latest CFU publication, *AgriZim*, which was started in 2010. Correspondence with Rook, 23 March 2010; interview with Wood, 19 May 2010.

25 *The Farmer*, 24 August 1995, p. 26.

26 *Rhodesian Farmer*, 26 October 1973, p. 3.

27 *The Farmer*, 27 May 1999, front cover.

28 Ibid., 24 August 1995, p. 26.

29 Winkfield mentioned that due to financial difficulties in the mid-1980s, the magazine downscaled and started only producing a bi-weekly magazine. However, the members of the CFU demanded the magazine to return to a weekly publication, and as soon as it could manage this, *The Farmer* reverted to a weekly publication schedule. Interview with Winkfield, 1 October 2009.

30 Interview with Wood, 5 October 2009; interview with Winkfield, 1 October 2009.

31 Wood confirmed this in her interview. Interview with Wood, 1 October 2009. In addition, in 1982 *The Famer* carried an article entitled 'How Much Does the Average Farmer Know?', which stated that there was an assumption that (white) commercial farmers were 'amongst the most knowledgeable in the world' and sought to test how true this was. Questionnaires were sent to commercial farmers on tobacco, maize, beef, dairy and general farming issues. Whilst the article realised there were numerous limitations with the exercise, it did reveal that the commercial farmers' answers to the maize, beef, dairy and general questions all scored very poorly. Only the tobacco scores were comprehensive. This article and the responses recorded reveal the lack of specialist expertise and knowledge. *The Farmer*, 12 April 1982, pp. 23, 25 and 27.

32 The 'tag line' is taken to be the text describing the magazine on the front page.

33 In the CFU's annual financial reports, the MFP Trust is shown to have been formed on 5 July, 1982. At the CFU, I was only able to see the statements from 1992-2000, but all confirmed the establishment date of the MFP Trust. See The Commercial Farmers' Union of Zimbabwe and Affiliated Organisations, 1992-2000.

34 Correspondence with Rook, 12 July 2009. For more on the merging of farming unions in Zimbabwe see Bratton, 1994, pp. 9-37. This is also discussed in Chapter One.

35 Correspondence with Rook, 12 July 2009.

36 Ibid.

37 There were seven editors before Dudley Dickin: Sir Humphrey Gibbs (1940–46); Douglas Holland (1946–53); Anthony Cullen (1953–55); Frank Clements (1955–58); Tony Morrison (1958–61); Clive Thompson (1961–64); Peter Dearlove (1964–65); Frank Clements (1965–67); and Peter Dearlove (1967–68). *Rhodesian Farmer*, 26 October 1973, p. 2.

38 Murungweni's official title was Production Editor. In practice, however, Wood was the editor of the magazine during this time.

39 Dickin had arrived in Rhodesia in 1964 to edit the magazines *Shell Farmer* and *Shell African Farmer*. Before that he was senior reporter and sub-editor of the *East London Daily Dispatch* in London, UK. *Rhodesian Farmer*, 16 August 1974, p. 3.

There is no mention of Duggan's background in the magazine.

40 This is also analysed in more detail in Chapter One.

41 See Chapter One. Also, see Phimister, 1987, p. 52; Riddell, 1978, p. 13; Stoneman, 1981.

42 Godwin and Hancock, 1993, Chapters Two and Three.

43 *Rhodesian Farmer*, 9 February 1973, p. 7. Also, see *Rhodesian Farmer*, 17 December 1976, p. 33.

44 Grundy and Miller, 1979, pp. 132-41. This publication contains a list of all white farmers killed during the Liberation War. See Chapter One.

45 Part of this was the establishment of the RNFU's life assurance scheme, publicised in the *Rhodesian Farmer* and in co-operation with The Old Mutual insurance firm. An article on the policy stated, 'death benefits will be paid for any cause INCLUDING WAR, ACTS OF WAR AND TERRORIST ACTIVITY'. *Rhodesian Farmer*, 10 May 1974, p. 5.

46 *Rhodesian Farmer*, 9 February 1973, p. 7.

47 Caute, 1983, pp. 48-9, 183 and 287. Also, see some of the state propaganda issued by the RF government, for example, Ministry of Information, Immigration and Tourism, 1978. Godwin and Hancock also talk of the RF's propaganda in portraying the guerrilla forces as inept, murderous and cowardly. See Godwin and Hancock, 1993, pp. 115-6 and 311-2. See Chapter Four for more discussion on the framing of guerillas, dissidents and war veterans by white farmers.

48 *Rhodesian Farmer*, 23 November 1973, p. 9.

49 Ibid., p. 11.

50 Selby, 2006, pp. 89-106.

51 Correspondence with Rook, 4 March 2011.

52 Grundy and Miller, 1979, pp. 132-41.

53 Caute, 1983, p. 78.

54 Selby, 2006, pp. 89-106; Godwin and Hancock, 1993, p. 258.

55 In particular see the Banket and Umtali meetings reported on in the *Rhodesian Farmer. Rhodesian Farmer*, 9 December 1977, pp. 7 and 9.

56 Ibid., 2 December 1977, p. 3.

57 Ibid., 9 December 1977, p. 9.

58 Ibid., 2 July 1976, p. 7.

59 Ibid., 18 November 1977, p. 3.

60 Ibid.

61 Ibid., 6 January 1978, pp. 11 and 15.

62 Ibid., 23 December 1977, p. 3.

63 Ibid., 7 April 1978, p. 3.

64 Ibid., 6 January 1978, p. 3.

65 Ibid., 7 April, 1978, p. 3. Such staunch advocacy to ensure that compensation could be paid outside the country could easily be read as something that undermined white farmers' claims to patriotism and commitment to 'their' country.

66 *The Farmer*, 4 August 1978, p. 3.

67 Godwin and Hancock, 1993, p. 226 and footnote 57.

68 *The Farmer*, 4 August 1978, p. 3.

69 For more on the failure of the black and white farming institutions to merge, see Bratton, 1994.

70 *The Farmer*, 5 January 1979, p. 3.

71 Ibid., 28 March 1980, p. 3.

72 Hills, 1981, pp. 198-7.

73 *The Farmer*, 4 January 1980, p. 3.

74 As Chapter One has shown, Mugabe faced a difficult task in running Zimbabwe after 1980. Ibbo Mandaza pointed out that, 'Mugabe would have to begin the delicate task of nation-building in an atmosphere of intense suspicion and even hostility on the part of those he had defeated at home; against the covert threats of military, political and economic destabilisation from South Africa; and with the pervasive threat of economic and political blackmail by the imperialist powers that had been the undertakers of the Lancaster House Agreement but were now seeking to keep the new state in line.' Mandaza, 1986, p. 42.

75 What follows is a longer extract of Mugabe's independence speech: 'Henceforth you and I must strive to adapt ourselves, intellectually and spiritually to the reality of our political change and relate to each other as brothers bound one to the other by a bond of comradeship. If yesterday I fought you as an enemy, today you have become a friend and ally with the same national interests, loyalty, rights and duties as myself. If yesterday you hated me, today you cannot avoid the love that binds you to me and me to you. Is it not folly, therefore, that in these circumstances anybody should seek to revive the wounds and grievances of the past? The wrongs of the past must now stand forgiven and forgotten'. Raftopoulos, 2004, p. x. Also, see Mugabe, 1984.

76 Norman was very surprised by the appointment. In fact he has said that he initially refused the appointment and had still not accepted the role when it was announced by Mugabe. See Selby, 2006, p. 114. Also, see *The Farmer*, 21 March 1980, p. 5.

77 *The Farmer*, 11 August 1980, p. 19. Mugabe gave similar messages of support to commercial farmers in his 'Foreword' to the MFP Trust's *Zimbabwe Agricultural and Economic Review*. Mugabe, 1982, pp. 4-5.

78 Correspondence with Rook, 12 July 2009.

79 Correspondence with Rook, 4 March 2011. There were allegations of misappropriation of funds and nepotism leveled against Miller.

80 For examples of disaffection within Zimbabwe and of corruption in the land reform process, see Palmer, 1990, p. 175 (in particular footnote 43). For a more general insight into increasing levels of corruption in government, see Muzondidya, 2009, pp. 182-3.

81 *The Farmer*, 12 August 1985, p. 11.

82 Ibid.

83 *The Farmer*, 4 November 1985, p. 28.

84 Ibid., 27 January 1986, p. 5.

85 Ibid., 5 May 1986, pp. 9 and 11. The report also looks at suggestions by Mvurwi farmers that state funds be put aside to help finance the 'construction of farm workers' housing'. Another farmer asked about the dismissal of farm labour. The article summarised, 'While 95% of farm workers were "hard working, decent chaps" did the five-year development plan have anything in it for the 5% of workers holding the country

back? / Mr Mugabe said he saw no reason why lay workers could not be dismissed provided correct procedures were followed and he said that the lazy man had no place in Zimbabwe. / Mr Laurie said that the 5% comprised a "real problem as these workers influenced others"'.

86 *The Farmer*, 10 September 1987, p. 1.

87 Ibid.

88 *The Farmer*, 24 March 1986, p. 11; 2 July 1987, p. 7; 24 March 1988, p. 1; 12 May 1988, p. 10; 25 February, 1988, p. 10.

89 Ibid., 7 January 1988, p 1.

90 Ibid., 11 February 1988, p. 1.

91 Ibid.

92 Ibid., 13 July 1989, p. 9.

93 Selby, 2006, pp. 146-53; Palmer, 1990, pp. 174-81.

94 This approach became more pronounced as the 1990s progressed, as will be demonstrated later in this chapter.

95 *The Farmer*, 8 February 1990, p. 1.

96 Alistair Syme's editorship is not given the same analysis as the others' because it was too short to have any dramatic influence on the publication, serving only from 1990 to 1991. However, he did serve at a very dramatic time, with the end of the Lancaster House Constitution and the start of governments plans to introduce compulsory acquisition.

97 *The Farmer*, 24 August 1995, p. 26.

98 Interview with Wood, 5 October 2009.

99 *The Farmer*, 24 August 1995, p. 26.

100 There were calls from some sectors to reinstate the 'Message From the President' column. However, these were rebuffed by Wood and her editorial team. *The Farmer*, 24 August 1995, p. 26. Interview with Wood, 5 October 2009.

101 *The Farmer*, 2/9 January 1992, p. 7; 2/9 January, 1992, p. 7. The 'Farm Woman of the Year' title was intended for someone who '*excels in their contribution to the rural community*' (emphasis in original) and was accompanied by a Z$5,000 (US$800) cash award. 'Nominations are open to all members of the CFU ... who may nominate any woman living on a large-scale commercial farm.' Kerry Kay (the wife of Iain Kay mentioned in Chapter Two and later one of the founding members of the organisation Justice for Agriculture (JAG)) was the first winner of this title. *The Farmer*, 17/24/31 December 1992, p. 3.

102 *The Farmer*, 31 July 1997, p. 20.

103 Ibid., 24 August 1995, p. 26.

104 Interview with Wood, 5 October 2009.

105 *The Farmer*, 24 August 1995, p. 26.

106 The CFU and Affiliated Organisations, 1994. The reasons why the magazine stopped receiving subsidies from the CFU is unclear and none of my informants have offered any insights into this.

107 The CFU and Affiliated Organisations, 1992–1997.

108 The CFU and Affiliated Organisations, 1992–2000.

109 Interview with Wood, 5 October 2009.

110   *The Farmer*, 19/26 December 1991, pp. 10-13. Wood commented that this article received a serious reaction from the farming community and that the CFU received hundreds of complaints over it. Many within the CFU heavily criticised Wood for publishing it. Interview with Wood, 5 October 2009.

111   Moyo has argued that the racial bias of the white farming attitudes expressed itself most fully in reference to the land reform issue: 'White farmers believe that they, not the state, should decide on land designation ... (but) such decision making powers in designating land undermines the legitimacy of the elected government in adjudicating the land problem ... it is a pretence that land grievances do not exist or are irrelevant in implementing land designations. Most interestingly it demonstrates an arrogance that only makes sense in racial parlance.' Moyo, 1994, p. 8. During the early 1990s, the CFU hired Professor Michael Bratton as a consultant to assess the organisation's political engagement and structural integrity. He apparently reported that the racial exclusiveness of the CFU was its biggest and greatest threat. Selby has stated that a copy of this report exists in the CFU archives. Selby, 2006, p. 242.

112   Ibid., pp. 241-4.

113   This was such a central theme in *The Farmer* over this period that it was addressed in practically every issue.

114   *The Farmer*, 11 May 1989, p. 3.

115   CFU, 1991. This report was the final nail in the coffin of the working partnerships between the CFU and the other black agricultural unions in Zimbabwe. This is discussed in Chapter One. See Bratton, 1994, pp. 19-20.

116   *The Farmer*, 2/9 January 1992, p. 1.

117   Ibid., 30 January 1992, p. 1.

118   Ibid., 30 January 1992, p. 9; 30 January, 1992, pp. 9-12, and 13.

119   Ibid., 6 February 1992, p. 1.

120   Ibid. In the next edition of the magazine a letter was published entitled, 'Too Late to Trust?', drafted by Ian Smith. Smith stated that, 'this government has been a complete failure, it has fulfilled out worst possible fears, and in so doing has fast created a situation of open resentment, at all levels of our society'. Tellingly, the letter was accompanied by a note from the editor stating that 'In a separate letter Mr Smith said he was writing the above letter as an ordinary farmer', and offered to pay for publication of the letter as an advertisement if it was considered unprintable. / No letters are considered unprintable if they are signed, do not contain defamations, obscenities or sectarian religious beliefs.' This is clearly a radical change from the attitude of the 1980s during the Gukurahundi years. *The Farmer*, 13 February 1992, p. 14.

121   *The Farmer*, 20 February 1992, p. 1.

122   Ibid., 20 February 1992, p. 3.

123   Ibid., 6 August 1992, pp. 12-3. This same article also commented on the 'decade of public silence' on the land question by commercial farmers that had preceded this meeting in January 1991. Also, see Selby for an overview of this meeting. Selby, 2006, p. 201.

124   *The Farmer*, 26 March 1992, p. 3.

125 Ibid., 6 May 1993, p. 7.

126 Ibid., 17/24/31 December 1992, p. 3.

127 For a brief sample of articles on AIDS in the early 1990s, see *The Farmer*, 13 April 1989, p. 9; August, 1991, p. 27; 28 November 1991, p. 8; August 6, 1992, p. 9.

128 *The Farmer*, 31 August 1995, p. 21; 9 November 1995, pp. 12-3; 9 November 1995, p. 14; 22 August 1996, p. 30.

129 For example, see *The Farmer*, 16 September 1993, pp. 11 and 13. The article ended with the plea, 'they deserve a better deal, after all, their sweat helped build the country'. It is only in this context that credit is given to labour for their input; at all other times it is the 'hard work' of the farmer himself that has made the farms and the country a success. For more on this discussion see Chapter Five.

130 For example, see *The Farmer*, 8 September 1994, p. 21; 8 August 1996, pp. 28, 29 and 31.

131 For example, see *The Farmer*, 16/23 December 1993, p. 21. In the article, Brian Oldrieve a farmer from Hinton Estates Farm in Bindura, argued that the only solution to the negative press white farmers were getting about their wealth was 'to increase prosperity on other side of fence' (or the communal lands), so as to make them 'more productive and diminish the contrast by increasing their productivity where they are'. At the same time he warned white commercial farmers that they 'should not isolate themselves and think that because of their high level of productivity they are indispensible'.

132 *The Farmer*, 16/23 December 1993, pp. 24-6.

133 Ibid., 24 August 1995, p. 26.

134 Ibid., 17 October 1996, p. 32.

135 Ibid., 7 November 1996, p. 10.

136 Ibid., 14 November 1996, p. 14.

137 Heroes' Day is a national holiday in Zimbabwe established after independence to commemorate and remember those who lost their lives in the Liberation War. It is celebrated on 11 August.

138 *The Farmer*, 29 August 1996, p. 14.

139 Ibid., 12 September 1996, p. 14.

140 When Wood took over in July 1991 the staff were: Production Editor: Felicity Wood; General Manager and Coordinator for Advertising, Marketing and Distribution: Michael Rook; Accounts: Kate Woods; Circulation: Derek Kapenga; Smalls Advertising: Rose Goto. When she resigned as editor in July 1997 the staff were: Editor: Nicholas Holme; Production editor: Maud Murungweni; Chief Reporter: Charles Kabera; Assistant Advertising Manager: Rose Goto; Accounts: Kate Woods; Circulation: Derek Kapenga; Origination: Costa Chirambaguwa, Peter Kawondera, Isaac Nyagura; General Manager MFP Trust: Michael Rook; Editorial Director MFP Trust: Felicity Wood.

141 As with Alistair Syme's editorship, Nicholas Holme's is not discussed in any detailed way because his tenure was too short to influence the nature of the magazine.

142 *The Farmer*, 27 May 1999, p. 9; May 1999, pp. 9 and 11.

143 Interview with Wood, 5 October 2009.

144 Correspondence with Rook, 4 March 2011.

145 Correspondence with Brian Latham, 21 April 2010.

146 Interview with Wood, 5 October 2009.

147 There were several letters from white farmers to *The Farmer* attesting to this. In particular see the letters from Ian Smith, which are discussed at length later in this chapter.

148 Selby, 2006, Chapters Four and Five.

149 *The Farmer*, 27 January 2000, p. 7.

150 Ibid., 17 February 2000, p. 5.

151 Selby, 2006, p. 277.

152 *The Farmer*, 2 March 2000, p. 23.

153 Raftopoulos, 2004, p. 13.

154 Freeman, 2005, pp. 147-72; Phimister, 2008, p. 212.

155 Raftopoulos, 2009, pp. 230-1.

156 *The Farmer*, 2 March 2000, p. 9.

157 The white farmers used the word 'invaded' to describe the land occupations. As discussed in Chapter Two, there are a number of terms used by the various protagonists to describe the land occupations (my term). Invasions and invaders were the terms preferred by *The Farmer*. Worby, 2001, p. 476, footnote 1.

158 *The Farmer*, 2 March 2000, p. 9.

159 Blair, 2002, p. 70.

160 For more on squatter movements and land occupations, see Alexander, 2003, p. 88; Moyo and Yeros, 2005.

161 *The Farmer*, 16 March 2000, p. 3.

162 Ibid., 6 April 2000, p. 5.

163 The land invasions radicalised more than the farmers' voices. For academic voices fervently supportive of the land reforms/invasions see Moyo and Yeros, 2005. For an exiled voice strongly against the reforms/invasions see Godwin, 2006. The interesting thing about Moyo and Godwin is that both used to be well respected for their balanced assessments of political situations in Zimbabwe. For a discussion on both see Pilossof, 2008b.

164 Harold-Barry, 2004, p. 269.

165 For more on one of the most outspoken critics of the CFU's stance see the letters of Catherine Buckle, available on her personal website. http://www.cathy-buckle.com [accessed 24 June 2010]. Also see her books, Buckle, 2001; Buckle, 2002. These are discussed at length in Chapter Five.

166 *The Farmer*, 30 May 2000, p. 1.

167 Ibid., 11 May 2000, p. 3.

168 Ibid., 16 March 2000, p. 1.

169 Ibid., 4 May 2000, p 4.

170 This was clearly not the case however. Not only were there numerous civic and political organisations opposing Mugabe and ZANU-PF, but these groups often sought to forge alliances with the CFU and white farmers to consolidate forces. The CFU refused all of these advances. Interview with the director of a

human rights organisation, Harare, 4 April 2009. See Chapter Six for more on this.

171 For the multiple dimensions of the Zimbabwean crisis, see Hammar and Raftopoulos, 2003, pp. 4-9. This dogmatic vision of a solitary cause to the Zimbabwean crisis is one of the most interesting aspects of white farmers and their continuing isolation.

172 *The Farmer*, 28 November 2000, p. 5.

173 Ibid., 5 December 2000, p. 1.

174 Ibid., 28 November 2000, p. 5.

175 Ibid., 23 March 2000, p. 11; 16 March 2000, p. 15.

176 Ibid., 20 June 2000, p. 4.

177 Ibid., 18 July 2000, p. 5.

178 Ibid., 26 September 2000, p. 3.

179 Ibid., 18 September 2001, pp. 12-13; 28 August 2001, p. 7.

180 The form of diplomacy resonates with that of the South African government and their attempts to mediate with Mugabe and his government. For more on this, see Phimister, 2005b, pp. 271-91.

181 *The Farmer*, 13 February 2001, p. 1.

182 The only indication of the closure was a small advert in the issue before which stated that MFP trust was closing due to 'restructuring'. *The Farmer*, 26 March 2002, p. 9.

183 *The Farmer*, 2 April 2002, p. 8.

184 As stated earlier, Winkfield started up a magazine called *Countdown* after *The Farmer*'s closure, but this failed to attract the advertising it needed to survive and only produced 13 editions.

185 A survey carried out by Target Market Research on behalf of *The Farmer* found that 80 per cent of readers had a positive response to the magazine's political coverage and that 87 per cent rated the magazine excellent or good in terms of editorial content and coverage of pertinent issues. *The Farmer*, 23 January 2001, p. 13.

186 Correspondence with Rook, 12 July 2009.

187 Interview with Wood, 5 October 2009; interview with Winkfield, 1 October 2009.

188 Interview with Winkfield, 1 October 2009.

189 In particular the closing down of the *Daily News* offices. See Nyarota, 2006; Chuma, 2004, pp. 133-6.

190 Cooper, 2008, p. 195.

4

Discursive Thresholds & Episodes of Crisis
The Liberation War, Gukurahundi
& the Land Occupations

People protect themselves through silences as well as through speaking.
– Carolyn Nordstrom.[1]

Introduction

The Farmer magazine played a central role in framing and constructing the political interactions of farmers. It was used as a vehicle for the union to speak to and for the community, and the community relied on it as an avenue of communication with the union. Although the degree to which the magazine performed these two distinct functions varied according to the shifting political and social context (and in no small part to the editor in charge) sustained patterns can be discerned in *The Farmer*'s publication and production. Furthermore, it provides immediate access to the language and discourses employed in farming circles.

This chapter will explore how the farming community reacted to three important and highly traumatic episodes in the country's recent history: the Liberation War in the 1970s, the violence of Gukurahundi during the 1980s, and the 'fast-track' land reforms in the 2000s.

This analysis is based on *The Farmer* for two main reasons. First, it offers valuable information about how the farming hierarchy framed these events and how they wanted them to be spoken of and understood. Second, the magazine provides frequent indications, in letters and interviews, about how farmers at large reacted to these events. Many commentators and observers have failed to connect the reactions farmers have had to the events after 2000 to earlier episodes of violence in Zimbabwe and how farmers reacted at those times. This chapter seeks to do just that.

The Discursive Threshold

The term 'discursive threshold' is most commonly associated with Gillian Whitlock and her use of it in discussing various forms of life writing. Whitlock asked, 'when does autobiography become active in the politics of identity?' She argued that a 'discursive threshold must be reached before autobiographic writing appears as an agent. This is clearly not the case for each individual autobiographical act'.[2] As such, discursive threshold will impact other forms of writing, public engagement and vocalisation beyond acts of life writing. The concept as it relates to life writing will be explored in more detail in Chapter Five, but is used here to expand on these foundations of the term and apply it to other forms of farming discourse-making.

A threshold is a point of beginning or entry. It is something that, when crossed, represents change or at least alteration. When prefaced by discursive, it creates a term that seeks to identify an occurrence after which a new form of discourse comes into the public domain. As such, a discursive threshold is achieved when, after a certain occurrence, there is a noticeable and palpable change in the discourses employed by an actor (be that an individual or a group). Such a threshold involves the waning of one discourse and the growing acceptance and use of another one. New discourses build upon elements that have been covertly or privately disseminated, but once the threshold has been passed, emerge into the public domain to receive widespread and popular recognition. As Kay Schaffer and Sidonie Smith explain:

> Local movements that 'go national' or 'international' often generate climates that enable the reception and recognition of new stories, attaining what Gillian Whitlock refers to as a 'discursive threshold' .... Emergent in communities of identification marginalised within the nation, such movements embolden individual members to understand personal experience as a ground of action and social change. Collective movements seed local acts of remembering 'otherwise,' offering members new or newly valued subject positions from which to speak and to address members of their own community in acts of solidarity. They also offer members of the dominant community occasions for witnessing to human rights abuse, acknowledging and affirming the rights of others. Through acts of remembering, individuals and communities narrate alternative or counter-histories coming from the margins, voiced by other kinds of subjects – the tortured, the displaced and overlooked, the silenced

and unacknowledged .... Individuals and groups may also engage in narrative acts of critical self-locating through which they assert their cultural difference and right to self-determination, or they may imagine leaving the past behind for a new social order or a newly empowered collective subjectivity.[3]

Two discursive thresholds of major importance occurred in the period under examination. One is a silencing threshold that seeks to 'leave the past behind' and the other is a reawakening or a renewed attempt to assert the 'right to self-determination'. The first was independence in 1980. The election of Mugabe and the introduction of a black national-ist government necessitated a shift in the language white farmers used to employ to discuss and refer to black leaders and political parties. The language of the war was quickly abandoned as farmers sought to adapt to the new political context and ensure their survival. However, the problematic process of national unity after 1980 resulted in many of the divisive discourses linked to the trauma of the war being ignored and unresolved. The discourse changed, but this masked or silenced underly-ing divisions. This is illustrated in *The Farmer* magazine in a number of interesting ways. The second discursive threshold was the year 2000 and the start of the land invasions. These events reinvigorated much of the language and discourse of the Liberation War and offered the opportu-nity for these discourses to re-emerge and become potent once more. Events after 2000 resuscitated many of the fears of dispossession and exile evident in the 1970s, but which were paved over in the 1980s and 1990s. They also created audiences, both local and international, recep-tive to those anxieties. Furthermore, they opened the way for farmers to express themselves in ways they had been unwilling and unable to do after independence. *The Farmer* shows how these changes unfolded and how these spaces were opened up.

Attempting to identify the specific moment of a discursive shift, such as when a certain term or phrasing becomes accepted in public arenas, is often both impractical and self-defeating: the new discourse is never entirely new and will always feed off elements that existed before. What changes is how these new ways of understanding gain popular and politi-cal currency. As a result, it is important to identify the circumstances that enable this shift to take place. This chapter explores the impact of the discursive thresholds identified and how these relate themselves in the magazine. The purpose, according to Hideki Richard Okada:

is not to reify 'historical background' or to be concerned with how a text [such as *The Farmer*] can be read as simply 'mirroring history,' but to examine why a narrative should enact a particular reappropriation of 'history.' The examination of a particular discursive threshold, by allowing a convergence of various intertextual and narrative aspects, can help trace the narratological (and/or ideological) perspectives of the text in a way that neither so-called literary, nor historical foundationalist readings are able to do.[4]

It is this approach which underpins the examination of *The Farmer* in this chapter, and which offers a critical discussion on the discursive thresholds identified and how these impacted on the other forms of expression analysed in Chapters Five and Six. As Okada pointed out, there is a critical need to understand and explore how other forces impacted on a particular reaction to a threshold. Not only are the contexts important, but also how interactions are formed and disseminated.

There is merit in locating changes in the way people or groups talk about events. In their study of white society during the 1970s, Peter Godwin and Ian Hancock stated:

> There are considerable rewards for paying more attention to what Rhodesians actually said and did. Their language, rituals, and symbols are fertile sources for their political culture .... For, by exploring the Rhodesian language ... [historians] can draw conclusions about the level of White ignorance, political sensitivity, and sophistication. They might also locate the deeper recesses where individuals and groups hid their fears and superstitions about the unknown Africa and the allegedly unknowable African mind.[5]

The same can be said for white farmers after 2000. There is a great deal to be gained from a detailed and historical analysis of the discourses employed, rather than simply observing their reappearance. This chapter looks at three key episodes of violence and how they have affected the discourses that have emerged. It looks at the politics of *The Farmer* and the Commercial Farmers' Union of Zimbabwe's (CFU) representation of violence against farmers and how this was dictated by the prevailing contexts in which they were immersed.

The Liberation War, Gukurahundi & the Shifting Discourses of Violence and Victimhood

The Liberation War had a huge impact on the farming community as a whole. In terms of the immediate and physical realities, farmers were often on the front line of the conflict and were frequent targets for attack by the guerrillas.[6] While the physical threat was highly uneven, with the vast majority of farming deaths, attacks and desertions occurring in the outlying border regions, the threat of land expropriation espoused by the nationalist movements affected the entire community. This threat was constant throughout the war and was intensified by the coming of independence to other parts of Africa, and the failures associated with these developments in the eyes of the farming community.[7] These fears and concerns were a constant part of the white social fabric and were intensified by the arrival of independence across the continent. 'Memories' of Mau Mau were often evoked, as were those of violence against white settlers in Belgian Congo and Mozambique.[8] With the increasing inevitability of the end of white rule by the late 1970s, the sense of trepidation became ever more apparent.[9]

With the coming of independence, the avenues for the expression of the fear of black rule became remarkably narrow. The public discourse became instead one of hope, reconciliation and rejuvenation. This process was facilitated by Mugabe's reconciliatory approach to white farmers, which revealed that, in practice, there was little for white farmers to fear under his rule. The white farming community and hierarchy actively participated in this new approach. As one would expect, this process is easily identifiable in *The Farmer*. However, the change in discourse had a number of other interesting effects on the remit and approach of the magazine. One of the most important of these was the issue of violence and farming deaths. How these issues were covered in the magazine in the 1970s was radically different to how they were addressed in the 1980s. This shift has important ramifications for the approach to and coverage of the violence after 2000.

The 1970s and the 'War'

The *Rhodesian Farmer* offered no direct coverage of the traumas experienced by the farming community during the guerrilla campaigns of the 1970s. While 'security concerns' were often raised in the magazine, the obvious fact that these 'concerns' were directly responsible for increasing numbers of farming deaths was not stated. It is a denial that the magazine followed consistently throughout the 1960s and 1970s. Reports of attacks on white farmers were conspicuous by their absence. Even when Pieter Johannes Andries Oberholzer, a farmer from Melsetter (Chimanimani), was stabbed to death at a roadblock ambush in 1964 (becoming the first white Rhodesian to be killed by African combatants since 1897) the *Rhodesian Farmer* made no mention of his death.[10] Two more farmers were killed in 1966, but as before, their deaths were not reported.[11] From then until 1973, 'terrorists' killed no other farmers in guerrilla activity, but in the early 1970s the liberation war started in earnest.[12] The starting point of the new campaign came on 21 December 1972, when guerrillas attacked Altena farm in Centenary. While no one was killed, those injured became the first white casualties of 'the renewed guerrilla war'.[13] From this point there was an obvious 'change from the sporadic, and militarily ineffectual, actions of the Sixties, to protracted armed struggle'.[14] The *Rhodesian Farmer* kept such events out of the magazine. Indeed, the only report of a farming death that was directly attributed to 'terrorist action' was that of Peter Purcell-Gilpin and his son Alastair in 1979 in a two-paragraph article.[15]

It must be stressed that this was not because farming deaths were uncommon. As *The Farmer at War* documents, from 1964 to 1979 over 270 members of the Rhodesian National Farmers' Union (RNFU), or their families, were killed over this period.[16] These figures do not represent farmers killed on active military duty, only those killed in ambushes on their farms or elsewhere.[17] As John Mckenzie points out, in the small tight-knit farming areas the deaths of white farmers had significant impact: 'In the small white rural community ... the loss of a single life brought a new sense of urgency to security matters, and prompted organised agriculture to redouble its attempts to ensure farmers' safety from attack'.[18] Security concerns and the deaths of farmers were a key concern to the RNFU and the RF government.

Although direct commentary on death was avoided, there were numerous indications of the worsening situation within the *Rhodesian Farmer*'s pages. For instance, when atrocities did start to escalate after 1973, both the government and the RNFU acted swiftly to offer farmers support to stay on the land. Two of the most obvious of these measures received ample coverage in the magazine. The first was a detailed summary and appraisal of the government's terrorist compensation bill.[19] The second was lengthy coverage of the RNFU's life assurance scheme.[20] As the *Rhodesian Farmer* illustrated, this new scheme was directly tailored to cover the loss and damage under the banner of 'terrorism': 'one very important feature [of the plan] – which will not go un-noticed, nor unappreciated by the farming community – is that the death benefits will be

paid for any cause INCLUDING WAR, ACTS OF WAR AND TER-
RORIST ACTIVITY'.[21] Death and injury due to 'terrorist' activity was
clearly an increasing concern for much of the farming fraternity and this
plan sought to appease those apprehensions.

The only other indications the *Rhodesian Farmer* gave of the worsening security situation were adverts for and reviews of various forms of
security and defence. The first of these was published at the end of 1976,
which, at that point, was the worst year on record for white farming
deaths. It was a review of the new 'all-Rhodesian 9-mm L.D.P. semi-
automatic pistol'.[22] Lightweight and easy to handle, this was sold as the
perfect weapon for women and for household defence. Over the next few
years, more such adverts were published, from hand grenade screens to
landmine-proof vehicles.[23] Some of these adverts even appeared on the
cover of the magazine: in May 1978, Curtis, a fencing company, offered
'a FREE LDP PARABELLUM MACHINE PISTOL [emphasis in orig-
inal] with every security fence'.[24]

Why then did the magazine steadfastly refuse to directly acknowledge
violence and death? One might have expected that white farmers would
wish to highlight their plight during the war with a great deal of vigour by
publishing details of horrific deaths and atrocities carried out by 'savage'
and 'cowardly' terrorists. The protection of a sympathetic government,
one would imagine, would have given Modern Farming Publications the
freedom to relate the ordeals of the community without fear of reprisal.

The reasons were directly related to white attitudes to the war itself,
and white understandings of what was occurring in the 1970s. The 'Liberation War' was never framed as such by white media, the *Rhodesian
Farmer* included. As Anthony Chennells has noted:

> The war, when it came, could not be a war; it could only be a rebellion, which
> meant, in settler mythology, primitive space attempting to reabsorb civilised
> space, and it was as a battle against this reassertion of the primitive that the
> war was described and indeed fought. Their failure to understand what was
> happening around them was entirely predictable. Victims as they were of their
> own discourses, fostered over the years and kept ignorant by their media of
> developing ideologies among Black nationalists, the settlers ... had few means
> of correctly analyzing the situation in which they found themselves.[25]

There was therefore a widespread and general misunderstanding of the
war and the reasons for which it was fought. All black nationalists were
tarred with the same brush in *The Farmer* as foreign-trained peasants

who sought to sabotage the existing racial harmony in the country. There was no discussion or recognition of the war as a struggle for independence and there was no way this could be permitted to be expressed in white political discourse.

Because of this, the magazine sought to keep intact the image of farmers as resilient, determined masters of the land. Articles recounting their deaths and struggles would have countered this message. While the community could face 'security concerns', and lobby government to find solutions to those issues, the portrayal of death was transgressive, especially amongst such a small, isolated and identifiable group. 'Real farmers' did not 'die', and they especially did not die at the hands of inept and incompetent black peasants. The magazine therefore sought to negate, or at least soften, the impact of the war. Since the government and the RNFU were so keen to keep farmers on their land, publication of farming casualties would have had a negative impact on the morale of farmers and may have incited many more to leave their land. Whilst it is naïve to think that such stories would not anyway have spread within the community, by not making them a permanent feature of public expression, the magazine sought to keep the issue of violence confined.

The publishers of the magazine did however produce a book in 1979 – *The Farmer at War* – which attempted to illustrate how dramatically the war affected the lives of white farmers and the sacrifices that they had made to protect their land and livelihoods. It collected much of its material from the *Rhodesian Farmer*, but, as the title suggests, it was much more concerned with the process of the war and its repercussions. It championed the white farmers for what they had done for the country and what they had battled against:

> The Zimbabwe Rhodesian farmer is at war. He is in the frontline of this conflict, a top 'soft target' for the externally-based, Communist-trained terrorists whose aim is to remove whites from the country and destroy their influence which in 89 short years has been the key to economic and social development unparalleled on the African continent.[26]

The pictures in the book further indicate the aim of the publication. Dead 'terrorists' were shown, as were 're-educated terrorists', attacked homesteads, security forces in action, refugees and prisoners, child victims of 'terrorist' attacks, arms, dead cattle, voting in April 1978 and the celebrations of 'majority rule' at the formation of Zimbabwe–Rhodesia. The book was at once a call to arms, a lobbying for the defence of farmers, a morale booster and tourist brochure. This is evidenced in its acknowl-edgements, where thanks are given to 'The Rhodesia National Farmers Union (now the Commercial Farmers Union), Combined Operations, Ministry of Foreign Affairs, Ministry of Information, National Tourist Board, BSAP magazine, *The Outpost* [and] *The Herald*.'[27] The book also included a Roll of Honour of all the farmers killed by 'terrorists' during the 1960s and 1970s. It thus expressed the impact and cost of the war far more than the *Rhodesian Farmer* had ever done.

The coming of independence in 1980 radically altered the discourse and approach of the magazine. With the election of ZANU-PF, the farming community and the union found themselves under a black gov-ernment. As Chennells has commented, 'With Mugabe's victory at the polls both the discourse and the Rhodesia which had produced it were simultaneously swept away.'[28] The farmers and their media had to find new ways to report on themselves and the state. The negotiation of inter-action between farmers and government was fundamental to the creation of a new discourse. In the event, this meant that the farming community was keen to do all it could to secure its place in the new national order. Violence and death again played a central role. As the war ended and the new 'peaceful' era of independence began, white farmers had more to gain from reporting violence than they ever did during the war.

The 1980s and Gukurahundi

Mugabe's reconciliatory appeals to the white farming community fos-tered a convenient partnership, one that remained intact during the 1980s despite the violence that was wrought in Matabeleland. Some white farmers in Matabeleland found themselves the victims of 'dissi-dent' attacks, in which significant numbers of them were killed; in some areas the numbers were higher than during the Liberation War. For the farmers in the affected areas, it was as if the war had never ended, as they continued to live under the threat of violence and death. The distur-bances, and the government's response, were concentrated in the south of the country and had a massive impact in Matabeleland and the Mid-lands, where farmers were caught in the crossfire between state actors and 'dissident' forces. Their unforeseen acceptance by the ZANU-PF government meant that they were now part of the new national pro-ject. The Union took on its 'national' responsibility and endeavoured to ensure that positive messages of its support for the new government and their actions were expressed. This was done on numerous occasions and in various forms of print as the farming community and the new government constantly reaffirmed the partnership between the two. However, the rise in dissident activity in the countryside after 1980, and the resulting deaths of white farmers, meant the union found itself in the difficult position of advocating white farming rights and security, whilst seeking not to fracture its relationship with the government. The CFU felt that its best course of action lay in fully aligning itself with ZANU-PF, regardless of the government's abuses. It must be remembered that white farmers were not alone in this chosen path. As Phimister has illustrated, few questions were raised about the government's actions at this time by any national or international body, as the pursuit of racial reconciliation between black and white was viewed as far more important than the ethnic antagonisms of 'black on black' violence.[29]

The reconciliation extended to the whites after independence (including Ian Smith himself) was not extended to Mugabe's other political rivals, Joshua Nkomo and ZAPU. Tensions between the two men and parties, evident before the coming of independence, continued after independence, resulting in several armed skirmishes and deliberate manoeuvres by Mugabe to undermine and disenfranchise Nkomo and his party.[30] As a consequence, many parts of Matabeleland witnessed civil unrest and disobedience, as political and regional distrust, compounded by racial and ethnic tensions, intensified. Finally, in 1983, under the pretext that unrest in Matabeleland was being caused by forces loyal to ZAPU who refused to accept the election results of 1980, Mugabe deployed the newly trained Fifth Brigade and other military units.[31] What followed was a wave of violence that, from 1983 to 1986, claimed an estimated 20,000 lives, while 'hundreds of thousands of others were tortured, assaulted or raped or had their property destroyed'.[32]

Throughout this time, ZANU-PF propaganda maintained that there were large numbers of 'dissident' and 'rebel' forces roaming the country who were seeking to destabilise the country and who posed a very real threat to the fledgling democracy's sovereignty and integrity.[33] It is now widely accepted that such language and this framing of events had more to do with the political expediency of legitimating the scale of intrusion into the region than with the threat actually posed. Nevertheless, in a region so affected by the transnational interplay of states and actors, there was an element of truth to ZANU-PF's claims. In addition to the presence of ZAPU dissidents, rumours abounded of a Super-ZAPU force operating in the area. This Super-ZAPU was supported and trained by South Africa in an operation code-named 'Operation Drama'. As with attempts to destabilise other regional front-line states such as Mozambique and Angola, members of Super-ZAPU were trained to exacerbate the 'security situation already in existence'.[34] The South African government hoped to gain international currency by demonstrating the 'failures' of black rule and highlighting the deaths of white Africans.[35] According to the *Breaking the Silence* report, very little is known about the details of Operation Drama and it is thought that the force deployed probably numbered in the tens, rather than hundreds.[36] While there certainly were rebel ZAPU elements, 'the scale of the threat posed by dissident activity … was greatly exaggerated'.[37] Reports from the state-run news services frequently claimed that the rebels numbered up to 5,000, while the official government line was that there were around 1,000 heavily armed 'dissidents' in the country.[38] In fact the dissidents probably numbered 400 at most. Furthermore, they had remarkably high desertion and attrition rates, due to the harsh conditions of their existence and the forces massed against them.[39]

White farmers were often direct victims of dissident activity. By 1987, more than 50 farmers and their families had been murdered by dissidents.[40] *Breaking the Silence* acknowledges that it is:

> generally accepted by all parties that dissidents were responsible for all the murders of white farmers and their families in the 1980s. Between late 1982 and 1983, 33 farmers or their family members were murdered. While the impact of dissidents on civilians in the communal lands was perceived as less harsh by far than that of 5 Brigade, the impact of the dissidents on the small commercial farming communities was dramatic.[41]

The scale of violence and threat of attack that farmers in these areas experienced meant that they existed in circumstances similar to those they faced during the Liberation War. This is illustrated in a report on conditions in Matabeleland published in *The Farmer* in 1986. Under the title 'They Need Help', the article drew an obvious comparison to events of the war:

> Many farmers in other farming areas of the country have long since forgotten those dark days of the war and living under constant threat of attack. Thankfully those days are over [for most farmers] and farmers are able to concentrate on their essential occupations … / Consider then the plight of Matabeleland

farmers and their wives and families. / Spare a thought for farmers who still have to live like that.[42]

Not surprisingly, the events that so devastated the white farming communities in Matabeleland and Midlands received a great deal of attention in *The Farmer*. Concerns over security and stability had been constant themes in the magazine throughout the Liberation War, and the continuing rural violence after 1980 meant that such issues were never far from the magazine's view. However, there was a new tension to this coverage. During the 1970s, it had simply labelled all such activity as 'terrorist'. Now, with a black 'terrorist' government in charge, farmers and *The Farmer* had to find more nuanced ways of describing and reporting on events of rural violence. Thankfully for *The Farmer*, it was the government itself that provided the new discourse on these elements that solved the problems of identification.

Directly after independence, ZANU-PF began to disseminate anti-ZAPU and anti-ZIPRA propaganda aimed at discrediting them as legitimate agents of national liberation. This involved labelling all crime and robberies in Matabeleland as the work of 'dissidents' and 'bandits', terms that were quickly and unashamedly adopted by the CFU and *The Farmer*. They allowed *The Farmer* to define any disturbances in these provinces as caused by 'dissidents', and the magazine was now even keen to publish stories about the deaths of white farmers. The first was reported in March 1981. Four members of the Victoria East farming community had been gunned down in their homes and *The Farmer* outlined the CFU's deep concern at the loss of life and increasing lawlessness in the region.[43] Although the farmers were thought to have been killed by purely criminal elements, there were many references to the Liberation War throughout the article. For instance, the killers were 'armed with AK rifles – the standard weapon of guerrillas during the war'. The article hazarded a guess that the 'killers may have been guerrillas in the past'. Clearly, events and memories of that time were still fresh in the minds of the farming community; the article concluded that 'Lawlessness has been discussed at Cabinet level and the re-introduction of Agric-Alert in most of the countryside means, basically, that the community must stay alert as it did during the war which claimed hundreds of farming lives.'[44]

The next farm murder was a full year later, in May 1982. Brian Dawe, a Chinhoyi cattle rancher, was reportedly killed by three 'AK-waving "dissidents"'.[45] In what was to become a common lament of the CFU and *The Farmer*, the 'security situation' was now said to be the gravest concern for the white farming community. It was made clear that 'every representation on the matter that can be made has been made, including to the police and the National Army'.[46] By this time it was obvious that white farmers had become key targets of the 'dissident' forces.[47] *The Farmer* assigned all violence in Matabeleland and the Midlands to 'cowardly' dissidents and bandits.[48] This shift of discourse responded positively to the government's explanation for the continued violence in the region.[49] ZANU-PF's hostility to the dissident forces was such that *The Farmer* could use it to support white farmers' own calls for protection by the new black government. The death of white farmers augmented such calls and the magazine constantly highlighted the plight of white farmers in order to maintain the pressure. The farming representatives could now use the death of white farmers in ways they could not during the Liberation War. The national unity project depended on ZANU-PF defending the rights of its white and black citizens. Regardless of the fact that it was in the process of instigating a massive campaign of violence against the black population of Matabeleland, the government went to great lengths to be seen to be protecting white farmers, thereby preserving the façade of racial unity and harmony in the country.

The most dramatic change in the discourse employed by *The Farmer* after 1980 is that it began to speak of death and violence. Farmers now had the space to claim protection and defence. They were a fragile and highly susceptible group that needed constant affirmations of support from the new black government. This support was readily provided, and the government realised that it could use the attacks on white farmers to further promote their control over Matabeleland.

In *The Farmer*'s account of Dawe's murder, Mugabe's reaction to dissident-led attack was published alongside those of the farming hierarchy: 'I can assure you they [the dissidents] cannot escape the hand of justice. In due course we are going to rid this region of these elements which are committed to banditry.'[50] The vast majority of articles on the violence and killings in the region were accompanied by messages of support and acclaim for what *The Farmer* viewed as the government's evident commitment to resolving the security concerns in the region.[51] An in-depth feature about the region in 1983 noted that:

> The police and 5 Brigade members that we saw were turned out in clean kit, looked fit and were well armed. However ... the security forces are often

handicapped by a reluctance of victims or witnesses to report the incidents .... Government's heavy military commitment to the area leaves no doubt as to its intention to restore law and order.[52]

This understanding of government actions was in line with what was proclaimed by the CFU leadership at the time. For example, in 1984, the CFU president John Laurie was quoted in *The Farmer* as saying, 'The commercial farming sector is fully aligned with the Government's fight for stability and law and order.'[53] As the violence continued, his successor as CFU president, Bobby Rutherford, reiterated this sentiment, confirming that 'numerous meetings have taken place with ministers and members of the security forces, and I wish to assure you [the farmers] of their concern and their determination to see an end to the harassment and unwarranted loss of life.'[54]

When the security forces killed the notorious bandit, Gwesela, it was heralded as a great achievement:

The news that Gwesela ... has at last been killed has come as a great relief to many people, not least the people whom he and his gang have terrorised over the last few years. Farmers, farm workers, officials, tribesmen have all been victims of his ruthless and inhuman acts. / It is good that ordinary people realise that there is nobody who is above the law and that criminals will be dealt with.[55]

Occurrences such as this were reported with obvious relish in *The Farmer*, bringing a palpable sense of relief to the farming communities.[56]

However, there was a tension between the CFU sanctioned reporting in *The Farmer*, and those actually affected by the violence. Despite the *The Farmer*'s focus on the issue, many farmers still felt that the magazine greatly under-reported the extent of the violence. Regional newspapers often gave much greater weight to the events in Matabeleland, and offered farmers the space to deliver messages that were much more explicit about the violence. For example, the *Sunday Times* (South Africa) reported Mike Wood, 'president of the Matabeleland branch of the all-white' CFU, who said that, 'this is the biggest crisis we have ever faced in the area.'[57] Others warned that unless something was done to stop the dissident threat, 'there will be another war in this part of the country'.[58] Another report had a white farmer saying:

'Comparing the situation now to during the war, virtually all agree that things are now worse'. / 'At least then you knew that if you got revved,[59] there would be a reaction from the security forces or the farmers themselves. Now all you'll get will be some blundering around in the bush and "Sorry, tracks lost",' said one rancher .... The ideologically-indoctrinated Fifth and Sixth Brigades whose training was mainly the responsibility of North Korean trained instructors, are units which come in for the toughest criticism in the province. / Many farmers have experiences of verbal clashes with these soldiers, who seem to have an antipathy for whites. / Mr Wood said at Bulawayo that some units almost considered the farmers a hindrance. 'This attitude is completely unacceptable.'[60]

These voices carried in external newspapers could be far more radical than those reported in *The Farmer* because they could question the actions of the government. As long as ZANU-PF protected farming interests, the magazine and the CFU could offer no alternative explanation for events in Matabeleland, other than 'dissident violence' which the government was allegedly doing all it could to address.

On the few occasions when *The Farmer* did articulate concerns about government actions in Matabeleland, these primarily expressed dissatisfaction that the government was not doing enough to quell the so-called dissident threat. The first apparent dissension appeared in 1983 when, at the Cattle Congress, *The Farmer* reported that 'in a heated debate on security, law and order, particularly in Matabeleland, Government was accused of "covering up" the true situation'.[61] Tellingly, the same report revealed the extent of white farmers' awareness of government and Fifth Brigade activity in the region:

Mr Joubert [a farmer in the Bubue District, one of the worst affected areas] alleged that instead of hunting dissident gangs, troops are avoiding them. He claims that on several occasions, dissidents had ambushed Army personnel. Army units, said Mr Joubert, would not attack gangs of more than 15 dissidents and often avoided contact with smaller groups. / Mr Joubert angrily criticised the lack of response by Army and Police to reported sightings and alleged Army and Police units on the ground lacked the will and motivation to counteract dissident activity.[62]

The article labelled the drought affecting the country as 'a holocaust', with no evident sense of irony or understanding of the broader context of events.

Other reports followed a similar pattern, criticising only the scale and efficiency of government actions. For example:

It is now clear that, regardless of all measures adopted to date, the terrorist activities of the dissidents continue unabated. / We look to government to reach an agreement that will result in conditions that remove all local support from the dissidents and permit our whole population to go about their lawful business in peace.[63]

The resurgence of such activities is very distressing and unsettling for people in these regions and it damages productivity. / Where security forces have taken prompt action this is appreciated. However, I [CFU President Bob Rutherford] must stress the continuing need for firm action to deal with the perpetrators of such horrifying acts against innocent civilians.[64]

In a strongly worded address ... Mr Laurie [CFU President at the time] queried the effectiveness and discipline 'of some elements of the security forces'. / If there were some elements of the security forces in Matabeleland who were not able to control the security situation 'then I ask that they be pulled out to make way for those who can'. / 'The safety and protection of farmers, farm workers and other civilians must be achieved, enabling them to go about their lawful work without fear and in peace.'[65]

Laurie's quote, and the way it was framed in *The Farmer*, is very revealing. As reported in *The Farmer*, it comes across as reserved and measured. However, the same address was reported in other media, for example *The Star*. Their evaluation of Laurie's statement was far stronger:

War-weary, worried and angry, Matabeleland's white farmers have warned the Government of Zimbabwe that they will quit their land unless something is done about the ineffectiveness of the army in anti-dissident operations in the province. / Commercial Farmer's Union (CFU) president Mr John Laurie and farmers from the province made the point in no uncertain terms when they met the Minister of State responsible for Defence, Mr Ernest Kadungure, here at the weekend. / Mr Laurie told the minister that the farmers wanted a full military inquiry into the failure of military follow-up operations after the killing last week of Figtree farmer Mr Ian Birchall. The CFU delegates also said they wanted ineffective army units pulled out and replaced with those who could do the job properly.[66]

This illustrates the difficulty the farming union faced in promoting its own cause whilst simultaneously seeking to be part of the new 'inclusive' nation.

As *The Farmer* sought to balance its reportage and representation of the government, farm murders continued to mount. In August 1987 it reported that 'well over 40' farmers or members of their families had been killed in Matabeleland and Midlands 'since Independence at the hands of murderous dissidents'.[67] A month later, John Norvall became the '50th [to lose his life] since 1980'.[68] *The Farmer* gave details of the vast majority of these murders, including a great deal of coverage of the murder of 16 missionaries near Esigodini, in Matabeleland.[69] Yet it was constrained by its desire to appease the government and stay on the right side of the political elite. As Mike Rook, who was General Manager of MFP Trust, explained:

> there was a policy of reconciliation during the 80s and a desire to play down events that would deter investment .... The overriding interest seemed to be to pacify the government of the day that was at the time supporting large-scale commercial agriculture.[70]

Despite the coverage of 'dissident' activity and other 'security concerns' in *The Farmer*, there was absolutely no mention of the mass violence carried out by the Fifth Brigade against the people of Matabeleland.

For the victims and survivors of Gukurahundi, statements such as 'the rule of law' and the 'cruel and inhuman acts' solely of the dissidents are totally at odds with their experiences.[71] More than just an isolated episode of 'tribal' violence, ZANU-PF's campaign in Matabeleland was a concerted and deliberate attempt to destroy the opposition's regional base. As such, it illustrated that ZANU-PF still operated much as it had done during the Liberation War. It was still overwhelmingly 'hierarchical and authoritarian' rather than democratic and inclusive. It was highly 'militaristic, vertical, undemocratic, violent and repressive', and continued to conduct politics 'though the barrel of a gun', a practice that became all too evident after 2000 with the rise of the MDC.[72]

The CFU and *The Farmer*'s deliberate and complicit silence on the issue needs further explanation. Considering the extent of the government's operations in Matabeleland, it seems unlikely that farmers would not have had some indication as to what was actually taking place. As the comments by Mr Joubert on the intricacies of Fifth Brigade movements make clear, some white farmers had very detailed knowledge of events in the region. Yet *The Farmer* never confronted the issue.[73] To understand why, Rook provides revealing retrospective arguments. With regard to the coverage of Gukurahundi, he claims that 'the extent of the deliberately motivated genocidal [sic] policies then being perpetrated by the 5th Brigade in Matabeleland were at the time successfully shaded by government propaganda'.[74] However, he admits that this was not the only reason for the circumspect reporting: '*The Farmer* then and later was sometimes subject to censorship by CFU. The degree of censorship was dependent on who was holding the Presidency at the time, and who was serving on the all powerful Council.'[75] During this time, one of the CFU presidents was Rutherford, who was described by the CFU Director at the time as 'a card carrying political harlot, who spent more time with government than with his members'.[76] Having survived the coming of majority rule, it is clear that the CFU wished to preserve its cosy relationship with the new government. Offering criticism of its approach in Matabeleland would have put that partnership in jeopardy, so the CFU muzzled *The Farmer* and forced it to toe the CFU and party line.

Changes in the political environment allowed a new discourse to emerge in *The Farmer* after independence. With the threshold of black majority rule having been crossed, the CFU worked hard to secure a partnership with the new government. White farmers could now portray themselves as victims of the dissidents (unlike during the Liberation War) and could actively and publicly call on government for support and protection. As a result, they were complicit in the violence wrought by Gukurahundi.

The political changes following independence had a massive impact on the discourses employed by the farming community. It gave them the tools to proclaim a victim status, which would be refined and reinforced with the violence of the land reforms after 2000. However, because it was protected and encouraged by the ZANU-PF government during the first decade of independence, the farming community gained a sense of confidence that allowed it to withdraw from the public arena and retreat to its own insular world. While the 1990s brought some changes to this approach, it was only after 2000 that there was another major shift in the farming discourse. After the signing of the Unity Accord in 1988 and the capitulation of ZAPU, the security situation was resolved. The threat of violence dissipated and farmers could withdraw further from public engagement. Confrontation with the government escalated during the 1990s, but there was no obvious movement toward any form of organised violence. However, this changed dramatically with the emergence of the MDC, following the Constitutional Referendum in February 2000 and the start of the land occupations. These events resulted in a new wave of violence that was markedly different from the threats farmers had faced in the past, and which represent another important discursive threshold.

2000 & After: State-Sponsored Violence & the Reformed Victimhood of White Farmers

By 2000 *The Farmer* had a much greater degree of editorial freedom than it did during the 1970s and 80s. The editorial staff used this space to full effect when the land occupations began, and reported openly on events in the countryside. This initial approach was curtailed somewhat in the second year of the invasions, partly due to increasing pressures from the CFU for the magazine to tone down its reporting, but also because it had become clear by then that the land occupations were not fleeting occurrences that would quickly dissipate. These land invasions were very different in character from earlier episodes, where popular localised occupations occurred independently (and were often suppressed by the state): white farmers were now direct targets of the state. The realisation that they were under attack reinvigorated the often racist white farming discourses of the 1970s that had lain dormant since the immediate aftermath of independence. Now these discourses had widespread domestic, regional and western support, as well as the evidence on which to reassert underlying beliefs about the true nature of black rule and Mugabe.[77]

The Farmer capitalised on these opportunities and set about recasting farmers as 'reformed victims'. The reason for use of this term is that the overwhelming majority of coverage white farmers received from the international press (but not in the rest of Africa) portrayed them as innocent victims of Mugabe's desperate attempts to hold onto power.[78] The prime example of this is Christina Lamb's book, *House of Stone*, which illustrates this reforming process extremely well.[79] According to her narrative, the white farmer she focuses on, Nigel Hough, was a racist, often employing terms such as 'munt' and 'kaffir' and making derogatory statements about black people in general, but he undergoes a racial reassessment in the 1990s and by the time of the land occupations in 2000 had no racial bias or prejudice whatsoever.[80] As part of this reformed victim portrayal, white farmers were rendered as people who led simple lives and who continued farming for the good of the country. Crucially, the contemporary white farming community was disassociated from that of the 1970s, understood as a racist, bigoted elite who had enriched themselves at the expense of the rural peasantry.[81] The white farmers of 2000 had apparently reformed themselves and had truly become part of Zimbabwe.

If they had been racist, they no longer were; they were now seen as true sons of the soil who belonged to Zimbabwe in any and every way.[82] Land inequalities were dismissed as faults of the government's misrule, and no attempt was made to discuss the inequalities of wealth. This international sympathy was gratefully identified by *The Farmer* and had a significant influence on the way it reported on events after 2000.

The violence and terror wrought on the community was certainly of a scale white farmers had never before experienced. The trauma of the Liberation War and Gukurahundi were surpassed by the land invasions, which eventually spread across the entire country. This wholesale onslaught fundamentally undermined the foundations of the white farming community. This was of course what many white farmers in the 1970s had predicted was going to happen after independence. The intervening two decades of relative peace (certainly in Mashonaland if not Matabeleland) and prosperity did nothing to placate those fears.

The farm occupations became the staple content of the magazine for the next two years. Even before the more horrific violence began in earnest, images and memories of the Liberation War and the violence of Gukurahundi were evoked. For instance, a 9 March report on farm violence claimed that 'the "war vets", many too young to have fought in Zimbabwe's bush war' had 'invaded' farms in northern Zimbabwe.[83] This sentence captures the essence of white farmers' attitudes towards the land occupations. 'Invasion' became the standard description, and was adopted by national and international media.[84] The dubious credentials of the 'war veterans' were also highlighted. Although this scepticism had been expressed since 1997, with the government's compensation payments to war veterans and the corruption that ensued, it was cemented in 2000. The term 'bush war' used in this sentence is saturated with racial undertones that are implicitly dismissive of the struggle for independence. For those who subscribe to the 'bush war' view of the conflict, a 'war veteran' was in fact a cowardly 'terrorist', rather than a soldier worthy of the title and fighting for a legitimate cause. While it is indeed debatable how many of the land occupiers were war veterans, the use of the term by white farmers and in *The Farmer* became laden with mocking and insulting overtones.

This easy recall of the 1970s and the related sense of victimhood expressed itself in other ways. On 16 March 2000, Brian Latham wrote in his 'Leader' column that anyone seeking to understand these events:

should also take note of the parallels between the present situation and the situation the country faced in 1979. Back then, South Africa and Portugal closed the taps, forcing Smith to capitulate – and right now there is every sign the taps are being closed again, this time by South Africa and Britain.[85]

The implication is that ZANU-PF would not have won the 'war' were it not for outside assistance. White farmers are reminded that foreign intervention did not aid their cause then and they should not rely on it now.

Images of other attacks on whites in Africa were also evoked: 'Chenjerai Hunzvi's Zimbabwe National Liberation War Veterans' Association (ZNLWVA) has threatened to wage a Mau-Mau style war against [white] commercial farmers in Zimbabwe.'[86] As Richard Winkfield often stated in his 'Bottom Line' column, the disaster occurring in Zimbabwe was a typical manifestation of the broader decay of the continent.[87] In April 2000, Winkfield played on the speeches of Mugabe:

> In April 1982 the Prime Minister of Zimbabwe said: 'No sane political leader, and I believe we are sane, can, even in the absence of constitutional provisions offering racial safeguards, fail to recognise and appreciate the existence and worth of the community so sizeable and so culturally and economically strong as our white community by adopting policies that deny them right of representation in the governing institutions of the country.' (The Herald, 7 April 1982). / Exactly 18 years later our nation and more particularly our commercial farming community is being systematically bludgeoned into oblivion by lawless thugs under the command of a self styled 'Hitler' who has the tacit approval of the same person who in 1982 had given so much hope to the new Zimbabwe. / In his own recent words 'white farmers are enemies of the state'. What has gone wrong and how long will the madness last? These same questions must have been asked by the Jews and Gypsies in Central Europe under the vicious heel of the Nazis just 65 years ago, which was the beginning of the holocaust which lasted just 12 years.[88]

White farmers' capacity to present themselves as a victim group was aided by ZANU-PF's own radical language surrounding the land invasions, with the language of the Second Chimurenga reignited for this Third Chimurenga and the need for a final solution to the land problem.[89] These attempts to equate their situation to that suffered by Jews under Nazi rule reveal just how threatened this group believed it was. As has been noted, the furore white farmers managed to whip up over the land invasions even resulted in Genocide Watch (an international organisation established to predict, prevent, stop, and punish genocide and other forms of mass murder) opening a case study on white farmers.[90] *The Farmer* continually suggested this parallel in the last two years of its publication. In 2001 Latham wrote:

> Mugabe and his henchmen (to borrow a phrase) are intent on whipping up racial hatred in Zimbabwe ahead of a presidential election that should fall between January and March next year. He is using the same sort of language, and adopting similar tactics, to those being used by Mr Adolf Hitler against Jews when the Nationalist Socialist Party was attempting to consolidate its power.[91]

It should be remembered that, while the vast majority of farmers were forced from their land, only eleven white farmers were killed between 2000 and 2004 (and not all of these in actions sanctioned by government).[92] However, the Nazi-type violence referred to by *The Farmer* concerned actions against white farmers, not the wider farming community (including black farm workers). Over the same period, hundreds of farm workers and MDC members were killed by government forces. The recent JAG reports confirm the fact that the overwhelming majority of violence on white farms was suffered by farm labourers.

However, *The Farmer* continued to promote the isolated sufferings of white farmers and emphasise their victim status. As during the Gukurahundi years, the magazine published details of white farming attacks and deaths, but the new political context meant that it could push the boundaries of its coverage further. It began to include images of beaten farmers as well as lurid details of farming deaths. As the magazine no longer felt the need to protect its relationship with the ruling elite, it was explicit in this coverage.[93] The brutal murders of Martin Olds, Allan Dunn, David Stevens, Tony Oates and Henry Elsworth were all covered during 2000. Many of the more brutal assaults, such as those carried out on Iain Kay, Richard Bedford, Richard Melrose, Roy Bennett, Marshall Roper and Keith McGaw were also reported on in detail, often including photographs of the battered farmers, as well as direct attribution of the violence to ZANU-PF and its supporters. The most graphic of these was the attack on Roper. He had been slashed across the face with a machete and his wounds were shown in a full-page colour photograph.[94]

With the increase in violence and the death of white farmers, it is perhaps understandable that the magazine resuscitated the imagery and language of the Liberation War. However, it never attempted any reflective or critical review of its own position regarding earlier episodes of state-sponsored violence. There was never any recognition of the complicated relationship between the magazine's earlier refusal to report on the government's involvement in the Gukurahundi massacres, and its identification of the current violence as proof of ZANU-PF's misrule and authoritarianism. The painful memories of Gukurahundi, which the magazine had worked so hard to avoid attributing to government, now became a key point of its focus. After the murder of Martin Olds in April 2000, *The Farmer* reported: 'Illegal land invasions by Zimbabwe's so called war veterans began slowly in Matabeleland, but last week's brutal and cowardly slaying of Nyamandhlovu farmer Martin Olds created tension not seen since the Five Brigade massacres in the 80s.'[95] Later, when Allan Dunn was killed, the magazine stated that:

> It was a political murder and we must assume it was sanctioned, as we must assume the other murders, the rapes, the arson attacks and the assaults have been sanctioned. / Zimbabwe cannot afford another Matabeleland, another infamous Gukurahundi massacre of the innocents on its hands.[96]

Unprepared to speak out when white farmers were not the direct victims of ZANU-PF's violence, *The Farmer* now sought to illustrate a longer trajectory of government misrule which needed to be stopped, for the sake of the whole country, and not just their own immediate futures. The magazine never admitted its complicity in the previous violence, but its sudden association with a claimed fellow victimhood is entirely ahistorical and reveals the silences and forgetting central to white farmer discourse.

In an interesting parallel with the government's attacks on ZAPU in the early 1980s, the government accused Matabeleland farmers of harbouring weapons of war, resulting in a police and CIO 'blitz to search for arms of war on commercial farmers in Matabeleland region' in June 2000.[97] Such actions made it easy for the farming fraternity to manufacture connections and shared injustices. This is reflected in letters published by *The Farmer*. In August 2000, Diana Charsley quoted at length the graphic testimony of a pregnant woman who was hit in the stomach with the butt of a gun wielded by a uniformed Fifth Brigade soldier:

> The unborn child broke into pieces in my stomach. The baby boy died inside. / It was God's desire that I did not die too. The child was born afterwards, piece by piece. A head alone, then a leg, an arm, the body – piece by piece ...[98]

Charsley's justification for citing this testimony was that 'the man who sanctioned incidents like the one ... is the same one who is responsible for the current suffering'. The lack of other contextualisation shows that Charsley claims a direct connection between the sufferings of white farmers in the 2000s and those of the Ndebele in the 1980s. The magazine's decision to publish the letter, and the horrific account it contained, was part of a clear strategy to connect the two events. Later in 2000, David Tyndale-Biscoe also commented upon the horrors of Gukurahundi in a letter. However, the ironic prophecy of his conclusion was probably lost on him:

> As president [Mugabe], he can also keep the curtain down on the genocide wrought on the civilian Matabeleland population by his 5th Brigade in the early 1980s. Power is so intoxicating. / What is so unsettling for us southern Africans and potential foreign investors is that our SADC leaders seem mesmerized by Mugabe's artful talk. / When you sup with the devil, please be sure to use a long spoon.[99]

Tyndale-Biscoe offers no view on the length of the farmers' own spoon, but it is clear that by 2000, white farmers saw no contradiction in using the horrors of Gukurahundi for their own purposes.

While the 'genocide' of Gukurahundi was evoked, many declared Mugabe's actions against white farmers to be another genocide, or at least an 'ethnic cleansing'.[100] Yet most of these claims were utterly unconnected with events that were taking place. White farmers were certainly attacked, but they represented a very small proportion of the white population of Zimbabwe (around five per cent).[101] In addition, farmers had very little understanding of wider happenings in the countryside, of who was involved and who was suffering, and made little apparent effort to find out. On the same letters page where claims of ethnic cleansing were brandished, two writers absolved farmers of any responsibility for the problems in the country, and blamed 'the people' for not standing up to ZANU-PF and Mugabe. The first described a mock boxing match between 'R Magabe [sic] – No gloves, no rules' and 'A Farmer – 40oz gloves – Queensbury Rules'. In the ensuing fight A Farmer gets pummelled by a series of low blows, which the referee (Mr CFU) tries to stop, but is totally ignored by R Magabe. The fight ends in this way:

> Blue [A Farmer] desperately wants to take off the gloves but is restrained by the tearful Referee
>
> Red [R Magabe] swaggers to the centre of the ring and proclaims himself

Champion of Zimbabwe

Boos from the audience

Moral: Since neither the referee nor the Judges can restrain Red, only the Audience [The people of Zimbabwe] can intervene and forcibly get rid of this dictator.[102]

The message is clear. The farmers alone have been putting up a fierce, but clean and noble, stand against Mugabe. As Latham later wrote:

So far farmers have maintained the moral high ground and gained immense respect for facing their crisis with courage and honesty – and so far farmers have not compromised their integrity by dealing or negotiating outside the law, or with people acting outside the law.[103]

In taking this stance, farmers simultaneously committed themselves to continuing their personal fight, and absolved themselves of any wider responsibility. It illustrated a division between farmers and 'the people', a division that was often compounded by a lack of compassion for circumstances of the wider population. In a letter next to that depicting the boxing match, Disllusioned [sic] stated:

the people voted for what they wanted; they want ZANU-PF, this is what the people want so let them have it .... If the people say they were frightened, I know they were, but their vote was a secret; where is their courage and pride. I say again, let them have ZANU-PF, I am ashamed of these people, I am disappointed in these people, after six months of hardship, and pure hell, I say to these people 'you voted, now you live with it.'[104]

As the Human Rights NGO Forum has shown, those who voted against ZANU-PF were targeted with extreme force once the results were known. The brutality of ZANU-PF's election campaigns and its ability to enforce its political agenda were, however, dismissed as irrelevant. These letters make it clear that many white farmers believed the fight against Mugabe could only be fought by black Zimbabweans.

The government-sanctioned violence and the 'failures' of the 'people' created the space for farmers to publicly criticise the state of the nation and the ineptitude of black rule. *The Farmer* acknowledged this by publishing a string of letters extolling the virtues of the colonialists, the failures of 'African' leadership and the downward spiral in Africa since the coming of independence.[105] Brian Cawood claimed:

The Afrikaner in general and the Boer in particular had been persecuted by the British for centuries. Now the descendants of these same people are being persecuted once more together with their brotherhood of fellow farmer. / Whilst it is acknowledged that the 'Broederbond' and its formation of affirmative action (Apartheid) was to lead to an evil regime it was not without a noble cause in its inception. / There is no difference with the concept of African nationalism, affirmative action and resettlement to Afrikaner Nationalism of 50 years ago.[106]

This and other messages of colonial apology and romanticism were given life by the discursive threshold of 2000. In an attempt to uphold white farming virtue and right, letter writers and *The Farmer* sought to identify with a glorious past that was threatened with extinction by ZANU-PF'.

In 2001 the magazine put more effort into portraying the effects of the fast-track land reforms on black farm labour, but it was still overshadowed by the coverage of attacks on white farmers. The last death it reported was that of Terry Ford in March 2002.[107] The magazine blamed ZANU-PF for the killing, and laid out its understanding of the attack:

> The lessons to be learned are there for all. The government will attempt to do to the entire country what it did to Matabeleland in the eighties – but it will fail. Crushing Matabeleland was relatively simple; it is sparsely populated, home to a minority group (that at the time enjoyed little popular support) and out of the public eye. On top of that, it was unfashionable to denigrate Mr Mugabe at the time. He was a liberation hero and the darling of the west, a so-called 'pragmatic Marxist,' surely an oxymoron. / The situation could hardly be more different now. Mr Mugabe is despised around the globe for his brutality, while his political opponents, far from being an ethnic minority is [sic] sparsely populated and arid provinces, are right under his nose [the MDC].[108]

Accompanying the story were images of Ford's dead body. This was the first and last time the magazine carried such potent and shocking images of a farmer 'slain in cold blood by suspected ZANU-PF supporters and war veterans.'[109] These accusations and graphic portrayals of death gave the CFU a clear reason to close the magazine down. In effect, the CFU was trying to silence farming dissent. It felt that its objectives were being jeopardised by changes in discourse and the public airing of opposition. As such, the demise of *The Farmer* was 'an attempt at closure through silence of an inadmissible discourse'.[110] However, by this time the CFU had lost the support of much of the farming community and its attempts to close the space for public engagement were unsuccessful. Forms of expression that had become unfashionable, such as the memoir, became popular again; oral testimonies, particularly by evicted white farmers, became staple news material for the international media.

Conclusion

The discursive thresholds of 1980 and 2000 marked crucial shifts that were articulated in *The Farmer* by the way it chose to portray issues of violence and death. The foregrounding of violence in the 1980s was part of an attempt to recast farmers as an endangered species. However, this message, while made plausible by 'dissident' activity in Matabeleland, was tempered by the magazine's unwillingness to question the role and action of government force in the region. When ZANU-PF turned on the farmers after 2000, *The Farmer* rediscovered the violence of Gukurahundi and tried to present white farmers as fellow sufferers in the long battle against Mugabe's misrule. Violence and murder were constant themes in the magazine because it no longer saw the need to placate government. In addition, longstanding fears of black rule, swept aside in the name of reconciliation after independence, were reinvigorated and given expression.

Notes

1 Nordstrom, 1997, p. 84.
2 Whitlock, 2000, p. 146.
3 Schaffer and Smith, 2004, p. 4.
4 Okada, 1991, p. 60.
5 Godwin and Hancock, 1993, p. 11.
6 Selby, 2006, p. 78.
7 See many of the editorials produced by Bernard Miller in *The Farmer* mentioned in Chapter Three.
8 Caute, 1983, p. 289.
9 For an urban expression of these fears, see *Property and Finance*, a monthly magazine published for white business which claimed a readership of over 70,000. It was radically right wing and frequently published material on the atrocities of black rule. For example, one article related the story of a white woman giving birth: 'For family reasons, a European woman had to go back to Mozambique recently. / While there, she gave birth to a child. A Black doctor was in attendance. / As soon as he had delivered the child, the doctor drowned it in front of the mother's eyes. He remarked: "There are far too many White children in the world, anyway"'. *Property and Finance*, June, 1976, p. 2.

10 His death was included in the 'Roll of Honour' in *The Farmer at War*. Grundy and Miller, 1979, p. 137. For more coverage of Oberholzer's death and the fallout from it, see Ranger, 1997.

11 Those farmers were Mr J.H. Viljoen and his wife in Gadzema in 1966. Grundy and Miller, 1979, p. 139.

12 Chennells, 1996, p. 102.

13 Godwin and Hancock, 1993, p. 86. Also, see McKenzie, 1989, p. 192.

14 Martin and Johnson, 1981, p. viii. McKenzie noted that these first attacks in Centenary certainly caught white farmers there unawares, as they did the government. McKenzie, 1989, p. 197.

15 See the 'Roll of Honour' in Grundy and Miller, 1979, pp. 132-42; *The Farmer*, 9 March 1979, p. 3.

16 For a yearly breakdown of farming deaths, including name and region, see Appendix Five. The numbers claimed in Grundy and Miller were: one dead in 1964, two in 1966, seven in 1973, six in 1975, 31 in 1976, 52 in 1977, 115 in 1978 and 58 in 1979. Grundy and Miller, 1979, pp. 132-42.

17 According to Selby, farmers accounted for more than 50 per cent of white civilian deaths during the war. Selby, 2006, p. 78.

18 McKenzie, 1989, p. 257.

19 *Rhodesian Farmer*, 9 February 1973, p. 7; *Rhodesian Farmer*, 17 December 1976, p. 33.

20 Ibid., 10 May 1973, p. 5; *Rhodesian Farmer*, 24 May 1974, p. 9.

21 Emphasis in original. *Rhodesian Farmer*, 10 May 1973, p. 5.

22 Ibid., 3 December 1976, p. 19.

23 Ibid., 7 January 1978, p. 11; *Rhodesian Farmer*, 10 March 1978, supplement; *Rhodesian Farmer*, 10 March 1978, p. 7; *Rhodesian Farmer*, 17 March 1978, p. 9.

24 The advert appeared in the *Rhodesian Farmer*, May 19 1978, front cover.

25 Chennells, 1996, p 104.

26 Grundy and Miller, 1979, p. 13.

27 Ibid., p. 145.

28 Chennells, 1996, p. 129.

29 Phimister, 2008, pp. 199-218.

30 Muzondidya, 2009, pp. 178-9.

31 Phimister, 2008, p. 200.

32 Ibid.

33 Catholic Commission for Justice and Peace in Zimbabwe (CCJPZ), 1997, pp. 40-5. Much of the discussion that will follow relies heavily on this report, which was republished under a different title in 2007. As Phimister explained, 'the investigation's detailed findings were as shocking as its recommendations were far-reaching. But in the event, they were simply ignored by a government so certain of its hitherto unchallenged authority that it anyway permitted publication of Breaking The Silence inside the country. Those Zimbabweans who thought that the report, read in the wider context of the apparent precedent set by neighbouring South Africa's Truth and Reconciliation Commission, heralded a new era of openness, were soon disabused of any such foolishness. Starting in 2000, and for many of the same reasons which had

underpinned the massacres in Matabeleland, Mugabe's murderous regime embarked on another violent political adventure. By the end of 2006, with no end in sight to this enduring crisis, concerned activists in the region decided that the time was right for Breaking the Silence to be republished. With a forward by Archbishop Pius Ncube, and an introduction by Elinor Sisulu, it is now available as Gukurahundi in Zimbabwe'. Phimister, 2009, p. 472. For the republishing of the report, see CCJPZ, 2007.

34 CCJPZ, 1997, p. 30.

35 Dzimba, 1998. Dzimba spectacularly overestimated the intrusion of South African forces in Zimbabwe and, as a result, reproduced much of ZANU-PF's rhetoric and propaganda of the early 1980s. For alternative views, see Hanlon, 1986; Martin and Johnson, 1986.

36 CCJPZ, 1997, p. 30.

37 Phimister, 2008, p. 198.

38 *Sunday Times*, 22 January 1984, p. 1; CCJPZ, 1997, p. 37.

39 CCJPZ, 1997, p. 37.

40 Selby, 2006, p. 170. Dissidents claimed that they 'murdered those white farmers they perceived as hostile, without a clear redistribution policy'. See CCJPZ, 1997, p. 40.

41 CCJPZ, 1997, 38.

42 *The Farmer*, 10 March 1986, p. 10. See another article along the same lines a year later, *The Farmer*, 3 September 1987, pp. 12-3. Much is made of the dissident threat, the carrying of firearms by all family members and of reports of more white farmer murders, 'yet another senseless, wicked act by criminals who are the scourge of the country'.

43 *The Farmer*, 30 March 1981, p. 3. The farmers listed as killed were Mr Abraham Barend Roux and his wife Margaret, Fort Victoria, Mrs Helena van As, aged 70, and her grandson Philip, aged 20, in Fort Victoria's Eastern farming district. The article mentioned another farmer killed in Umtali (Mutare) a week before: Mr John Patrick Franklin, aged 36, on his farm Greater Sisal.

44 *The Farmer*, 30 March 1981, p. 3.

45 This was the first murder in *The Farmer* to be attributed to 'dissident' activity. *The Farmer*, 10 May 1982, p. 9.

46 Ibid.

47 The land issue was a key concern for the dissidents, as was targeting hostile or well-known racist white farmers. See Alexander, 1998, pp. 164 and 168; Ranger, 1999, p. 251.

48 For example, see *The Farmer*, 16 July 1984, p. 7.

49 Immediately after Mugabe's victory, an editorial in *The Farmer* congratulated him on it and on the fact that the 'obscene war' had ended. It went on to say, 'While incidents of banditry and thuggery, particularly in the farming areas, poses a real threat to the return of normality, these pale when compared with the war situation pertaining this time last year'. *The Farmer*, 28 March 1980, p. 3.

50 *The Farmer*, 10 May 1982, p. 9.

51 Ibid., 25 February 1985, p. 5.

52 Ibid., 25 April 1983, p. 5.

53 Ibid., 27 February 1984, p. 7.

54 Ibid., 3 September 1987, p. 7.

55 Ibid., 26 November 1987, p. 1.

56 CFU branch chairman for the Midlands, Mr Klaas Folkersten stated, 'I think the farmers should congratulate the security forces – there is generally a feeling of relief in the area.' *The Farmer*, November 26 1987, p. 3.

57 *Sunday Times*, 22 January 1984, p. 1.

58 *The Star*, 2 June 1983, p. 2.

59 In white farming parlance 'revved' has a number of meanings that range from minor irritations to full-on attack. In the Liberation War setting and the security concerns in Matabeleland in the 1980s, it would most likely have meant coming under attack (from direct fire or ambush) by guerrillas or dissidents.

60 *The Star*, 6 June 1984, p. 4.

61 *The Farmer*, 20 June 1983, p. 3.

62 Ibid.

63 *The Farmer*, 15 October 1987, p. 1.

64 Ibid., 1 December 1986, p. 5.

65 Ibid., 4 June 1984, p. 3.

66 *The Star*, 4 June 1984, p. 2. The Star was published in South Africa, and would have been much less concerned with the Zimbabwean government's reaction. As a result it could be (and was) much more explicit about events in Zimbabwe.

67 *The Farmer*, 27 August 1987, p. 3.

68 Ibid., 3 September 1987, p. 3.

69 Ibid., 3 December 1987, pp. 1, 3. For a list of all those killed in Matabeleland during the 1980s and reported in *The Farmer* see Appendix Five.

70 Correspondence with Michael Rook, 23 and 24 April 2009.

71 For more on black experiences of Gukurahundi, see Werbner, 1991; Werbner, 1996; Werbner, 1998; Zhira, 2004, pp. 61-77. For insights into the region immediately after the signing of the Unity Accord in 1998, see Ranger, 1989.

72 Freeman, 2005, p. 165; Phimister, 2008, p. 212.

73 For a discussion of the extent to which farmers were aware of the events of Gukurahundi, see Selby, 2006, pp. 172-5.

74 Correspondence with Rook, 23 and 24 April 2009.

75 Ibid.

76 Selby, 2006, p. 177.

77 The question arises of whether white farmers' views had changed in the first decades of independence and reverted once the land occupations began in 2000, or were largely constant but unexpressed between 1980–2000. I think the analyses of *The Farmer* in this chapter and the previous one, together with the discussion of the farming novels in Chapter Five, shows that the farmers largely retained the prejudices and biases that expressed themselves so evidently after 2000.

78 For example, see Blair, 2002; Hill, 2003; Meredith, 2003. Due to the extent of violence enacted on white farmers it is not surprising that their fate has received sympathetic coverage, both in local independent press and international media. However, what is surprising is the sheer quantity of that coverage, given the small number of

white farmers and the actual scope of violence they have been exposed to. To illustrate this, I carried out a search using Google and compared the findings of "farm workers" AND Zimbabwe, "land reform" AND Zimbabwe, and "white farmers" AND Zimbabwe. Farm workers received 5,700 hits, land reform 21,000, and white farmers over 827,000. These simple findings illustrate that white farmers received an embarrassing avalanche of attention. All searches carried out on Google, 22 March 2008.

79 Lamb, 2006.

80 Hough is quoted as saying, 'I was soon aware that farming was extremely hard work and that without endless supervision the munts would do nothing' (emphasis in original, p. 41); and, when talking about going to the same school as black people; 'I guess we were thinking about the munts we had on our farms, recalled Nigel, how they smelled and stole things and how our parents always said the black man couldn't be trusted. We knew that blacks were way behind in civilization' (emphasis in original, p. 51). Lamb herself uses the word 'native'; 'As usual the platform was packed with natives hoping to sell sodas and biscuits' (p. 49). Yet even after 1999 Hough stated, *'Blacks didn't understand that you needed to start off small* [in business] *and build up, they wanted to be big right away, and also when they did make money they spent it on flash cars and things rather than reinvesting, so very few were getting anywhere'* (emphasis in original, p. 168). The change in his attitude is not outlined in any great detail and there is no direct affirmation that he is not 'racist' any more. As the last quote illustrates, there are still overarching judgements made by Hough of what 'black' people are and are capable of. Lamb, 2006.

81 Caute, 1983; Godwin and Hancock, 1993.

82 In Lamb's account of Nigel Hough and his life in Zimbabwe, she quotes him as saying, after a confrontation on his farm in 2002, 'Funnily enough, I had never been called a racist, even though there were times when I was.' Many of Hough statements on blacks are laden with paternalistic and racist overtones. Lamb, 2006, p. 252 (see pp. 51, 141, 168 and 238 for other examples).

83 *The Farmer*, 9 March 2000, p. 2.

84 Willems, 2004.

85 *The Farmer*, 16 March 2000, p. 1.

86 Ibid., 30 March 2000, p. 5.

87 For example, in March 2000 Winkfield stated, 'The extraordinary events of the past few weeks that are slowly ripping apart the fabric of our country is simply the ongoing story of Africa.' *The Farmer*, 30 March 2000, p. 25.

88 *The Farmer*, 27 April 2000, p. 41.

89 Mugabe, 2001, pp. 40-2, 93, 96-101.

90 The Justice for Agriculture (JAG) Trust and the General Agricultural and Plantation Workers Union of Zimbabwe (GAPWUZ), 2008, p. 14.

91 *The Farmer*, 23 October 2001, p. 3.

92 See Appendix Five for the list of white farmers killed between 2000 and 2004.

93 Correspondence with Brain Latham, 21 April 2009.

94 *The Farmer*, 3 October 2000, pp. 18-9.

95 Ibid., 27 April 2000, p. 5.

96 Ibid., 11 May 2000, p. 1. These events were also labelled as political killings, put-

ting the blame squarely on ZANU-PF. When a prominent Kwekwe farmer was murdered in 'an ambush at his farm gate by unidentified gunmen', the suspicions were that it was a politically motivated killing. Tim Henwood, CFU president, said 'this was not a random criminal act – the murder of Henry Elsworth represents the ultimate political intimidation against farmers and is a desperate reflection of the depths of lawlessness to which we have sunk'. *The Farmer*, 19/26 December 2000, pp. 5 and 9.

97 Ibid., June 27 2000, p. 8. For the 'discoveries' of arms on ZAPU properties during the 1980s, see Alexander, 1998, pp. 155-156; Alexander, McGregor and Ranger, 2000, pp. 180-96.

98 Ibid., 15 August 2000, p. 4.

99 Ibid., 14 November 2000, p. 3.

100 Ibid., 12 December 2000, p. 2.

101 Selby, 2006, p. 63.

102 *The Farmer*, 12 December 2000, p. 2.

103 Ibid., 19 September 2000, p. 7.

104 Ibid., 12 December 2000, p. 2. 'The people' was a very popular motif. In January 2001 Eyes Wide Open stated in a letter that 'There is no pride or dignity in this path to self destruction, and only the people can open their eyes and stop it.' *The Farmer*, 2/9 January 2001, p. 2; 20 November 2001, p. 2.

105 Ibid., 2/9 January 2001, p. 2; 30 January 2001, p. 3.

106 Ibid., 3 December 2001, p. 7.

107 Ibid., 19 March 2002, p. 11.

108 Ibid., 26 March 2002, p. 1.

109 Ibid., p. 6.

110 Chennells, 1996, p. 104.

5

The Consolidation of Voice
White Farmers' Autobiographies
& the Narration of Experience after 2000

The heavier the burden, the closer our lives come to the earth, the more real and truthful they become.
– Milan Kundera[1]

Introduction

This chapter looks at memoirs written by white farmers since 2000. They are one of the key ways that the farmers have chosen to relate the ordeals they have been through, and as a result provide an insight into their understandings of place, race and belonging within Zimbabwe. Such understandings of the past have a major impact on people's beliefs and outlooks.

For Edward Said, 'How we formulate or represent the past shapes our understanding and views of the present'. It also allows us to think about how people pit 'versions of the past against each other'.[2] Both Paul Cohen and Luise White have shown how texts often compete with each other to represent the past for certain groups or agendas.[3] 'The past', or the events that did or did not happen, are no longer what is primarily at issue. Rather it is how beliefs of that past impact on the actions and reactions of the protagonists.

Said remarks on this in a way that is remarkably apt for the Zimbabwean context:

> More important than the past itself, therefore, is its bearing upon cultural attitudes in the present. For reasons that are partly embedded in the imperial experience, the old divisions between colonizer and colonized have re-emerged ... which has entailed defensiveness, various kinds of rhetorical and ideological combat, and a simmering hostility that is quite likely to trigger devastating wars – in some cases it already has.[4]

Discourse & Myth

Much has been made of the rhetoric employed by Mugabe and his supporters to exonerate their actions in the countryside, but the same attention and critique has not been applied to how white farmers and their supporters frame discussions over land issues.[5] Ironically, what emerges from the following analysis is that the discourse of the white farmers is just as rooted in the past as that of ZANU-PF.[6]

For Michel Foucault, a discourse was 'groups of statements which provide a language for talking about a particular topic at a particular historical moment'.[7] Nicholas Dirks expanded on this, saying that discourse is 'about the conditions under which the world presents itself as real, about the way institutions and historical practices become regimes of truth and of possibility itself'.[8] Zimbabwe's white farming community has such 'regimes of truth', that inform and mould their responses to the land reforms.

The literary reaction of farmers to the land occupations has been considerable. Novels, memoirs, autobiographies, countless opinion pieces, articles and letters as well as websites have been dedicated to telling their story. But the context of the writing has not been confined to recent events. The space has been opened up for the telling of farming or pastoral experiences reaching deep into the past. Thus the discursive threshold of 2000, marked by the land occupations and state-sponsored violence, implies two things.[9] Firstly, it is a point that allows such writing to come to the fore, containing sentiments and beliefs that previously had few avenues of expression. For example, the fears of the farming community about life in independent Zimbabwe were seemingly shelved once Mugabe adopted such a pacifying and reconciliatory tone with white farmers.[10] Secondly, these works have become agents in the identity politics of the white farmers, cultural artefacts of the community that represent their beliefs, and their understandings of their history and of their place in independent Zimbabwe.

Indeed, as Andrew van der Vlies has noted:

> Many scholars have explored the role of books and writers in the construction of postcolonial national identities, and there is by now a large body of work in the field. Timothy Brennan, for instance, observes that nations are 'imaginary constructs' whose existence depends on 'an apparatus of cultural

fictions in which imaginative literature plays a decisive role'; Homi Bhabha suggests that the 'repetitious, recursive strategy of the performative' informs the 'conceptual ambivalence' of national identity – that it is literally a case of 'writing the nation'.[11]

This 'writing of the nation' is important in the Rhodesian/Zimbabwean case. Rhodesia, as a place and as a nation, no longer exists but it still has the capacity to capture the imagination and consciousness of many people across the world, not only of ex-Rhodesians but also of their supporters and sympathisers largely found in the white western world.[12] Many of the works reviewed here are an attempt to keep that 'imagined' community or nation of Rhodesia alive, and so it is not surprising that they contain a number of sensitive contradictions, or 'myths'. In his thesis on settler myths in Rhodesian literature, Chennells explained why he chose to employ the word himself:

> What I wanted was a word that would suggest beliefs and perceptions which were deeply held and felt by the [white] settlers even though in some cases they seldom articulated them. The word 'myth' seemed the most satisfactory term since it embodies both the rational and irrational levels at which man perceives the world .... Myth also suggests a perception that retains its validity regardless of changing circumstances. Perhaps most important of all for my purposes myth implies a collective perception and is basic to more complex formulations of ideology, to subsequent political programmes and to social attitudes. At the same time myth seems to have the capacity to be seen to be true even while institutional changes are enacted which contradict it.[13]

Chennells identified that myth is more than an individual belief. As Richard Slotkin has illustrated, myth is 'a narrative which concentrates in a single, dramatised experience the whole history of a people in their land. The myth-hero embodies or defends the values of his culture in a struggle against the forces which threaten to destroy the people and lay waste to the land.'[14]

The Importance of Literature & Autobiography

Literature has attracted increased attention from historians in the last 20 years.[15] Such historical investigation provides a wealth of information on cultural practices and codes, such as language, gender relations and identity formation. In exploring these currents, one is forced to offer an interpretation of authorial intentions. However, the autobiographical works of the white farmers commonly establish their agendas within the work, making this process an easier one to negotiate. These motivations have particular relevance to this chapter, for there is more to the writing than a simple expression of an individual story. There is a marked attempt to 'tell the other side of the story', or indeed an authentic 'real story'. In order to do this, these works engage with the 'history' of the issue written about, giving one an insight into ideas of the past and present constructed by the authors. Furthermore, when, as in this case, there are a number of works that have similar aims, emerging from the same set of circumstances, it allows a comparison of these ideas that gives a greater insight into the mentality and beliefs of the community in question. As Keith Thomas has observed, 'Quite apart from the purposes which literary texts have been meant to serve, they are historical objects in themselves'.[16] The collapse of Zimbabwe and the anxieties it awakened in the white farming community hark back to the era of white minority rule, and as a result this period has witnessed the writing of a number of stories about that time that have only now found the space and initiative to come to print.[17]

This chapter will focus on works written by white farmers only. These are, in order of publication date, Catherine Buckle's *African Tears* (2001) and *Beyond Tears* (2002), Richard Wiles' *Foredoomed is my Forest* (2005), Eric Harrison's *Jambanja* (2006), Jim Barker's *Paradise Plundered* (2007) and Ann Rothrock Beattie's *Tengwe Garden Club* (2008).[18] Other works written that comment or focus on the white farming experience will receive more limited mention. For example, a number of more established writers, such as Peter Godwin and Alexandra Fuller, have used the fast-track land reforms and the market they have created for white narratives from Zimbabwe, to produce their own works that piggyback on the rural landscape.[19]

Though there is a great deal of variation in the scope, intention and quality of these works, there is a remarkable overlap of ideology and justification that allows them to be grouped together as the latest evolution of Zimbabwean pastoral 'white writing'.[20] As J.M. Coetzee has illustrated in the South African context, it is possible to group these works as 'white writing' because they address themselves to European rather than African audiences. For Coetzee, 'White writing is white only insofar as it is generated by the concerns of people no longer European, not yet

African', but who nonetheless train their gaze to fit European or western epistemological frameworks.[21] This is another example of affirmative parochialism at work, especially with the case of white Zimbabwean (and Rhodesian) farmers.

This chapter's main aim is to explore the reaction of white farmers by probing what the published farming narratives iterate and elide, and some of the problems these proclamations and silences reveal. The disconcerting silences that play out alongside continuations with earlier (colonial) forms of pastoral or farm writing make the evaluation of these works an important part of deciphering white farming reactions to the events in Zimbabwe since 2000, and, more generally, of their role in independent 'Africa'.[22]

Writing Traditions & Authorial Intentions

Writing a memoir or autobiography is typically a deliberate and planned process that allows the author to consider choices of language, definition, chronology and structure. The authors are able to choose what story is told, and a result supply the reader with an insight into their ideologies and understandings. These insights are not restricted to individual assumptions; larger, grander assumptions can be extrapolated. As Ngugi wa Thiong'o stated, literature cannot help but reveal the power and class struggles in any given society. Whether the author is aware of it or not, his or her work will comment on the social, economic, political and ideological struggles in that society; it is inevitable. For Ngugi, all the writer can do:

> is choose one or the other side in the battle field: the side of the people, or the side of those social forces and classes that try to keep the people down. What he or she cannot do is remain neutral. Every writer is a writer in politics. The only question is what and whose politics.[23]

The choices the farmers make in their writing, such as in what language they deploy, how they frame themselves and those around them and how they comment upon their social, political and historic contexts, inform us not only of who they write for, but how they view themselves. What becomes evident is that they locate themselves as a distinct group and, as a consequence, are in their view the only ones able to fully comprehend what happens to their own. What they write is tailored for a limited number of distinct groups: the farming community, white Rhodesian/Zimbabwean communities of the diaspora, and international white/western audiences. What is also important to note is that of the works focused upon in this chapter, only those of Buckle have been published by a recognised publishing house.[24] The others are either published through some form of 'vanity press' (Wiles with Trafford Publishing and Beattie through online publishers, Lulu Press), or have been self-published, as is the case with Harrison and Barker. This means that what they have written has not gone through detailed editing processes and arguably represents the farming voice in a 'purer' form.[25]

This act of writing does not occur in isolation, but builds upon a 'tradition' of writing, in that there have been numerous earlier works by Rhodesian/Zimbabwean white pastoralists. However, this 'tradition' of writing is not born out of farmers reading and responding to other writing. Rather, it is their response to events around them that prompts the farmers to think, for whatever reason, that it is important for them to write their story. There is no reference to contemporary authors within these works. The only exception is Barker, who refers to Buckle as a great source for those looking for more detailed examination of events in the country.[26] This is interesting because, firstly, it endows Buckle with the ability to speak for the community. Secondly it shows how Barker is placing himself in a different category by focusing only on his story.[27] Harrison and Wiles do the same by expressly stating that they will only focus on events that have happened to them personally, and do so with no reference to other farming writers.

Chennells has shown that all of the myths that will be looked at in this chapter, such as those of the empty land, the hard-working white pastoralist and the lazy 'Africans', can be located in earlier autobiographical texts. D.M. Somerville, who moved to Rhodesia in the 1920s, wrote in his memoir, *My Life was a Ranch*, of the empty and 'unmapped lands' of Southern Rhodesia, which he and his employer, Lucas Bridge, exploited to make productive.[28] A.E. Bell, whose family moved to Rhodesia in the 1950s, also commented on the vacant lands: 'the Bell family ... bought a couple of farms, in particular Yale and Oxford, which were virgin land in every way!'[29] Wilfred Robertson, a rancher near Sinoia (Chinhoyi) during the first decades of the twentieth century, wrote that 'the background to my many years of ranching life in Rhodesia was the land itself, the twenty seven square miles of virgin bush, unaltered by man since the dawn of time.'[30] Images of vast, open, virgin lands found a deep resonance in the imaginations of the white settlers who came to Rhodesia. It was something that was 'natural' and ready for exploitation by the settlers who had the skills and civilisation behind them to make such a venture work.

Such beliefs in empty land deny the indigenous black populations a place of belonging, and the treatment of the 'native', when he does appear, varies. 'Africans' employed by the white man fit the model of pastoral paternalism, whereby they are completely subservient to the white man. For example, while Somerville acknowledges the contribution of black labour, he comments on how beneficial this work is for the 'native':

> During the years when Devuli Ranch was emerging from wildest bushveld into tamer pastoral country, the African native was an indispensible factor. Without him, we could not have made the ranch. / As the years had gone by, he has changed from a primitive man to a much more civilised being, with civilised wants and customs.[31]

Bell felt much the same way: 'We were lucky with our native employees; it was just like a big happy family'.[32] Even in the rare cases when the white farmer was not very pleasant, he still worked to control the 'natives' and distil awe in them. For example, Charlotte Truepeney in her book *Our African Farm* (1965) talks of the relationship between her uncle and his labour:

> But his old-timers, the men who had grown up on the farm or grown old in his service, were always there. He paid them as little as possible, illegally withheld payment if he felt annoyed, and habitually under-rationed meat, mealie meal and beans. Jacob, Lovemore, Manwari and several others remained whatever happened; their need for a chief was magnificently fulfilled by Uncle Alexander. Without any doubt they admired and feared his rages – to them a very proper display of might by a powerful being.[33]

Again, African subservience is stressed, as is the ability of the white man to control the 'African'. The flipside were 'Africans' who refused, or were too lazy, to work for the white man. Jeannie M. Boggie, who authored a number of accounts of life in Rhodesia, wrote in her *A Husband and a Farm in Rhodesia* that, 'Rhodesia is an inglorious little country of pests, and of incapable natives.'[34] The romance of the native as an untouched and uncivilised being waiting to be reformed by the civilised colonialist had long since worn off. He had become corrupted by worldly influences (such as Hollywood and alcohol). Robertson felt that:

> The native is losing his pristine freshness and cheeriness; the spreading upas-

tree of civilization – the canker that creeps outwards from the townships and big mines like ink on blotting paper – is turning him from an interesting savage to a detribalized 'nigger'. The old friendly relationship between rancher and native, sharing common primitive dangers and difficulties, is merging into the soulless contact between employer and labourer.[35]

This corruption by outside forces is blamed for the breakdown of the relationship between whites and blacks, thus absolving the whites of any wrongdoing or guilt, and is very similar to the way the white farmers framed the 'gooks' and 'war veterans' of later altercations between the races.

Predictably, nature plays a much larger part in these narratives than the 'African'. Robertson ends his book, after lamenting the decay of the country and the fall of the native, with: 'the air and the warmth and the sun, the pearly dawns and the crimson eves and azure midday sky that no economic conditions can destroy'.[36] Bell, in a poem on the back cover of her book, extols the virtues of Rhodesia:

A gem in the middle of Southern Africa,
A landlocked country with many blessings
You have the longest of rivers, Zambezi,
You have the biggest of mountains, Eastern Highlands,
You have the hottest and prettiest of bush, Lowvelds,
You have the most wonderful game park, Wanki National,
You have the most magnificent waterfall, Victoria Falls,
You have the biggest of manmade lakes, Kariba,
You have the greatest of mysteries, Zimbabwe Ruins,
But most of all, Rhodesia, you have people, who live and love there.
God Bless You All.[37]

It is the physical landscape that is most important to the white settlers. Regardless of political events, the country retains its image as a pastoral ideal.[38] In believing this, the authors show a short-sightedness and inability to connect to the political and social currents, not only within Rhodesia with the rise of African nationalism, but within the region and the continent.[39]

But these writings were not the only way in which discourse and tradition were passed on. In fact, earlier examples of pastoral writing might be the least common way for such disseminations because there was almost no reading tradition in white rural communities. As Chennells has noted with regard to pre-independence Rhodesian literature:

There is therefore nothing that can be called a tradition of Rhodesian writing, if a literary tradition involves a community of authors and critics who
are aware of what has been written before and contribute to and evaluate
new attempts to create a literature appropriate to local experience. On the
other hand what I could be certain of was that there were large numbers of
novels which embodied similar perceptions about Rhodesia. If novels written
by people with widely disparate backgrounds, shared the same perceptions
about the country, then another sort of tradition clearly existed. It was not
a self-generating literary tradition ... but it was a tradition that had emerged
from a certain conventional way of regarding Rhodesia which was shared by
settler and non-settler alike.[40]

So there must have been other traditions, or ways for farmers to learn the
discourse. Farming literature, such as the *The Farmer*, played an important part in this process. In addition, in place of a literary tradition, there
was an oral one.[41] Within the farming community there were a number
of mechanisms in place to ensure contact and integration. Events such as
the agricultural shows, exhibition days and farming congresses provided
such platforms on regional and state level. On a more local level, institutions like the country club were very important. These were all key places
where the white farming discourse was both formulated and propagated.

The white farmers who chose to write about their experiences set
themselves apart from the majority of their counterparts. By undertaking
to write about events they deem important, they perform a number of
important functions. Firstly, they give voice to the white farmers, many
of whom feel that their story has been ignored or misrepresented. As
Buckle states, she wrote *African Tears* to tell of events on the other side
of the farm fence, to let Zimbabwe and the world know what really happened.[42] D. Palamui-Poi wrote in his study of ethnic autobiography that
'the ethnic narrative presents an occasion for a subversive revision of the
dominant version of history'.[43] Here the competing history is that of
ZANU-PF, which has dogmatically maintained that white people do not
belong in Zimbabwe, and are outsiders or non-citizens.[44] These autobiographies and memoirs are a direct attempt to combat these notions
and prove belonging. Secondly, these works are not just for outside or
external audiences. They allow the community, regardless of how dispersed and fragmented it is, to see that there are still those from within
who are telling its story and extolling its virtues. Thirdly, these writers
are endowed with a particular responsibility. They are a select group of a

select group, one which has taken on the role of documenting community traumas. Various terms have been employed to describe such groups. Benedict Anderson's 'cultural entrepreneurs' is one.[45] However, the term that comes closest is Antonio Gramsci's 'organic intellectual'. For Gramsci:

> every social group, coming into existence on the original terrain of an essential function in the world of economic production, creates together within itself, organically, one or more strata of intellectuals which give it homogeneity and an awareness of its own function not only in the economic but also in the social and political fields.[46]

Every person and every action could be deemed intellectual:

> In any physical work, even the most degraded and mechanical, there exists a minimum of technical qualification, that is, a minimum of creative intellectual activity .... All men are intellectuals, but not all men have in society the function of intellectuals.

Gramsci went on to say that:

> Each man, outside his professional activity, carries some form of intellectual activity, that is, he is a 'philosopher', an artist, a man of taste, he participates in a particular conception of the world, has a conscious line of moral conduct and therefore contributes to sustain a conception of the world or to modify it, that is, to bring into being new modes of thought.[47]

What was important was how the group interpreted the actions of the individual. Whoever sought to shape and mould the thinking and outlook of the group could be termed an organic intellectual. Every member of the group had this capacity, even if it was not realised. The white farming authors perform part of this function of propagating the group's message and identity to those on the outside, as well as distilling information from the outside world to inform and shape the group's belief and ideologies. The very process of writing autobiographical texts involves the farming authors in this process; however, there are varying degrees to which they engage with the notion of being an 'intellectual'.

The author who fully appropriated such a role was Catherine Buckle. *African Tears* (2001) and *Beyond Tears* (2002) were the first farming books to be published and were issued while the fast-track land reform process was at its zenith. Read together, they cover her story of dislocation and forced removal along with a commentary on what happened to other farmers, their labourers, and those who have chosen to oppose the government. She considers a much wider range of issues than other authors, and deals with many of the more complex problems such as the implication of white farmers themselves in the post-2000 crisis. *African Tears*, however, centres on the experiences of her own family throughout 2000. Although their property, Stow Farm, was never designated for redistribution, Buckle and her employees were continuously harassed and threatened, at gunpoint on one occasion, until they shut down operations and left the farm. *Beyond Tears*, in Buckle's own words:

> is a sequel [to African Tears] and an eye-witness account of Zimbabwe's descent into total collapse and famine ... and outlines the systematic destruction of Zimbabwe by a government determined to retain power, revealing some of the horrors other farmers have endured and their desperate struggle to keep growing food for the country.[48]

Now living in Marondera, Buckle focuses her attention on the continuing meltdown in Zimbabwe but does so principally through a study of events in the countryside. She relates several of the more horrific abductions and murders, such as that of David Stevens, but also the tribulations of the MDC in daring to oppose Mugabe.

The other works are more introverted and focus predominantly on the experiences of the authors and their immediate families. Wiles' book, more a poorly edited publication of his personal diary than a conventionally recognised memoir, focuses largely on his own life from 2000 to 2004. Throughout the diary, he is primarily concerned with attempts to secure official protection for the 'forest' he improved and looked after on his property, in order to ensure its survival after his departure (either through forced removal or death). There is very little commentary on the larger scheme of events in Zimbabwe. However, this does not imply a shortage of commentary about the essential characteristics of 'Africa' and 'the African', which unapologetically repeats rhetoric from the colonial era.

Harrison takes a different approach. *Jambanja* is 'a true story', but 'like all stories, the storyteller is a part of it too. It is my story, my life, but I have told it from the outside.'[49] Thus he refers to himself as 'Harry' throughout the book and narrates events in the third person. In this way, he connects with many of the most prominent themes of Buckle and Wiles; however it sets his work apart because the line between fact and fiction, memory and imagination is harder to define.[50] Harrison also provides a great deal of background information. The first hundred pages document Harry's life from the age of 19 and his military call up in 1959, to the beginning of the fast-track land reforms in 2000.

Barker's *Paradise Plundered* is the complete antithesis of Harrison's book, in terms of both approach and content. He writes as if document-ing the only true and reliable version of events and makes no allowances for the problems of memory and recollection. The book is littered with references to every celebrity (however minor, and typically Rhodesian) that the author, or any member of his family, has ever encountered. Since his book starts with the arrival of his grandparents in Africa, this makes his work extremely long-winded. It is only on page 324 (of 363) that the fast-track land reforms are mentioned. For Barker, 'paradise' was Rho-desia. The book opens with a map of Rhodesia, and closes with a copy of the message Ian Smith inscribed to the Barkers in his autobiography, *The Great Betrayal*: 'To Jim and Judy, My respect to a wonderful family who have always supported the great ideal of our wonderful country. I. Douglas Smith.'[51]

Beattie's *Tengwe Garden Club* was published in 2008. Beattie is Amer-ican, and only settled in Zimbabwe in 1996, a mere four years before the land occupations began. Whilst on safari to Zimbabwe in 1995, she met and fell in love with Dave Beattie, a guide and farmer. Significant-ly, the way Beattie writes on issues such as the fast-track land reforms, and the politics of farm life, conforms in no small way with that of the other farmer writers. For a recent arrival to adopt so fully aspects of the white farming discourse, as well as accepting a number of their founding mythologies, demonstrates how efficient this group is at disseminating its ideologies. Bruce van Buskirk, an American who spent a year with a hunt-ing outfit in Zimbabwe, showed similar reactions and understandings to Beattie's, illustrating how outsiders who spend their time predominantly with white farmers create for themselves a view of the past and place.[52]

Myths & Themes

Despite the different backgrounds and approaches, a number of overlap-ping themes present themselves in these works. One set of myths centres on the motivations behind the fast-track land reforms and the authors' defences of their ownership and control of the land. Not surprisingly, all are severely critical of the reforms and the appropriation of their land and homes. For Buckle they were nothing but the desperate moves of a frantic dictator who has lost all popular support.[53] In accordance with this interpretation, Wiles states in his preface that:

> by 2000 Mugabe had lost popular support and his ZANU (PF) party had no prospect of winning a free and fair general election. Since the beginnings of history, a well-worn stratagem used by demagogues, when they wish to draw attention away from their own failings, is to identify a scapegoat .... The choice was made and the finger pointed at the white farmer.[54]

Barker, Harrison and Beattie make the same observations and the interpretation is that the land occupations have 'bugger-all to do with land – it's totally political'.[55] They identify the correlation between the land occupations and the political challenges Mugabe faced at the time.[56] However, for the farmers the land reforms were an attack on them, as white landowners, which, in essence, was a political tactic to win favour with the rural landless and poor. While this interpretation holds some validity, another factor is that the farm workers represented a huge voting bloc. The fast-track land reforms had as much to do with them as it did with white landowners.[57]

Regardless of who the main targets were, the assaults on white owned farms and their labour were, very often, undertaken with a certain amount of relish and zeal. What the farmers fail to register, is why the attacks on the white farmers fell on such fertile soil, for it is clear that many of those who supported the land occupations were not in the pay of government.[58] Buckle is the only one to admit that farmers have to bear some of the responsibility for events on the land:

> As farmers we were all to blame for the position we now found ourselves in as our lands were invaded. When the [compulsory acquisition] lists came out in 1997, we all made a lot of noise, offered alternatives and suggestions, but left it up to someone else to sort out. We assumed that somewhere along the line someone would step in and do this thing properly ... who would handle the highly emotive issue diplomatically and to the satisfaction of all. [59]

This tentative criticism sets Buckle apart from many of her contemporaries and all of the other writers and is another indication of her role as organic intellectual and her attempt to capture an essence of the larger picture. However, she falls short of recognising that there may have been genuine support for the government's land reform agenda. The only people she talks of as occupying her farm, the war veterans or ZANU-PF hired troublemakers, are presented as gullible fools swayed by Mugabe's rhetoric, or rent-a-crowd youths with no genuine interest in land or farming. Neither does she admit that white farmers attracted a great deal of hostility because of the isolated lives they led, their wealth and often because of their real or perceived racial prejudices.

Barker admits land 'had always been an emotive issue', and that 'There was no one, I believe, in the farming community that did not recognise the need for land reform.'[60] But these comments are sandwiched between his dismissal of land shortages in Zimbabwe, using a bizarre comparison with Germany, and a list of statistics supposedly showing that 80 per cent of land bought by white farmers was bought after independence, and with government consent. The sentiment feels insincere at best and this feeling of insincerity is reinforced when one looks at how Barker portrays the black people of Zimbabwe, land hungry or otherwise.[61] On the other hand, Wiles, in all of his 360 pages, fails to mention even once that land reform and poverty remained pressing concerns for a large proportion of the population, or that white Zimbabweans might bear any responsibility on account of their privileged status in the past.

Rather, there is much emphasis on demonstrating how tirelessly he, and other white farmers, worked to create their own success, most commonly claiming that this was effected from barren, untamed, uninhabited, and otherwise useless or unused bush. Wiles tells the reader, for example, that he bought his farm in 1963, but that because it was 'small', with little arable land, he was told that 'it would be hard to make a living. It took all of our savings and another 16 years to pay off our bonds', but 'by working hard we managed well enough.'[62] Buckle says of her property, Stow Farm, that it was 'located on poor, rocky soil and not suitable for cropping'. She continues:

> the farm was extremely run down and we know that we had a long road ahead of us to get it up and running .... Ian had no choice but to find work outside Zimbabwe and I ran the farm alone, continually living on the breadline in a collapsing and very dilapidated house.[63]

Regardless of her questionable definitions of 'breadline' and 'dilapidated', Buckle's insistence that white farmers owed little of their existence to anything other than their own hard work and commitment is clearly evident. The following quotes are from Barker, Beattie and Harrison respectively, but could have come interchangeably from any of the books:

> Thirty-eight years earlier there had been nothing – not fields, no buildings,

no standing water – just three thousand three hundred acres of untamed bush .... We had fought for this land in every sense of the word, stumping the fields, planting the crops, erecting houses, barns and sheds, building dams and conserving the wildlife.[64]

Andy [her father-in-law] had purchased the land from the British government in 1961 and had carved his farm out of a tract of land that was two thousand acres of thick African bush. He built roads, dams, houses, fences, workshops and tobacco barns. He built a successful farming enterprise over the next forty years.[65]

Everything that had gone into developing the land – the years of work, sacrifice and involvement counted for nothing.[66]

Many white farmers did work hard (although some very conspicuously did not), but all depended on other factors for their success.[67] None of the writers mention anything of the considerable support and assistance white farmers received from the Rhodesian state in establishing farming businesses and enterprises.[68] At that time, most of the land deemed to be of prime agricultural use was reserved for whites, and aspiring white farmers were supplied with an array of subsidies and state benefits in order to establish themselves.[69] Indeed, there were numerous other benefits the Rhodesian state offered out to its European populations, rural and urban, to stay and fight the cause.[70] Nor do they mention the favourable treatment white farmers continued to receive after independence as the land reform process faltered and failed to achieve its ambitious plans.[71] White farmers, and particularly the tobacco farmers, were vital to the country's economic prosperity, and were thus protected by the new (black) Zimbabwean government, despite land inequality remaining a pressing concern.[72] None of the writers mention the scale of profits they made from their farming ventures, but they give indications of their wealth when detailing the holidays they went on and the luxuries they bought, including planes, boats and cars.[73]

These myths of hard work and empty land are accentuated by the fact that no mention is made of unsuccessful white farmers, or of the vast tracks of underutilised land that were widespread in white land holdings.[74] As Roger Riddell has shown, during the 1960s and 1970s white farmers received large subsidies from the government, which resulted in a significant number of inefficient and incapable white farmers remaining on the land. For example, in the 1975/76 season, 4,023 of 6,682 (60 per cent) white-owned farms were not profitable enough to pay income tax;

five per cent of farms accounted for 50 per cent of the land and produced 48 per cent of the output, while 72 per cent of European farms covered 23 per cent of white land and contributed only 21 per cent of the total output.[75] This inefficiency would have decreased after 1980 as the subsidies dried up, but the independent government's decision to not impose a land tax allowed white farmers to retain their land holdings even if they were unproductive.[76] As Angus Selby has shown, white farmers, as a unit, are not unified by their work ethic, productivity or success.[77]

However, it is important to recognise that (often unwarranted) claims of productivity and hard work on barren, 'empty' lands serve as defences of ownership, place and belonging that have a long tradition in Zimbabwe/Rhodesia. Robin Palmer, Ian Phimister, Dane Kennedy and William Wolmer, amongst others, have all commented on the progress of white agriculture in Rhodesia and how those involved have framed discussions on land and ownership to defend their position and place.[78] These myths served the important function of allowing white farmers to live at ease with the scale of their land holdings, and to believe that they had done no wrong by buying into a system that so obviously segregated black from white. These beliefs in the honesty of the system were reinforced by ZANU-PF's lack of political will to redress the agricultural and land-holding system it inherited. This in turn allowed the space for white farmers to feel so wronged by events after 2000.

One of the most damaging results of this white myopia concerning hard work and empty lands relates to farm labour and black rural populations. Whatever hard work and capital was put into the farm, the farmer was utterly dependent on the cheap labour, and exploitation, of black workers to make their enterprises viable and successful.[79] Despite the impression created in these writings 'African' intrusion into European or white life was not minimal. As Kennedy reflects, every aspect of life involved labour to be undertaken by an 'African': 'Africans cultivated Europeans' fields, herded their livestock, harvested their crops, worked their mines, nurtured their gardens, swept their floors, cooked their meals.'[80] Yet, despite this constant contact, these writers do all they can to write it out of the record.

The arrival of independence had several implications for the white farming community, not least regarding the legitimacy of their land ownership. Wiles, Harrison, Barker and Beattie's family-in-law all bought their farms in Rhodesia. Buckle bought hers during the 1990s and, as the law required, received a certificate of 'no present interest' from the government.[81] Her indignation at the radical reforms after 2000 is thus in a sense more 'legitimate', but this does not stop her from collaborating and aligning herself with whites who owned land before 1980. She has no qualms about defending all white farmers, whether they owned land before independence, or continued to hold racist prejudices or 'Rhodesian' world views. She is adamant that the farmers should not be blamed for the actions of their forefathers.[82] This logic ignores the fact that independence had only been achieved 21 years previously, and many of the repressive actions against black people taken by the settler state remained in place until the very end of white minority rule.[83] This oversight is quickly forgotten, however, when the arrival of independence plays (unpredictably) to the white farmers' advantage. The well-versed response is that the majority of white farmers (some estimates put it as high as 80 per cent) bought their farms after 1980, and thus carry none of the historical baggage or guilt that came with owning pre-independence farms.[84]

It is true that a vast amount of land did change hands after independence (which the government failed to capitalise on), but the extent of those land transfers is difficult to assess.[85] The statistic of 80 per cent is questionable, however. According to the 1997 acquisition list of 1,471 properties, about 65 per cent were bought after 1980.[86] This figure is still very high, but not the 80 per cent that many white farmers claimed. In the interviews analysed in the next chapter, farmers were often asked when and how they acquired their farms. Of the 29 who gave details of when they bought or inherited their farms, many had multiple title deeds. A total of 44 title deeds were mentioned. Of these 29 were bought before 1980 and of the 15 bought after independence 8 were added to existing farms under consolidated title deeds. What this tentatively points to is that while land was bought after independence, it was often added to already existing farming enterprises.

What further complicates these figures is the way in which the land changed hands, and who the buyers and sellers were. Many of the farmers interviewed inherited their land, thus whilst it may have changed hands this was not a transaction carried out on the open market. (11 of the 29 white farmers interviewed acquired their land in this way.) Furthermore, many farms were owned as company assets and were sold via share transfer or a sale of the company and not the land. Again, the land may have changed hands but not on the open market.[87] The issue of land transfers and sales after 1980 is more complicated than many white farmers have made out, and particularly the writers discussed in this chapter.

The further set of myths contained in these writings revolves around overly romanticised visions of the farm setting and life before the land invasions started. This not only refers to the land and locale of the farm, but also includes an idealised view of race and labour relations. For example, in *Beyond Tears* Buckle reminisces about her son's life on the farm:

> Whenever I went out of the door on the farm Richard [her son] and his [black African] friends piled into the back of my truck, knowing they were heading for thrills and excitement. Wherever I went the children followed, guaranteed both drama and fun .... There was always laughter.[88]

Even more explicitly, Buckle states later that 'this little piece of our heaven was to be for Richard and it broke our hearts to think that we might lose it all for someone's political survival'.[89] Generally, all connections and happy memories of the farm revolve around the land and nature, and take on almost religious and spiritual connotations. Wiles talks of his protected forest in terms of a sacred Garden of Eden he has worked to create and preserve for over 15 years. Throughout his book he empathises more with his trees and pets than he does with any (black) human figures. For example: 'I always called it "my" forest because it was my personal and passionate concern.' He continues, 'I fear that my many, many "children" will perish. As I write this, most, I expect, are already dead. In God's name, I tried my best for them-I really did.'[90]

For Buckle too, trees represent a deep emotional point of connection with the farm. On returning to the farm after her eviction, she notes that:

> Many of the trees that had always been landmarks were gone or showed signs of being stripped of their wood. The huge lucky bean tree in the top field that should have been covered with crimson winter flowers had most of its branches missing, hacked off for firewood. My eyes burned with tears as I remembered how many hundreds of times I had sat under that tree ... the shock was beginning to sink in and I tried hard to bury all the memories that those trees held for me.[91]

Harrison shows a similar affinity for the trees. He 'felt quite proud of them he had to admit; after all, nothing pleases the heart more than a planted tree. It is there forever.'[92]

This connection with the land, and the beauty of the farm and its setting, creates problematic contradictions for the farmers. They have a difficult time reconciling these images of heaven with the barren, desolate pieces of land they inherited. Their calls for protection and sympathy have a much greater impact if they own and work a piece of land that no one else wants, or that has nothing to offer but agricultural productivity (which, of course, no one else can maximise quite like they can). However, when relating their memories, they cannot help but comment on the beauty and idealism of the farm, both in setting and lifestyle. The 'silence about the place of the black man in the pastoral idyll', in terms of both his presence and work, illustrate that the connections to these little pieces of subjective 'heaven' show more about the desires of the farmers and their attachment to the land than any glib arguments about feeding the country or serving the nation.[93]

The white farmers connect more with the landscape than they ever do with the (black) people living there.[94] This is by no means a new feature of white writing from and on 'Africa'; Chennells, Coetzee and David McDermott Hughes have all discussed its roots.[95] What is surprising, however, considering the position in which the white farmers have found themselves, is that they did not try to enhance the many positive aspects of relations between themselves and their labour to strengthen their claims of belonging and place. Instead, where connections to the 'local' or 'African' people are made, it comes over as paternalistic. Paternal/maternal relationships are better than overtly racial ones, but as Charles van Onselen illustrates, they were very often 'predicated on structured inequality that required the perpetual adolescence of the junior partner. It left [blacks] with no room for either psychological or economic growth.'[96] Thus the post-eviction romantic visions of the farm spill over to glorify the relations between the farm workers and the farmers.

In these writings, the labourers had no problems or worries; they are presented as happy, industrious workers who were always content under their benevolent employer. Consider this passage from Wiles about his faithful cook, Makosa:

> I have always said that Makosa should have been born fifty years earlier. He was a devotee of the white man. Loyalty towards the mzungu [white man] he served and a desire to serve each and every white person who came to his boss's home was his raison d'être. He loved to be appreciated and in turn he was appreciated most warmly. Our visitors always exchanged a friendly word with him. Makosa was meant to live in Rhodesia, never Zimbabwe.[97]

How far Makosa would have agreed with these remarks we will never know, but such condescending paternalism permeates Wiles' book. Unfortunately, this is the better side of his reactions to 'Africans' (for which read 'black people'). There are many descriptions in the book that one cannot read in any other way than the racist ramblings of a bitter and vindictive man whose ideas and outlook are cemented in archaic, colonial visions of Africa. There are numerous examples throughout the book, but one will suffice:

> My own scenario is but a miniscule representation of the total scene in Zimbabwe and indeed the whole of Africa. There is absolutely no hope that Africans will succeed in putting together anything worthwhile. They are unable to anticipate. They cannot administer. Responsibility is still a foreign word. Whatever they touch ends in ruin.[98]

In this discourse, the white farmers have done all they can for 'Africa' and the 'African', yet have not been shown the respect and acknowledgement they deserve. Instead they have been shunned and victimised as outsiders and undesirables while 'Africa' destroys itself. There is no discussion of their wealth and living standard in comparison to the 'Africans' around them. In this frame of understanding wealth is attainable by Africans if only 'they' put in sufficient effort. Much of Harrison's writing describes the black man in the same way. Consider this comparison of the work ethic of whites and blacks:

> This [hard working] attitude of the Commercial Farmer was in total contrast to the cultural handicap that the Africans in the main experience, and is very similar to the Tall Poppy Syndrome. / People whose performance was obviously better that their fellows faced severe risks of reprisals. As a result, nearly every black Zimbabwean was on a never-ending quest for mediocrity. / This was a cultural handicap of immeasurable severity and it might help explain how whole races have managed to remain backward despite contact with more advanced societies, while others like the Japanese, could leap ahead and even outpace their teachers.[99]

These beliefs have a logical connection to the myths about the land. As with the descriptions of barren and empty land that white farmers made plentiful, they are a justification of position and ownership. Whites, because of their hard work, oversight and investment, have legitimate claims to all they own because they can utilise it to its maximum potential. Blacks, on the other hand, lack the skill to make the most of the resources around them, nor do they have the initiative or capacity to make what the white man has of the land. They do not deserve it.

For Chennells there is a direct link between ideas of the empty landscape and the inability to see or relate to the black people found there:

> Judith Wright has remarked, 'Before one's country can become an accepted background against which the poet's or novelist's imagination can move unhindered, it must first be observed, understood, described, and as it were, absorbed. The writer must be at peace with his landscape before he can confidently turn to its human figures.' By persisting in seeing their landscape as vast and untouched, the settler novelists misrepresented it. They observed and described it accurately; they did not understand it and they denied its essential qualities. The myth was important to them and this is perhaps one reason why so few of them are ever able to adequately describe its human figures.[100]

Coetzee describes this process as a 'failure of love', because, while the beauty of the land is so exalted, the people who live there, the blacks who are part of it, are ignored. The writing that emerges from this is 'a less than fully human literature, unnaturally preoccupied with the power and the torsions of power, unable to move from elementary relations of contestation, domination, and subjugation to the vast and complex human world that lies beyond them.'[101]

As a result, in order to keep distinctions clear between black and white, any discussion of inept, lazy and unsuccessful white farmers is avoided, as is any consideration of unutilised land. Neither are any illuminations offered on farmers who abused or mistreated their labour. Where such observations are made it is with the caveat that this minority marred the reputation of the vast majority of farmers who were fair and conscientious. But the abuse of labour seems to have been much more widespread than a few 'old time outsiders' of the farming community. As material from the interviews has shown, racial and derogatory sentiment towards black Zimbabweans was common, if not widespread.

Direct examples of racism, such as those of Harrison and Wiles above, confirm these suspicions. However, it is not merely in such obvious cases that these sentiments are evident. Consider the way black people are referred to in the other works. Barker, while talking of the war years continually refers to the guerrillas as 'gooks' or 'terrs'.[102] Furthermore, there is obvious relish in his tone when he writes of shooting, attacking, hunting down and killing 'gooks'.[103] On one occasion when his farmstead was under attack during the war, Barker proceeded to shoot at the guerrillas while his son, Gary, fetched fresh ammunition. Gary said:

> 'Mom, this is unfair.' 'What is?' 'I'm doing all the work, and dad's having all the fun.' [For Barker this was] Pretty good stuff for a fifteen-year-old, undergoing his baptism of fire![104]

The wartime killing of 'gooks' and 'terrs' was acceptable, even for teenagers, and there was no apparent realisation that the guerrillas were human too, fighting and dying for a cause very real to them. Below Barker recounts an episode where they had to move a load of 'dead terrs':

> The helicopter ... returned with a cargo net slung under the aircraft to transport the dead terrs. There were seven altogether and we put four in the net on the first load. One of the bodies was burning from a phosphorous grenade, so we put him in the second load. On the way to Karoi he burnt a hole through the net and 'dropped in' on Mrs Jacobson's garden party. Completely unfazed, Ruth phoned the police and said, 'If you are missing something, it's at the bottom of my garden.' / These were indomitable ladies, who, when asked somewhat breathlessly by a lady reporter what 'precautions' they took, Liz Searle answered, 'Oh, we're not worried, we are all on the pill!'[105]

What these descriptions show, is that once the black man has decided to take a stance and remove himself from the subservient position under white control, he can be totally dehumanised. The qualities that endow him with feeling, emotion and life are denied and he can thus be treated as the native savage. Later, Barker laments the loss inflicted by war: 'What a terrible Christmas it was – wives becoming widows, children becoming fatherless, and all of us losing good friends. There is no glory in war – but there is a lot of sadness and misery.'[106] However, there is no concern for the loss and suffering of 'Africans'.

This lack of empathy jars with the farmers' apparent connection to their labour. All the writers here claim a real bond with their labour, but as has been shown, this is a very prescriptive relationship. It is also clear that when blacks are no longer part of the labour force they are the enemy, who can be treated as the 'gooks' and the 'terrs' were. War veterans and land invaders were treated as such after 2000 and the terms 'gook', 'terr' and *'mujiba'* – terms intimately associated with the liberation war – were reinvigorated to describe them. Furthermore, other description of blacks, and where they live, have troubled geneses. Harrison talks of African 'tribes', as do Wiles and Barker. Harrison and Barker also continue to call the Communal Areas the 'TTLs', or Tribal Trust Lands, despite the fact that this name was changed at independence. It shows how doggedly these farmers have hung on to definitions, descriptions and ideologies of Rhodesian heritage regardless of changes that have been affected or implemented in independent Zimbabwe.

The use of the word 'tribe' is a prime example. As John Parker and Richard Rathbone explain:

> The idea of 'tribe' is connected with the language of empire …. The use of the word 'tribe' to describe African societies emerged from a desire to commend the nation-state while suggesting the inherent inferiority of the other. It also served as a moral justification for colonial conquest. In one short word, it connoted primitive polities that were less developed than nation-states, cultures that had yet to be illuminated by the insights of the Enlightenment, technologies untouched by modern science, religions that were superstitious rather than spiritual.[107]

Chennells expressed the same view when reviewing Ian Smith's autobiography. He noted that Smith:

> refers to blacks as 'tribesmen', a word that suggests they are outside the common run of humanity – although sometimes he uses 'African' to mean black …. This was a liberal usage in the 1950s and 1960s but inappropriate at the time when Smith was writing [1980s] and when whites, quite correctly, were insisting that they too were Africans.[108]

The white farmers, by and large, fall into the same contradiction while wishing to claim to be 'African' themselves.

In this regard, Beattie's book gives a remarkable account of labour and race relations. As a foreigner, her understandings of black people and labour relations would have been informed by her recent experiences on the farm, and she would have 'learnt' the right way to act from the post-independence white farming community that she became part of.[109] She also employs the terms 'tribe', 'native' and 'TTL' in her work, which show exactly what version of Zimbabwe she was exposed to and took on board. The following comments give a startling insight into her conditioning:

> I was keenly aware of the rank smell of body odor of the natives, who have no regard for personal space and crowd each other to the point of touching. I was blown away by the nauseating stench that hit me as I approached the kapenta [dried fish] section, apparently a favorite of the locals.[110]

> One day, Dave walked in to find me struggling to move a heavy piece of furniture and looked at me in disbelief. 'The staff is getting bored. Why don't you

give them something to do?' he said. I then asked them to move the furniture (using lots of hand gestures), and they were genuinely pleased and proud to be helping. To my surprise, they addressed me as 'Madam!' Not until later did I discover that it was a traditional practice of the natives to address their employers as 'Boss' or 'Madam'. I even had to learn to refer to Dave as 'the Boss' when speaking to my staff.[111]

I learned that no part of the cow went to waste – any off-cuts were sold as either 'ration-meat', a sort of stewing beef which I bought for the staff, or 'pets-meat', which was the absolute dregs and too nasty to even feed the dogs in my opinion. In the end I also bought them ration meat, for the pets' meat was way too smelly![112]

Without the deterrent of cleaning up, entertaining large crowds was relatively easy. I learnt that if I did not come out of my room until eight o'clock the next morning, all signs of the previous night's revelry would magically disappear! My staff grew accustomed to my penchant for throwing parties over the years and were always rewarded with leftovers the next day.[113]

I was impressed and amazed at the way they [the farm labour] lived ... A fire had to be lit for cooking, and laundry was all done by hand. The only source of light was candles and torches, and there was no refrigeration. One of their delicacies is sour milk – they love it! My staff was always delighted when our milk would go rotten after several days in the fridge.[114]

Dave related stories of [black] women actually giving birth right there in the field, and returning to work the next day with the baby on her back, of course! When I questioned this practice, Dave told me they actually chose to work in that condition, not wanting to miss a day's wage.[115]

The farm workers come across as simple, greedy and savage, hardly better than the family pets. The simplistic acceptance of them 'choosing' to work whilst giving birth shows no understanding of what would force a woman to do such a thing. Beattie shows the reader what were common practices on her farm and its ordering of labour and race relations. But these practices are never questioned, and where they are, such as with the pregnant women in the field, the answers are accepted and no blame is placed on the farming or wage system.

These observations contradict the statements, such as those by Beattie, that it is only recent events that have created a disjuncture between the farmer and his labourers. She stated, 'I hated the rift Mugabe had created between the races'; Barker and Buckle likewise accuse Mugabe of playing the race card.[116] Racism only seems to exist now, when directed at the white farmers, but no consideration is given whatsoever to the historic and continued racial bias evident within the farming community.[117] These notions, coupled with those emphasising the empty land they have made productive, are not merely apologist accounts for white farmers, often trying too hard to clear their history and justify their position. They are narratives that seamlessly adopt a range of assertions and themes that not only marred colonial literature about and from 'Africa', but also provide clues as to the audience these works are written for.[118]

Only Buckle, and to a certain extent Harrison, shows any real affinity with the black population. She makes constant reference to one of her employees, Jane, with whom she has an obvious bond.[119] More significant, however, is that both books conclude with an examination of the wider political, economic and social situation in Zimbabwe. *African Tears* ends with a chronology of events in Zimbabwe from October 2000 to December 2000.[120] At the end of *Beyond Tears*, Buckle includes another chronology, from January 2001 to June 2002. In addition, she includes a list of 145 victims of the political violence since March 2000, including commercial farmers, MDC activists and farm labourers.[121] Although her focus is predominantly on white farmers and her own situation, she makes a conscious effort to include transgressions against her labour and the wider black population of Zimbabwe.

Harrison is the only other author who really connects with his workers. For example, after the farm has been designated he writes a reference letter for Cloud, his chief tractor driver. After writing a basic letter of recommendation he then reflects and wishes he had added to the letter:

He could dribble a ball from his own goal line through the opposition of any team, making George Best look like an amateur, and was captain of the unbeaten Maioio soccer team for 25 years before his age caught up with him. After his retirement, we were beaten with monotonous regularity.

He was the local saxophonist in our dance band and lead soloist. During his time, he was the biggest womaniser I had ever met, and was reputed to have the biggest dick in the compound. Many a time I had to back him up as the compound committee wanted to take his balls out with a badza. I must have saved his bacon at least a dozen times.

But when it came to work, he was in a league of his own; he could make a tractor talk. He was in fact – a legend!

Cloud lived a simple life, doing just what he was tasked for – no more, no less. He enjoyed his Chibuku and smoking pot – usually followed by a night's hard work with one of his three wives or anyone else's that caught his fancy.

His 10 children worshipped him.

He is now unemployed, thanks to the land reform policies.[122]

There is a real sense that Harrison knew, and liked, this man and that during their time working together they had built up a very real relationship. Beattie, Barker and Wiles recount nothing like this. Rather, where relationships with black Africans are mentioned, they are premised on subservience and an adherence to the authority of the white man. However as we have seen above, Harrison still has some fundamental beliefs of the 'African' that mar the extent of his connection to the black labour on his farm. Harrison also carries a 'Roll of Honour' at the end of his book. However, in contrast to Buckle's, it only records white farmers killed since the start of the fast-track land reforms, although he does note that his list 'does not reflect those who have died of stress, nor the hundreds of farm workers who have died due to the Land Reform program'.[123] Curiously, Harrison's appendix begins with a list of honours won by Rhodesian troops in World War One and World War Two.[124] Why this is done is not immediately made clear, but it illustrates a fundamental connection to the memory of 'Rhodesia' and its glorified past. The placement of this list at the end of the book, as with Barker's book ending with a personalised note from Ian Smith, gives an insight into the target audience of these books and who the authors imagine to be their main readers.[125] Such practices also hark back to the 'Roll of Honour' found in *The Farmer at War*.[126]

Audience

These approaches to writing and the choices made in portraying and discussing the situation in Zimbabwe give a clear indication of who the white farmers imagine to be their audience. The way they talk of 'Africa', 'Africans' and the land, inherent with all its colonial predecessors, creates a double edged sword; while it helps the farmers generate more sympathy from the western world, it also serves to further alienate whites from the 'Africa' (and the 'African') they wish to adopt and call home.[127] Crucial to this process is viewing 'Africa' as one place, where one can talk of the 'African', the land, despair, and suffering as universal norms belonging to one place that allows the white man to understand it, no matter where the point of entry is. This is why 'Africa' and the 'African' is placed within inverted commas throughout this book, because it is not something that is explored or questioned in any form in these accounts. Africa is not a homogeneous entity that can be talked of as 'a thing'; neither are the 'Africans', though black Zimbabweans are continuously talked of in this way.[128]

Apart from this being a problematic way of looking at the continent and its people, such a viewpoint is also a strategic marketing tool, because 'Africa' sells. Westerners can relate to and identify 'Africa', not necessarily Zimbabwe, Malawi, Chad or any other remote 'African' country of indistinct blackness. Binyavanga Wainaina, in a scathing satire on 'how to write about Africa', offered this advice:

> Always use the word 'Africa' or 'Darkness' or 'Safari' in your title .... Note that 'People' means Africans who are not black, while 'The People' means black Africans ... In your text, treat Africa as if it were one country ... Don't get bogged down with precise descriptions. Africa is big: fifty-four countries, 900 million people who are too busy starving and dying and warring and emigrating to read your book. The continent is full of deserts, jungles, highlands, savannahs and many other things, but your reader doesn't care about all that, so keep your descriptions romantic and evocative and unparticular.[129]

This rationale is clearly evident in all the works looked at, and is exemplified in the title of Buckle's *African Tears*.[130]

It is hard to imagine this way of writing speaking to black Zimbabweans, or 'Africans'. This is especially true of Barker, who opens and closes his book with references to Rhodesia. He and Harrison use forewords from other whites who obviously sympathise with their recollections and ideologies and there is no evidence of black readership, or even the attempt to consider writing for it.[131] The exceptions once again are Buckle's books, both of which open with forewords by prominent black Zimbabwean journalists, Trevor Ncube, editor of the *Zimbabwe Independent* at the time, and Bill Saidi, the assistant editor of the *Daily News*.[132] This is yet another example of how Buckle has managed to distance herself from much of the insular and narrow-minded writing of many of her contemporaries. Far from writing for Zimbabwean audiences, the other books are intended for European, or white audiences, both in Africa and abroad. More precisely, they are aimed at an external Rhodesian audience. It is tempting to call this an 'imagined' audience, and in some sense it is. It ostensibly constitutes whites who fled Zimbabwe during and after the war of independence, so it is one that is no longer grounded in any cohesive national or collective entity. However, it is also a very 'real' audience, in that it exists as 'something' to write for. Luise White has shown this process at work regarding literature produced on the assassination of Herbert Chitepo. In 2002 Peter Stiff reissued a version of his study of Chitepo's death. The fact that since this 'new' work was a 'near-reproduction of the 1985 text suggests that this is a memoir for an imagined Rhodesian audience, one in which the exploits of a white man – trained in the SAS no less – are the subject, not history or politics or even the context of those exploits'.[133]

There are a number of what can only be described as Rhodesian websites that promote and distribute these books. The most notable are: Bushveld.NET, which claims to be 'Southern Africa's unique books portal: covering Rhodesia/Zimbabwe and surrounding countries'; Rhodesiawassuper.com, which sells a range of Rhodesian memorabilia; and Rhodesians Worldwide, which acts as a news centre, a networking site and a memorabilia shop.[134] Bushveld.NET carries the books of Buckle (listed under Politics), Wiles (Politics), Beattie (Autobiography) and Harrison (both Politics and Autobiography). The importance of these categorisations is not immediately clear, but since Harrison, Buckle and Wiles are all listed under Politics, it would seem that they are treated as more than just personal life stories. Again they are given the quality of an authentic organic intellectual who can inform a wider audience about the 'real' situation in Zimbabwe.

The books on these sites are not listed because of their literary merit but because of their subject matter, Rhodesia and Rhodesians. Even if events appear to have taken place in Zimbabwe, the framing of the writing and the discourse used makes it obvious what doctrines are adhered too. But as Chennells informs us, there is a great deal to be garnered from these writings: 'A bad novel allows us to glimpse the soft underbelly of a society'.[135] Furthermore:

> A novelist who deals explicitly with political events in his society and who accepts unquestioningly the conventional attitudes and prejudices around him is likely to produce a bad novel, for what he has selected as significant will be based on attitudes characteristically superficial, ill-informed and therefore inaccurate. Almost by definition, a bad novelist lacks the imaginative ability to recognize and convey complexity; he will lapse into polemic, ignoring the fact that part of man's bewilderment arises from his recognition of mutually exclusive but apparently valid versions of reality .... He will fail to register the social and economic issues and forces that make these ephemera take the various forms they do. More dangerously he will be partisan and treat sympathetically

only one side of what may be a many-sided confrontation, in which all sides have some sort of validity even if it is only in the myths and rationalizations with which members of the various groups defend their positions.[136]

These criticisms can be easily levelled at the most recent farming auto-biographies, in which the founding myths of the community are accepted in their entirety with almost no critical engagement. It is this exact process however, that makes them so appealing to Rhodesian audiences, imagined or otherwise.[137]

Considering Chennells' and Selby's comments on the lack of a cohesive white identity, why then does this farming voice appear so consolidated in the written form? Despite the range of reactions, understandings and experiences of the land occupations there is a notable solidarity of voice and agenda in the memoirs and autobiographies that have emerged. There are a number of possible answers. Firstly, the need to defend their lifestyles and land holdings is an integral part of the writings and farmers are well equipped to do this using myths such as the empty land, the lazy natives and their own hard work. Secondly, traumatic experiences, such as those of the land occupations, can have the tendency to radicalise people's reactions. So, falling back into 'Rhodesian' ways of thinking and expression is partly a reactionary move, but also one that the farmer may find familiar and easy to do. The nature of the events that have wrought such wholesale destruction on the white farmers and their way of life has created a cohesion in the discourse and language used to describe these events. Written responses can be seen as displacement activity responding to political impotence. Considering also that the farming 'community' still exists in some sense, with networks that allow farmers to communicate to each other, there is a pressure to conform to that voice. With the hardships that have occurred, any move away from the 'community' could be seen as an attempt to criticise it. Since this loss of community is exactly what they are lamenting, it is not surprising that there is a lack of differentiation. The reality of belonging to that farming community, however dispersed it is, dictates much of what the farmers then feel they can say about it.

Conclusion

As Chennells asserts, one has to be careful when analysing autobiographical writings to question the space between 'autobiography as representative cultural history and singular story of individual.'[138] The cohesion of myth and ideology shown in the latest evolution of white farmer writing makes it possible to pinpoint a 'representative cultural history' that is connected to and shared within the farming community.

A crucial part of the narrative is a longing for a return to 'the good old days'. As Stephen Clingman has commented, 'it is my feeling ... that if anyone, anywhere, feels truly 'at home', they are not paying attention'.[139] The 'home' that white Zimbabweans, and white farmers perhaps most of all, thought they had secured in Zimbabwe seemed so certain to them. When these homes were taken from them it induced a massive crisis of identity. The positions they held, the farms and properties they owned, and the 'Africa' of which they had felt such a part, had gone. This is not to dismiss or demean the terrible experiences that Buckle, Wiles, Harrison, Barker, Beattie and others have had to endure. For any person, in any place, these would have been traumatic events. What my analysis is intended to suggest is that, just as traumatic has been the dislocation with the 'Africa' of their imagination. Regardless of how flawed and misunderstood that construct has been, it is a myth that remains potently charged and dictates much of their thought, remembrance and action.

Notes

1   Kundera, 1984, p. 5.
2   Said, 1994, pp. 2-3.
3   Cohen, 2003, p. 74.
4   Said, 1994, p. 18.
5   For analysis of Mugabe's and ZANU-PF's framing of the land reforms, see Hammar and Raftopoulos, 2003, p. 19; Raftopoulos, 2003.
6   Raftopoulos, 2007, pp. 181-2.
7   Foucault quoted in Hall, 1997, p. 44.
8   Dirks, 1996, p. 34.
9   Whitlock used the term when answering the question, 'when does autobiography become active in the politics of identity? A discursive threshold must be reached before autobiographic writing appears as an agent. This is clearly not the case for each individual autobiographical act.' Whitlock, 2000, p. 146.
10   See Chapters One and Three for quotes from Mugabe of this apparent reconciliation. Also, see Selby, 2006, pp. 113-4.
11   Van der Vlies, 2007, p. xi.
12   This ability of Rhodesian and Rhodesians to attract attention will be considered in more detail below with a discussion of audience.

13 Chennells, 1982, p. xviii.

14 Slotkin, quoted in Haarhoff, 1991, p. 164.

15 For commentary on the increasing use of literature by historians, see Harvey, 2005, pp. 1-5.

16 Thomas continued: '[works of literature] are human artefacts with as much history as any other artefact'. Thomas, 1988, p. 14.

17 For proof of this, one only needs to look at the number of books published (or republished) after 2000 on Rhodesia and the Rhodesian war. The best place to do so is on websites dedicated to Rhodesian audiences such as http://www.booksofzimbabwe.com, http://rhodesiawassuper.com and http://www.rhodesia.com. All sites accessed 21 February, 2009.

18 Buckle, 2001; Buckle, 2002; Wiles, 2005; Harrison, 2006; Barker, 2007; Beattie, 2008.

19 The most prominent works from these authors that connect to issues of land are Fuller's *Don't Let's go to the Dogs Tonight* and Godwin's *When a Crocodile Eats the Sun*. Fuller, 2003; Godwin, 2007. For discussion on Godwin and Fuller, see Pilossof, 2008b; Harris, 2005.

20 The term, 'white writing' is by no means problem-free and using it creates a distinct grouping of literature that might be better understood or critiqued if read along with other works from Zimbabwe. For more on this, see Primorac, 2003. Since the books considered here are such personal accounts, and possess a number of repeated themes and overlaps, there is a strong case for regarding them as a distinct group.

21 Coetzee's focus is purely South African, but I feel that the observation remains valid for the white writers from Zimbabwe looked at in this chapter. Obviously, despite some similarities, there is a great deal of contextual, historic and linguistic difference between South African and Zimbabwean 'white writing'. Furthermore, 'European' in this sense essentially means an outside white audience. The use of the word European is not to essentialise European audience but to illustrate who these white authors imagined their primary audience to be. Coetzee, 1988, p. 11.

22 The use of 'Africa' and 'African' by all of the authors considered in this chapter will form one of the substantial critiques of their works. The use of the inverted commas serves to remind the reader that these terms and their use are not unproblematic.

23 Ngugi, 1997, p. xvi.

24 Buckle's first book, *African Tears*, was first published by Covos Day and she writes in *Beyond Tears* of her anxieties about waiting for it to be released. See footnote 139 for more on Buckle's experiences with her publishers.

25 It is possible then to see these works as more 'genuine'. Nkosi, when talking of white South African literature, stated, 'Because so many South African writers in English have sought to publish abroad, the character and identity of South African literature [has been largely] determined somewhere else, by people outside of the community in whose name the writer claims to be speaking,' Nkosi, quoted in van der Vlies, 2007, p. 4. This sets up an interesting dichotomy between those works published in Zimbabwe (Barker and Harrison, or even in Africa with Buckle being published in South Africa) and those published overseas (Wiles and Beattie). While this local self-publishing may allow a more 'authentic' voice to emerge, it also denies the authors the space to disown

their words. The ideas and beliefs propagated are fully their own and they have to face up to them if there are serious questions raised, as this chapter will do. However, wherever these books are published, the question still remains of who they are/were published for.

26 Barker, 2007, p. 333.

27 Ibid.

28 Somerville, 1976.

29 Bell, 2005, p. 7.

30 Robertson, 1935, p. 3.

31 Somerville, 1976, p. 153.

32 Bell, 2005, p. 115.

33 Truepeney, 1965, pp. 64-5.

34 Boggie, 1959. Also, see Boggie 1938, and 1966.

35 Robertson, 1935, p. 209.

36 Ibid., p. 211.

37 The book appears to have been written long before the publication date (2005) yet no alterations have been made to the manuscript. Not only do all the names still have the Rhodesian spelling, but there is a confusion of tense, which suggests that 'Rhodesia' still exists. Consider the third last line which states, 'But most of all, Rhodesia, you have people who live and love there'. Understandably, Rhodesia may have existed when the poem was written but placing it on the back cover is another example of a wish to return to the glory days of a perfect Rhodesian past. Bell, 2005, outside back cover.

38 Coetzee (1988:5) comments on the pastoral contradictions in South Africa, which applies to the early Rhodesian settler literature. 'Pastoral in South Africa therefore has a double tribute to pay. To satisfy the critics of rural retreat, it must portray labour; to satisfy the critics of colonialism, it must portray white labour. What inevitably follows is the occlusion of black labour from the scene: the black man becomes a shadowy presence flitting across the stage now and then to hold a horse or serve a meal. In more ways than one the logic of the pastoral mode itself thus makes the incorporation of the black man – that is, of the black serf, man, woman, or child – into the larger picture embarrassing and difficult. For how can the farm become the pastoral retreat of the black man when it was his pastoral home only a generation or two ago?'

39 For more on this myopia, see Caute, 1983; Godwin and Hancock, 1993.

40 Chennells, 1982, p. xv.

41 There is a certain amount of irony in this assessment, particularly considering the southern African context and the disdain with which colonial regimes had for the unwritten histories of black populations.

42 'I wrote African Tears because I wanted all Zimbabweans, of all colours, to know what it was like on the other side of the farm fence. I wanted the world to know what this "peaceful demonstration" was really all about, to see beyond the colour of my skin. I wanted to tell the other side of the story.' Buckle, 2001, p. ii.

43 D. Palamui-Poi quoted in Chennells, 2005, p. 133.

44 Raftopoulos, 2003, pp. 230-5.

45 Anderson, 1991.

46 Ransome, 1992, p. 188.

47 Ibid., p. 187.

48 Buckle, 2002, 15.

49 Harrison, 2006, p. 9.

50 One of the two most prominent examples is where one of his workers, Lillian, has a sexual encounter with the war veteran leader on his property. Harrison was obviously not present at the scene. Harrison, Jambanja, pp. 150-2. Likewise, in an account of a meeting in the Reserve Bank between several leaders of the ZANU-PF hierarchy, during which the 'Comrades' discuss the downfall of the white man and how to ensure his total destruction. Harrison, 2006, p. 252.

51 Barker, 2007, p. 364.

52 VanBuskirk, 2006.

53 Buckle, 2001, pp. 11-12.

54 Wiles, 2005, p. 7.

55 Harrison, 2006, p. 177.

56 Ibid., pp. 119-20; Barker, 2007, p. 332.

57 See Chapter Two. Also, see Zimbabwe Human Rights NGO Forum and the Justice for Agriculture (JAG) Trust, 2007, p. 10; Zimbabwe Human Rights NGO Forum, 2001. At the same time Mugabe and ZANU-PF argued that the 'racist white farmers' were influencing their farm labourers to vote for the MDC. Thus the land occupations and fast-track reforms were part of the process of 'liberating' the countryside. See Mugabe, 2003, pp. 92-101. The articles written by Richard Winkfield in *The Farmer* about mobilising his workers to vote add a certain credence to these arguments put forward by Mugabe. See *The Farmer*, 2 March, 2000, p. 23.

58 See Worby, 2001. In the same volume, see Alexander and McGregor, 2001; Rutherford, 2001, pp. 626-51.

59 Buckle, 2001, pp. 11-2.

60 Barker, 2007, p. 332.

61 Ibid. Beattie and Harrison carry almost identical observations. Beattie, 2008, p. 110; Harrison, 2006, pp. 119-20.

62 Wiles, 2005, p. 8.

63 Buckle, 2002, p. 13.

64 Barker, 2007, p. viii. He states elsewhere that 'about a hundred acres had been used in the past by miners to grow maize but this was now covered in re-growth and had reverted to untamed bush .... Much of the land was what we called goat, or baboon, country – very broken and not much use even for grazing.' Ibid., p. 106.

65 Beattie, 2008, p. 33.

66 Harrison, 2006, p. 9.

67 On farmers who were not renowned for their hard work ethic, see Clements and Harben's description of 'Meikles veranda farmers'. Clements and Harben, 1962, p. 76.

68 For the establishment of white agriculture and processes of land alienations from 1890 to 1950, see Palmer, 1977; Phimister, 1988. Both works illustrate how white farmers and landowners managed to overcome a difficult start and secure themselves on the land through the establishment of a range of racially biased laws. As yet there is no comparative, consolidated work on white agriculture and landholding from World

War II to independence. For an overview of the literature on the later period of white rule, see Alexander, 2007, pp. 183-98.

69 These subsidies and benefits are addressed in Chapter One. Also, see Riddell, 1978, pp. 11-12; Phimister, 1987, p. 52. As the twentieth century progressed and the face of agricultural activity changed, namely with a shift towards tobacco production, a variety of soils, not necessarily deemed 'the best', became fashionable. The black inhabitants of these areas were swiftly moved to make way for tobacco production. See Palmer, 1977, chapters seven and eight. After independence, the white farming community used the fact that they owned these 'less fertile' soils to defend their land holdings.

70 For example, Barker writes extensively on his experiences as a pilot during the war in the 1970s. 'You may wonder, under these impecunious circumstances, how we could afford to run our aeroplanes – well, the government paid for the use of our planes at an hourly rate, and also paid for all damages incurred, which it incurred while it was on duty. This rate was particularly generous in that it not only covered all the flying expense but our living expenses as well.' Barker, 2007, p. 221.

71 For an overview of land reform in the 1980s, see Palmer, 1990. For land discussions in the 1990s, see Moyo, 1995.

72 See Moyo, 2000b. However, there have been numerous studies undertaken that suggest that land, in and of itself, was no longer a pressing concern for much of the population. For example an Afrobarometer study carried out in 1999 stated that, 'In Zimbabwe, the scene of several months of political conflict and violent clashes over hundreds of farm invasions, only 1.1 percent of the Zimbabwean respondents told us in September/October 1999 (before these invasions began) that land was one of the most important issues requiring government action.' Mattes, Bratton, Davids and Africa, 2000, p. 38.

73 For example, both Barker and Harrison owned planes. Barker took numerous holidays to South Africa, the UK and the USA, as did Beattie. There are also constant references to cars, boats, fishing holidays and other 'expenses', which seemed to be just a natural part of a farmer's lifestyle. Yet when it came to the labour, often it was too expensive to pay them more and famers had to 'watch' their spending. A perfect example of this is when Baker had to pay the Statutory Instrument 6 (SI6) redundancy package to his labour when he left the farm. 'We had to pay out Z$26 million (US$ 0.07 million). To put this into context, we could have bought six lovely houses in Harare for that amount.' Barker, 2007, p. 360. Buckle is not of the same breed. She and her husband had a much harder time making the farm a 'viable' enterprise.

74 Only Buckle refers to unsuccessful white farmers. In response to the governor accusing white farmers of using their money against the government, Buckle retorted, 'Perhaps also the governor did not see or know any of the white farmers who actually struggled to make a living, had huge debts with banks and finance houses and drove around in second-hand, rusting pickup trucks.' Buckle, 2001, pp. 34-5.

75 Riddell, 1978, pp. 11-12.

76 Palmer, 1990, p. 179.

77 Selby, 2006, p. 10.

78 Palmer, 1977; Phimister, 1988; Kennedy, 1987; Wolmer, 2007.

79 A remarkably candid comment from the Government of India on Rhodesia from the 1930s still applies to the situation of post-independent Zimbabwe: 'The real wealth of the country and the real assurance of financial stability lies in the native ... it is the difference between the commercial value of his labour for the white man, and the very low rates the latter pays him, which constitutes the real wealth of the country.' Kennedy, 1987, pp. 148 and 235. For more on black farm workers, see Rutherford, 2002.

80 Kennedy, 1987, p. 148.

81 As Palmer has pointed out, though, these certificates of no present interest were only valid for a year. Palmer, 1990, p. 170.

82 This sentiment is typified by a poem, written by Pauline Henson, that Buckle quotes: 'White Africans don't need a yellow star / for you know just who they are. / They don't need that badge of shame / for you know just who to blame / for what they did / (one hundred years ago and more). 'The men with no knees' / that's what people called them when they came. / Grabbing land and laying claim / to all, in Queen and country's name. / They're the ones who stole the land / back when / CJ and his 'gallant' band / came rolling up across the plains / with their bibles – and their rifles – and / their wagon trains / (one hundred years ago and more). / But that was then – this is now. / Shall we live forever in the shadow of the past? / Blaming, shaming, holding on to hate / to see it stay and sour all our days? / Their children and their children's children/ must they forever pay? / (one hundred years ago and more)' Buckle, 2002, pp. 118-19. The overriding narrative of victimhood allows no space for blame to be placed on the shoulders of white farmers. Wiles echoed much of this same sense of victimhood and blame: 'White men and women began settling and WORK-ING as farmers in 1890. Those who have followed in their footsteps are now being evicted as being undesirable aliens. Yet in that SHORT period the African population has expanded to twelve million – a twenty-fold increase. Should four thousand white farmers be condemned for that? / It is said that one in three of that population have HIV or AIDS. Are the farmers responsible for that too?' Wiles, 2005, p. 359.

83 Indeed, the entrenched system of agriculture, plus Mugabe's message of reconcili-ation, allowed white farmers to enjoy the privileges bestowed upon their position long after independence.

84 A report by the Zimbabwe Human Rights NGO Forum and the JAG Trust, claimed that by 2000 over 80 per cent of white farmers had bought their land after independence. Zimbabwe Human Rights NGO Forum and the JAG Trust, 2007, p. 9. Barker uses the same statistic. Barker, 2007, p. 332. So too does Michael Auret in his recent autobiography. Auret, 2009, p. 103.

85 *The Farmer* carried lists of farm sales in the early 1980, but gave no indication of how comprehensive these lists were. This practice stopped after a few years.

86 The list was reproduced in full in *The Farmer*, 4 December 1997, pp. 23-75. How-ever this list was riddled with mistakes and misprints. See Appendix Six for a table and graph of title deeds from the 1997 lists.

87 The process of share transfer is mentioned in the interviews with Farmer 3 and Farmer 26. The inheritance of farms is discussed in the interviews with Farmer 1, Farmer 2, Farmer 4, Farmer 7 and Farmer 22. See interview with Farmer 1, 14 June,

2007, Harare; interview with Farmer 2, 12 May 2007, Harare; interview with Farmer 3, 2 March 2007, Harare; interview with Farmer 4, 5 April 2007, Harare; interview with Farmer 7, 2 July 2007, Harare; interview with Farmer 22, 19 June 2007, Harare.

88 Buckle, 2002, p. 19.

89 Buckle, 2001, p. 102.

90 Wiles, 2005, pp. 13-14. This connection to his trees, or 'children', is so strong that any action that threatens their existence is overly dramatised. For example when one of the war veterans who settles on his farm dares to raise an axe to one of his beloved 'children', Wiles' narration of the episode makes clear his fervent attachment to them: 'Simukayi [the war veteran] is obsessed with the thought of killing and the power that he has been given to threaten death is very real and meaningful to him. To watch him axe down a beautiful tree with obvious relish (as I have done) is a horrifying experience. He is a destroyer of life, a purveyor of death, a servant of Satan.' Ibid., pp. 48-9.

91 Buckle, 2002, pp. 161-2. Part of this nature connection includes pets and animals on the farm, whose fate is far more pressing than any other (black) inhabitants on the farm.

92 Harrison, 2006, p. 66.

93 Coetzee, 1988, p. 81. For more on Coetzee's discussion on the pitfalls on the white pastoral writing see pages 78-81. As for the comments about feeding the nation, an oft-repeated claim by Buckle was that white farmers just wanted the chance and opportunity to 'get on with the business of growing food for Zimbabwean stomachs.' Buckle, 2002, p. 20. However, there is plenty of evidence to illustrate that black farmers were capable of producing enough food the feed the country. Furthermore, over the 1980s and 1990s, white farmers had shifted a great deal of their energies to horticulture and wildlife, which were much more economically viable. Moyo, 2000b.

94 Beattie continually marvels at the 'natural' scenery around her farm and in Zimbabwe at large. 'Conservation' plays a major part in the pastoral debates and silences. Wiles, Barker, Buckle and Harrison all claim to be protectors of Zimbabwe's natural heritage and that without their control of the land, that ability to 'conserve' will be lost. However, as Hughes has shown with regard to conservation and white Zimbabwe, there a remarkable 'ambiguity in the entire enterprise of conservation: between an ideal of the wild and the merely pretty.' Hughes, 2006b, p. 827.

95 Chennells, 1982, Chapter Two; Coetzee, 1988, Chapters Three and Four; Hughes, 2006a.

96 Van Onselen, 1996, p. 281.

97 Wiles, 2005, p. 318.

98 Ibid., p. 171. See also page 300, where Wiles comments, 'it is in the holding of principals, that to a large extent the African mind differs from the European'.

99 Harrison, 2006, pp. 102-3

100 Chennells, 2006, p. 191.

101 Coetzee, 1992, pp. 97, 98 and 61. Also, see van der Vlies, 2007, p. 134.

102 Barker admits that the term 'gook' only come into use in Rhodesia when American veterans, who used the word to describe the Viet Cong in Vietnam, came to fight for the whites in Rhodesia, essentially as hired mercenaries. Barker, 2007, p. 103. Another term often employed to describe guerrillas by Rhodesian forces was 'floppies'

on account of how they looked when dead.

103 There are numerous descriptions of dead 'gooks' and kills in Barker's text, many of them recounted with a disturbing amount of pleasure and detail. For example, 'The next day I had to fly to Mukkers to pick up the six bodies from the previous day's contact – the man with the orange trousers had a neat hole in the crown of his head. It was later learned that a further six had died of their wounds, with four others injured. Twelve dead and four injured seemed pretty good odds.' Barker, 2007, p. 233.

104 Ibid., p. 246. After the 'gooks' retreated, Barker yelled to them, 'You are not Matabeles – Matabeles are men. You are just *"matidzi ye imbwa"*, dog shit. You are many, I am one, come and fight.' This is another of the white settlers' founding myths, that the Matabele are more manly, more warrior-like and more respectable than the weak and subservient Shona. For more discussion on the construction of this myth, see Chennells, 1982, Chapter Two.

105 Ibid., pp. 138-9.

106 Ibid., p. 204.

107 Parker and Rathbone, 2007, p. 45.

108 Chennells, 2005, p. 137.

109 The Country Club was an important place of learning and socialisation for white farmers. Beattie mentions the gatherings at 'the Club' and how these were important occasions for the farming community. For mention of the club in the books, see Beattie, 2008, pp. 38-9; Harrison, 2006, p. 110; Barker, 2007, pp. 143 and 154.

110 Beattie, 2007, p. 22.

111 Ibid., p. 34. Beattie recounts a similar example when talking of the surfeit of vegetables on the farm: 'I learned how to deal with foods in bulk …. Some could be frozen, some had to be stewed and then frozen, some I made into soups, and some I just gave to the staff if there was too much.' Ibid., p. 62.

112 Ibid., p. 36.

113 Ibid., p. 64.

114 Ibid., p. 87.

115 Ibid.

116 Ibid., p. 132. Barker also blames Mugabe for 'the stirring up of race hatred'. Barker, 2007, p. 332.

117 See Buckle for a lament about the racism white farmers were exposed to. Buckle, 2001, pp. 34-5.

118 For more on the representation of Africa by prominent authors, see Achebe, 1989; Ngugi, 2004.

119 For example, see the assistance and advice Buckle gives Jane after she was beaten up. Buckle, 2001, pp. 123-8.

120 Ibid., pp. 235-41.

121 Buckle, 2002, pp. 202-6.

122 Harrison, 2006, p. 245.

123 Ibid., p. 271.

124 Ibid., pp. 269-70.

125 Barker, 2007, p. 364.

126 Grundy and Miller, 1979.

127 Most of the authors seem oblivious to the blanket problems caused by the terms 'Africa' and 'African'. Wiles though, in a bizarre revelation, recounts a passage where he asks an 'affluent', 'educated' and 'emancipated' 'African lady' he knew if 'Africans' would be hurt by the use of the term 'African Township'. She replied: 'Well, you know nowadays people are very sensitive. It is best to speak of high density suburbs ... In other words avoid the label "African".' Despite this warning, Wiles shows no concern about using the word throughout his book. Wiles, 2005, p. 260.

128 Such approaches invoke a way of looking at the world, and the imaginations and ideologies this process contains, so castigated by Said in his critique of Western understandings of 'The Orient'. See Said, 2003. For studies adopting the same approach but in the African context, see Mudimbe, 1988; Mbembe, 2001.

129 Wainaina, 2005.

130 Wiles' title – *Foredoomed is my Forest: The Diary of a Zimbabwe* [sic] *Farmer* – is problematic for another reason. He may not use Africa, but his failure to 'adjectify' Zimbabwe is an all too obvious reflection on the quality and content of the rest of the book.

131 Barker's book is introduced by a Peter W. Richards, while Harrison's is introduced by a Dr Colin Saunders and a Jeremy Lee. In addition it contains an epilogue from the economist John Robertson. Barker, 2007, p. v; Harrison, 2006, pp. 6-8 and 264-7.

132 Buckle, 2001, pp. ix-xiv; Buckle, 2002, pp. 7-12.

133 White, 2003, p. 73.

134 See Books of Zimbabwe Online, http://www.booksofzimbabwe.com [accessed, 21 February, 2009]; Lekkerwear, http://rhodesiawassuper.com [accessed, 21 February, 2009]; Rhodesians Worldwide, http://www.rhodesia.com [accessed, 21 February, 2009].

135 Chennells, 1977, p. 178.

136 Ibid., p. 177.

137 In this regard, the sales figures of Buckle's books show that there is a relatively large demand for them. Of African Tears, she writes that 'the original publisher was Covos Day Books in SA. They printed 10,000 copies which were sold out in the first 6 months. After a year when I became more and more anxious about not receiving any of my royalties or share of serial payments that I knew had been made to Covos, I began to put pressure on them. They declared bankruptcy, went into liquidation, never paid me a cent and the owner disappeared out of SA. (He is now back in SA, has opened another publishing company and carries on – apparently untouchable) Anyway I scouted for a publisher to reprint *African Tears*, found Jonathan Ball Books in SA who agreed to reprint only if I wrote a follow up book which they would print in tandem – hence *Beyond Tears* ... [the books have sold] mostly in SA and the region (Zambia, Namibia) but steady sales in UK (Africa Book Centre distribute for me) Aus [Australia] and some in NZ [New Zealand]'. *African Tears* has since been reprinted. Correspondence with Catherine Buckle, 22 April, 2008. For more on Rhodesian diaspora community and their memories and commemorations, see Uusihakala, 2008.

138 Chennells, 2005, p. 132.

139 Clingman, 2004, p. 61.

6

'Orphans of Empire'

Oral Expressions of Displacement & Trauma[1]

> 'Voices' are voices, not choruses; they cry in the wilderness of history and speak, apparently, to experience. They represent another kind of fantasy of authenticity, our access to the 'real thing'.
> – Megan Vaughan.[2]

Introduction

The interviews used in this chapter were conducted in 2007, after the closure of *The Farmer* magazine and the publication of many of the auto-biographies discussed, and they offer the possibility to investigate the 'oral traditions' (or oral practices) of the white farming community.

This book has sought to explore the 'authentic' voice of white farmers, to which the interviews provide a further point of access. This voice, however, is not treated as the spontaneous voice that is the implicit subject of much oral history research in Africa. Nor is it the presentation of disempowered and unadulterated voices which interrupt 'the flow of the historians narrative', the use of which Megan Vaughn has rightly questioned.[3] These oral accounts provide a very direct means to engage with the trauma of the land occupations. In order to write not simply an apologist account of white farmers in Zimbabwe, or a tirade against an unchanged group of racist neo-colonialists who deserved exactly what they had coming to them, this source requires sensitive handling. My aim is to portray what has happened to white farmers in their own words and understandings, and then to engage with this voice to locate not only some of the factual inaccuracies, prejudices and faults contained within those views, but also to show how they echo oral practices of the past.

The Justice for Agriculture (JAG) Interviews

The start of the violent land reforms in 2000 saw white farmers come under direct and escalating attack by forces loyal to President Robert Mugabe and ZANU-PF. As a result of the CFU's unwillingness to champion the case of evicted farmers in the early 2000s, because it believed any such action would have jeopardised whatever fragile relationship it had with government, JAG was formed in 2002 to advocate and lobby for white farmers who had been adversely affected by the fast-track land reforms. Its declared aim was, 'to safeguard and support people directly affected, in whatever way possible, and to document and expose the injustices and human rights abuses being perpetrated against them'.[4] Information relating to the fast-track land reforms (such as personal stories of eviction and human rights abuse, and databases of gazetted land and ZANU-PF beneficiaries) was collected by JAG. Most of this data was assembled on an ad hoc basis and there was a lack of follow-up and consolidation of the material.[5] Because JAG sought to remain 'apolitical', even whilst it criticised events in the countryside, it did not make political alliances with parties such as the MDC. Both the CFU and JAG conform in different ways to the apolitical and affirmative parochial approaches identified in Chapter Three.

In 2007, JAG, with the assistance of the Research and Advocacy Unit (RAU), a human rights research and documentation organisation, embarked on a project to document the traumas suffered by white farmers during the land occupations. This began with a detailed questionnaire survey, the findings which – based on evidence from 187 white farmers – were published in a report by the Zimbabwe Human Rights NGO Forum and the JAG Trust.[6] This report revealed the vast amount of violence associated with the land occupations, and the trauma suffered by both white farmers and black farm labourers.[7] The project ultimately gathered responses from over 400 white farmers, almost ten per cent of the total in 2000.

JAG and RAU then conducted detailed interviews with a sample of the white farmers who had completed the questionnaires, in order to augment the quantitative information gathered. These interviews were intended to provide qualitative insights into the farmers' experiences of the fast-track land reforms.[8] This necessitated detailing the violence and trauma experienced, the people and individuals involved and the overall narrative of evictions. Over 300 interviews have been undertaken and several reports have been published based on the findings.[9] I was involved in the establishment of the process and personally carried out over 30 of the interviews, most of which were conducted in conjunction with a co-interviewer, a woman who herself had been evicted from her farm; they form the core of this chapter.

The JAG project faced many difficulties. These revolved around issues of funding, infrastructure and expertise, but also the adverse political climate in which the interviews took place. The interview process started at the beginning of 2007, at a stage when ZANU-PF was deeply concerned to limit exposure of its abuses of human rights, and whilst land occupations and evictions were still taking place. With elections due in 2008, there were palpable political tensions within the country and both JAG and RAU faced the constant threat of investigation by the police or CIO.[10] Identifying farmers to interview was difficult; they could only be located through JAG and farming networks and many were worried about being recorded, or refused to participate at all. The covert nature of the project, as well as limitations of funding, meant it was limited in its scope and reach. All the white farmers interviewed while I was working on the project were residing in Harare at the time. This unavoidable discrepancy is replicated throughout the book, since the other sources examined are also heavily biased towards Mashonaland. *The Farmer*, for example, was published by the CFU's Harare office and all of the autobiographies were written by farmers from Mashonaland.

Whilst seeking to avoid the trap identified by David William Cohen, Stephan Miecher and Luise White whereby the 'politics of the collection of oral testimony [assume] precedence over the critical practices of analysis and interpretation of texts', there are nevertheless important points to raise about the JAG interview collection.[11] Firstly, the interviews were not undertaken for the purpose of this research. They were carried out by a white farming organisation with members of the white farming community for their own purposes of research and documentation. The interviewers were often from a farming background, or at least had farming connections.[12] Indeed some interviewees were so 'comfortable' that they had no qualms about using the racist or prejudiced language that pervaded white farming circles, which would not have found expression in other, less congenial circumstances.[13] There were still many cases where the interviewees were cautious about being recorded and would excuse themselves from revealing too much on tape.[14] This is highly beneficial for research purposes, in the sense that the interviews provide access to a richer and less constrained voice of white farmers than that captured by researchers from outside the community.[15] However, because the interviews have been recorded in this way, it raises ethical issues about their use. The other sources analysed in this book were all produced for public audiences; the interview collection was not. Indeed, considering the sensitive political climate in which it was collected much of the material had the potential to create negative repercussions for the interviewees. Because of these concerns, the informants have been kept strictly anonymous.[16]

JAG's willingness to offer the interviews to researchers is based upon its assumption that they will be sympathetic to its cause and will use the material to criticise the land reforms and occupations, and condemn the violence carried out against white farmers. While these issues are certainly apparent in the interviews, the research also opens the way for interpretations that would not please JAG or many in the farming community.[17] The analysis presented here has been undertaken to reveal white farmers' reactions and expressions, not to castigate them. Furthermore, it is hoped that the evidence presented in the previous chapters shows that the language of the interviews builds on practices and discourse that have a long history. Despite these caveats and problems, the interviews provide a rich source from which to garner deeper, more nuanced insights into white farmers' reactions to the land reforms and events since 2000. It is hoped that the analysis will confirm Charles van Onselen's observation:

> A rigorous, thorough, sensitive and talented oral historian using interview material of only average quality is always likely to produce a more convincing and reliable study than a mediocre orthodox historian using the finest documentary sources – and vice versa.[18]

The Oral Account

What follows is not a radical reconstruction of the land occupations and the experiences involved, but a reading of how white farmers have interpreted and expressed the events that took place.[19] While the unfolding of the fast-track land reforms is an issue that still requires more research and analysis, it has been looked at elsewhere and continues to attract scholarly attention.[20] Furthermore, it is questionable how useful the interviews would be for this purpose, as so many of them are lacking the necessary depth, clarity, and substantiating evidence.[21] These interviews, as a scarce collection, offer something else. Throughout this book, various sources have been used to show how white farmers interacted with and commented upon events around them and how these expressions have related to certain readings and interpretations of the past. The interviews are the latest expression, as it were, of the recent past and deserve particular attention as a product of a specific context and time.

Reading the interviews in this way does not mean exceptionalising them as oral accounts. Rather, the aim is to read them as part of a wider collection of white farming voice and expression, to create a fuller, more layered and developed picture of those revelations. Oral and written accounts are treated as 'equal but distinct forms of recording the past', an approach that is more common in non-African historiography, because of the hallowed place 'oral traditions' hold in the establishment of the discipline of African history.[22] As Alessandro Portelli has suggested, much can be gained from listening to oral accounts 'as the poetic, ritual representation of the meaning of historical experience'.[23] This chapter hopes to do precisely that with the JAG archive.

The material is presented as a 'thematic montage'.[24] Partly this is a reflection of the need to anonymise the interviewees, but also because it connects the material to the preceding chapters. This illustrates the connections and conformities found in the interviews and the formulaic elements used by white farmers to relate their experiences.[25] What must be remembered is that the interviewees drew in their testimony upon an already established (written and oral) account of white farmers and their history. As with the other sources looked at, there are points of contact and cohesion that present themselves in the interviews. This is not to deny the fact that there was a wide range of experiences amongst white farmers after 2000 – the accounts collected by JAG tell of evictions happening at different times and in different ways, which is important to keep in mind.[26] There is nevertheless a language, a manufactured tradition, and a way of talking about the events that makes itself apparent in the interviews. (For information about the interviewees, see Appendix Seven.)

The Trauma of Eviction

The psychological harassment, beatings, evictions and murder of white farmers not only affected the individuals involved; the attacks threatened the whole community and fostered extreme anxiety and fear. This process has been well reported and has received recent attention in several documentary films.[27]

The trauma suffered by white farmers influenced the interviews in numerous ways. For example, their failure recall events in chronological order, conflict between husbands and wives over what happened and who was involved, an unwillingness to talk about certain issues and, most clearly, emotional breakdown during the interviews themselves. As with the autobiographies examined in Chapter Five, the sense of loss and displacement are an intricate part of the narratives that it is impossible to ignore.[28] Farmers' dislocation from their homes, their past and their community, often accompanied by extreme physical violence and psychological trauma, were not only part of the recorded oral account, but the whole experience of undertaking the interview and data collection process.

Many farmers were open about the levels of trauma suffered, or were unable to hide the emotional scars their evictions had left. Farmer 3's experience included political intimidation, being barricaded in the homestead, gun battles, verbal and physical assaults and the killing of pets and animals.[29] During one confrontation, he believed his mother to have been shot by occupiers in a separate house on their farmstead:

> I went out to have a look ... and, there's a couple of these guys who had got through the fence, through my fence and were coming at me with shotguns .... It was the first time we have seen them actively with shotguns .... I chased these 2 guys with shotguns back out of the fence. I went and got my shotgun and I had a revolver ... then there was a shot at my mothers place and I thought, well I heard from my sister who was inside the house, she said on the radio that my mother had gone out and she had been confronted by three of these gooks ... this shot was fired and I thought well, now she's been, she had been shot and killed or she's been shot because it was just like one shot .... I was at my place ... so I thought I better go across there and see what was going on. So I got through my gate, and now I'm surrounded by all these people and they are just being pressed towards me, you know, causing a lot of trouble, throwing stones and all that kind of thing. And I'm trying to get

across there quickly to see what was going on without looking like I'm running away from the crowd that are there, so I am sort of moving away from them and they are closing in towards me shouting and screaming and all that, they were getting so close and I couldn't run so I turned back and I fired a shot into the ground which chased them away again. I subsequently fired a lot of shots into the ground to keep this crowd away …. I got to my mother's gate which was locked so now I was stranded …. I was on the radio saying please to let me in. I had to go right around the main fence … as I was sort of going around the fence there was the hanger which had an airplane inside it … two of these guys … were watching and as I came around the corner they were firing at me, so I just had to fire back at them and I don't know how, no one was, was, was hit. So, I had this big group coming along behind me, I'm sort of trotting along firing shots back at them and these guys are firing shots at me and I'm firing forward and feeding bullets in as fast as I can shoot them … anyway, it sort of calmed down because I just carried on going towards them … we were fairly close … say ten yards away, pointing guns at each other. They had this whole bunch of guns and I was aiming at them as well. [Getting emotional, tears in eyes] … my sister came out, opened the gate and let me in … so, we had this, both houses all surrounded, they had loud hailers, and they were just shouting, "Farmer 3, you are going to die today, Farmer 3 we are going to kill you, Farmer 3 get off this farm" …. Ya, we, subsequently we found there was, they had taken my mothers radio and her weapon …. My mother was fine, my sister and my mother and two kids were fine.[30]

Farmer 3's mother was not killed, but the murder of several other white farmers across the country had increased the fear that killings would and could happen. As he explained, 'the situation was at that time … Dave Stevens had been killed, Martin Olds had been killed … there was just so much violence at that time so, so to put it in that context we were expecting a hit in our area'.[31] Farmer 10, an elderly woman, supported this: 'you just lived in constant fear'.[32] For many farmers there was a constant threat of attack or abuse that made life on an occupied farm extremely difficult.

Farmer 13 was one of the most visibly traumatised of the farmers I interviewed. His narrative was barely coherent and he was almost unable to talk about what had happened. His neighbour was Terry Ford, who was killed in March 2002. On his farm he recalled, 'there was this one woman … [who was involved in Ford's murder] and she, she openly said, "I pulled the trigger" so you know … that was one of the great threats to me is that I'm going like Terry now'.[33] The murders acted as a form of psychological weapon to break the resistance of those who remained on the land.[34]

The invasions put great strain on marriages and family lives.[35] They were also the source of many health problems; heart attacks, strokes and other afflictions claimed the lives of white farmers in less dramatic and often unreported ways. Farmer 13 believed the land occupations were the cause of his wife's death:

> My wife definitely, I say, died through the trauma of all this .... Before I got the, you know, before moving, you know, we had hassles. All the next door neighbours were getting hassled and they were chanting past our gates and that. Odd one would come in and shout and she was just a bundle of nerves you know .... And then she had a heart attack in, she, 2000, June.[36]

Children were also severely traumatised by the processes of eviction, and a number of those interviewed made the point that their children had to attend school alongside those of beneficiaries of their family's eviction.[37]

Farmers seldom found ways to confront their feelings of loss. Farmer 24 thought he had found an opportunity to do just this long after his eviction. One of his workers had died on the farm, and he arranged to go and help bury her. After arriving, he was told a woman living there was pregnant and he offered to take her to the hospital. He related his feelings of going back to the farm:

> I went to the farm feeling quite excited. I'm going to bury, finally bury this damned thing, I'm going to put cement on the cemetery .... She was a girl who was a significant, sort of part of our life and the presence on the farm and she'd been very vociferous when [a war veteran] came ... she really cussed him ... but, anyway she died there and he would have nothing to do with her or anything. So, we left money for the grave and I thought, this is it, this is great, we're taking a woman, she's going to have a baby – new life – everything's going to be okay. And we got to town and found she'd left her bags in the back of the truck and the next morning we got a phone call from her father to say what can we do about the bags? So I sent my man back to Headlands with the bags and got news that evening that the baby had been stillborn, it was half rotten and she's in Jairos Jiri [a hospital for the disabled and handicapped] half paralysed, so ... It was really sad and really painful to me in the sense that I can't ditch this thing, that it kind of speaks what the land reform is – death of the past and stillborn present. And I really don't see that any good can come from the present situation. It's got to get resolved properly to sort it out.[38]

The experiences referred to above were some of the most violent. However, others (like those of Farmers 7, 12 and 23) were remarkable for the total lack of physical threat.[39] Farmer 7, an elderly woman, left her farm and moved to Harare in 2002 having not experienced any intimidation or violence.[40] These interviews confirm the analysis of Angus Selby and others, including that in *The Farmer* magazine, that there was a great deal of variation in the land invasions and occupations.[41] Despite the differences, there were (and still are) standard discourses for referencing the land occupations and evictions in the white farming community that make themselves evident in the JAG collection. The first of these tropes is the language of the Liberation War.

The Re-emergence of Past Discourse

The trauma of the evictions, and the manner in which the land occupations took place, reinvigorated earlier ways of talking about violence and attack that had connections to the Liberation War of the 1970s. These manifested themselves in several ways in the interviews. The most striking are those that replicate the way the guerrilla forces were discussed in white Rhodesian society. The derogatory terms of 'gook', 'terr' and *mujiba* that were commonplace in the white farming community and the armed forces became part of the vocabulary of the land occupations after 2000. Racism and prejudice find fuller expression in these oral accounts than in the written ones examined in the previous chapters.[42]

For instance, Farmer 3, when asked who were the people on his farm, replied, 'they were, were those, we call them gooks, vermin.'[43] The main war veteran on an occupied farm was described as 'the resident gook' in one interview. Farmer 1 said of the Deputy Police Commissioner in his area, 'He was very much on their side [the war veterans]. He was an ex-gook himself.'[44] Farmer 14 commented that 'every week we had a severe threat from [the settlers], or from [a particular war veteran] who was the sort of roaming gook [in our area]'.[45] Farmer 20 said he had taken a few of his labourers to work on another piece of land after his first invasion, but 'the gooks took over that, the war vets took that place over too'.[46] Farmer 32 also used the word:

> there's now a gook in the compound, one of the main stirrers, you know. Now he is organising all these beatings and all this sort of thing, you know retribution sort of thing in the compound, he's organising these beatings and he's organising what they should do next and all that … you know exactly where he's coming from, he's a snake, a snake of the first order, you know.[47]

As in the Liberation War, the use of the term 'gook' to label these individuals denies them status and negates the importance of the 'war' they fought and their actions in that war. The reinvigoration of 'gook' reveals not only a lack of recognition and acceptance amongst much of the white farming community of the causes and aims of the Liberation War, but also their racial prejudices by employing term.[48]

When 'gook' was not used, it was often replaced by an equally contentious word: *mujiba*. This term also has its origins in the Liberation War. A *mujiba* was a young boy who ran errands for the guerrilla forces.[49] In *The Farmer at War*, a young white farmer explained the role and significance of the *mujiba*:

> Discussing terrorist ambush tactics, Don said, 'They [the guerrillas] know what they are doing, the bastards. They have had contacts in the area. Usually, they pressure foremen or headmen. They also get their information through the mujibas ... they are the eyes and ears of the terrs. They are sometimes only 12-year-olds but they know everything. I don't know what the word *mujibas* means in Shona, but I believe it's messenger or something like that'.[50]

After 2000, white farmers used the term to describe the occupants and settlers on their farms. Farmer 2 said that on one occasion when his father was being threatened by the occupiers, 'My dad said, "I'm not buckling down to these bloody young *mujibas*."'[51] Farmer 15 also said that he kept calling the war veteran on his farm a *mujiba*.[52] Farmer 17, talking of the woman war veteran leader on the farm, said:

> Well, I saw her once being taken around in a little, little, um, 323 taxi. She had with her, her, I suppose her little *mujiba* group, her sort of bodyguards and one of them wore an AK magazine, uh, chest webbing and in that were beer bottles ... and when she needed a beer, he would pull out of the magazine pouch a beer and hand it to her. You can imagine how warm and horrible and hot it was .... She was a venomous, very evil person.[53]

Describing these people as *mujibas* denied them legitimacy as war veterans and called into question their role and standing in the new land movements. It also reinforced the white farmers' belief that the people invading their farms were too young to have been active combatants during the war. Mainly, however, the term was a belittling one, which questioned both the past of these new settlers, and their maturity. They were basically children, the pawns of ZANU-PF.

It is important to realise that the white farmers have been highly instrumental in creating the 'war vet' that has become the stock image of the land occupations in Zimbabwe since 2000.[54] Consider these selected quotations describing those who moved onto farms:

> The ridiculous nature of the whole exercise is that the pathetic little rabble caused so much trouble.[55]

> So I went outside ... to try and negotiate with these fools and they got hold of me and dragged me off .... At that particular time my brother drove in ... and he drove into this mess and he saw one little white man standing there with 1,000 heathens standing around him.[56]

> [my white manager was] singled out ... and they took him ... around the back and threatened to kill him and they said that we want to see your boss ... so I came out ... and I went in the yard and there were these terrible looking creatures there.[57]

> They [the occupiers] were the dregs of the TTL [Tribal Trust Lands, the colonial term for the Communal Lands].[58]

Frantz Fanon argued that 'the feeling of inferiority of the colonised is the correlative to the European's feeling of superiority. Let us have the courage to say it outright: *it is the racist who creates his inferior*' [italics in original].[59] The war veterans, portrayed as 'gooks' and *mujibas*, augmented by descriptions of their appearance and behaviour, are portrayed as inferior and as blights on the landscape of the farm.[60] This image has been reproduced in the international press, and has led to a consolidation of such negative stereotypes.[61] (However, some, such as Norma Kriger, have sought to nuance the portrayal of war veterans.[62]) To emphasise his point, Fanon quoted Jean-Paul Sartre, 'The Jew is one whom other men consider a Jew: that is the simple truth from which we must start. ... It is the anti-Semite who *makes* the Jew.'[63]

Twenty years after the end of the Liberation War, the white farming community was able to seamlessly fit the 'land invasions' into the paradigm of war. This was aided by the combative and military stance of Mugabe and many of the war veterans themselves, whose own attitudes to the 'land reforms' were based upon their hopes of resolving the perceived failings of the Second Chimurenga. However, while this certainly explains part of this reviving of war terminology, it does not explain the whole story. As Chapter Four explored in its discussion of the discursive threshold crossed in 2000, the ease with which white farmers fell back into the references of the 1970s speaks to a prevalent mindset in the community.

The enduring nature of such discourses suggests that there has been a limit to the 'decolonisation of the mind' for some (if not many) white farmers.[64] For the orphans of empire, the remnants of the colonial settler population that remained in the independent countries, this has allowed them to move beyond the unfounded claims of superiority colonial rule instilled. The language used to talk about indigenous populations has failed to move away from that of the colonial era. As Antjie Krog has commented:

> the first casualty of conflict is identity … literature on reconciliation identifies the 'turning away (of former adversaries) from each other' as a crucial point in reconciliation – redefining identity makes a new kind of relationship possible …. We are also redefining: how black is black, what is white? If redefinition is unsuccessful, a group may become frozen in a permanent quest for identity that often expresses itself in rigid and aggressive forms of ethnicity or nationalism.[65]

For the white farmers, the reversion to the use of terms such as 'gooks', 'terrs', *mujibas* (regardless of constant use of other problematic terms such as 'munt', 'kaffir' and the undifferentiated 'they' and 'these people') reveals the extent of their unreconstructed views.

For Krog, the Truth and Reconciliation Commission (TRC) established in South Africa after its 1994 elections has aided this process of redefinition, and in so doing the processes of reconciliation.[66] One farmer felt he had been denied his 'right to reconciliation' after the Liberation War, and that this had led to the resurfacing of many of the same problems, racial stereotypes and conflicts witnessed after 2000.[67] This failure to redefine themselves and others in the post-colonial setting, meant that white farmers remained trapped in a colonial past.[68]

'I paid my houts everything':
Labour Relations on White Farms[69]

Throughout the 1990s, government levelled many accusations at white farmers for their mistreatment of black labour and the lack of social welfare and development, and Rene Loewenson's studies have confirmed the inadequacy of nutrition, education and health care on commercial farms.[70] A report by the Farm Community Trust of Zimbabwe in 2001 found that only 59 per cent of children on commercial farms attended primary school. In addition, many of the farm schools were unregistered and operated with severely limited resources, resulting in very poor educational standards.[71] While some commercial farms operated primary schools, very few offered any secondary education.[72] Farm workers were not only neglected by their employers; their cause was also ignored by government who failed to demand any major improvements in their living and working conditions.[73]

Within the white farming community, the paternalistic attitudes that were so prevalent during the colonial era remained intact into the new millennium. Farmer 32 viewed the labour on his farm as 'his'; his blacks, his workers, his 'houts'.[74] Van Onselen has illustrated the articulation of these same beliefs in rural South Africa during the first half of the twentieth century. In that setting, Afrikaners proclaimed that the black man, be he a labourer or sharecropper, owned nothing. For van Onselen, 'Shorn of its Sunday finery, paternalism wore the undergarments of autocracy', and for all its 'many virtues in a harsh environment, paternalism was predicated on a structured inequality that required the perpetual adolescence of the junior partner.'[75] Even in post-colonial Zimbabwe farm labourers remained that junior partner. Furthermore, the racial prejudices against the land occupiers and war veterans was not reserved only for those groups. The same bias informed labour relations. As a result, much of the white farming discourse about black labour was infused with a problematic paternalism, as the interviews make patently clear.[76]

Every farmer was asked a variation of the question: 'Did you have good relations with your labour?' All replied that they had, at least at the beginning of the land occupations.[77] There is obviously a range of interactions that constitute 'good relations' in the minds of white farmers, and this was discussed in the interviews. The main interpretation given was that 'good relations' existed if the workers behaved in a manner that was not aggressive or threatening towards the white farmer. This interpretation did not necessarily include any reflection on how the white farmers treated their labour. Some, like the farmer who supplied the subtitle for this section, believed good relations could exist whilst still employing words like 'hout' and 'munt'.[78] Others clearly felt much more affinity for their workers. Farmers 24 and 29 demonstrated the strongest connections with their workforce and supplied a great deal of detail on their experiences, the suffering they endured and the loss they felt when they moved away from the farm. The labourers were often referred to by name and not just 'garden boy', 'driver' or some other title. Indeed Farmer 24's account above about the dead girl and the unborn child attest to the centrality of the farm workers in his vision of the farm. Farmer 29's wife also commented on how often their workers protected them during attack or assault:

> [My husband's] sight was not that good. He had a man who walked with him … his assistant … and when these people [land occupiers] arrived, all the drivers and everybody in the compound came and stood around Bruce. Just closed ranks around him and as [a woman war veteran] and [a] colonel came forward they moved back and forwards and it happened many, many times …. On occasions people would arrive at our fence on a Saturday afternoon and would start a fire and beat drums and that and all the women and children from the workers' village used to come. They used to come and used to stand, all the women and children with their heads looking down at the ground. And as the war veterans came towards the gate so the women and children would move and when they turned around and screamed the women would move back but they never left …. [One farm worker's wife in particular] never said a word, they never confronted them or anything but every time they heard the lorries and the drums and the fires, saw the fires the women and children used to come to the workers' village and very quietly get sticks and just stand, just stand, stand. Amazing people.[79]

Farmer 29 and his wife recounted numerous examples of their labour force going to extraordinary lengths to aid and assist them.[80] It was clear from this interview, if accepted as even an approximation of the real situation, that there was a very close and tight bond between them.[81] Every farm labourer discussed was addressed not by their job title, but by their own first name. It is no coincidence that neither Farmer 29 nor his wife used any derogatory or racial terms, either for their black farm workers, or the settlers and political beneficiaries that moved onto their farm. This is despite the fact that their eviction was one of the most violent and traumatic recorded.[82]

Many other farmers, however, recounted episodes where farm workers put themselves in danger in order to protect their employers. Farmer 25 recalled his workers circling around him when settlers threatened violence.[83] Others gave examples of the workforce actually chasing away occupiers or settlers, but this tended to take place early on in the land occupation period. Such tactics were abandoned as violence and intimidation against farm workers increased.[84] Other white farmers, while not citing specific examples, recalled how 'loyal' and 'fantastic' their labourers were throughout the occupations.[85]

While some farmers did have excellent working relationships and communications with their labour, many had little idea of what they suffered. Many farmers who claimed to have excellent labour relations, admitted that they did not know exactly what happened to their workers, in terms of violence and intimidation. A typical exchange is given below:

Interviewer: And you had pretty good relations with your labour?

Farmer 21: Oh yes.

Farmer 21's Wife: Oh yes, very.

Farmer 21: You say that now, but when you look back, if you look at the guys that you thought you could really trust, how they turned against you, you know. I think their intimidation, I always sort of thought back of that Goebbels in the Second World War, who did a very good job for the Germans and this Made [the Minster of Agriculture], who was in charge then did a very good job for ZANU-PF. They all turned and it's amazing some of the guys that you didn't think would, would er, you thought would turn against you didn't, like we got a phone call just the other day from one of the lighties [children] that I never liked, to phone to tell us that they were now moving the Modro curers off the farm as well. You know, that type of thing. With the blessing of the Ministry of Agriculture .... So what can you do about that, you know?

Interviewer: So, did your labour suffer quite a bit of intimidation and violence?

Farmer 21: My driver, my lorry driver and three or four other guys did, yes.

Farmer 21's Wife: Because they were the ones that stuck their heads out.

Interviewer: Initially?

Farmer 21: Initially .... And anybody who even uttered an other word, or showed any, any other opinion, they, I mean, I don't know what exactly went on in the compound, but I knew from that that they were definitely intimidated.[86]

'Good relations' did not mean that the farmers had to have detailed knowledge of the black farm labour experience. There is little in the JAG interviews about the experiences of farm workers during the land invasions. When Farmer 4 was asked if his labour were attacked or traumatised, he replied, 'I think they could have been traumatised a bit, but you never know with them. It wasn't like in some areas where they got beaten up.'[87] The farmers often felt that the accounts of their labourers were inherently unreliable. Their underlying attitude towards black people dictated their reaction to the sufferings of their labour, and the stories that they related. As Farmer 5 said, when asked if he had any source of information or contact with the farm after he left he said: 'It's not reliable, they just tell you, like all these Shona people, they only tell you what they think you want to hear and for that they want some sort of reward.'[88]

Farmer 21's interview also reveals the sense of betrayal felt by white farmers when their labour 'turned' on them. Such occurrences sometimes resulted from the government's introduction of Statutory Instrument 6 (SI6) in 2002, under which farmers whose land had been acquired by government were required to pay their farm labourers termination benefits, or 'retrenchment packages'.[89] These packages consisted of two months' pay, plus a month's pay for every year worked. Such payments were a massive outlay for the farmers, many of whom were already struggling financially. As Selby has noted:

> Gratuity packages for farm workers became a key strategy in breaking the alliance between farmers and workers .... Disenfranchised farm workers, vulnerable and traumatised, sought short-term security and increasingly turned on their employers, sometimes violently. Initially farmers refused to pay if they were undesignated, or had won court appeals, but as more conceded, so the process became a formality. In some cases farm workers conspired to ensure that farms were designated. Most farmers were forced to pay out in the end often to buy time to salvage possessions or equipment. Any mutual trust that had developed between farmers and workers was lost. It was an incredibly effective tool for government. The gratuities diminished the financial clout of the farmers and temporarily softened the blow for laid off farm workers, but perhaps most importantly it drove a wedge between the two groups and broke the remaining morale of many farmers.[90]

Many white farmers identified the SI6 packages as the dividing point between themselves and their labour. As Farmer 3 stated:

> you know what the package was? ... they would intimidate the labour to pressurise the farmers to pay a gratuity because the farmer was leaving and that was probably the thing that cracked the nut of the connection between the labour and the farmers. The farmers and the labour [were] very good until this happened and as soon as one person paid, the labour would then say ... to the neighbours, look we've just been paid a whole lot of loot and we've bought bicycles and got drunk and whatever, why don't you do the same. So that really split the labour with the farmer.[91]

Such statements also reveal an underlying paternalism: black labourers could not be trusted with monetary payout. Farmers 6, 7, 9 and 11 all claimed that it was the SI6 package that created a division between farmers and workers.[92] In fact Farmer 9 was violently confronted not by 'war veterans', but by his own labour demanding SI6 packages.[93]

Even Farmer 29, who had such good communications with and protection from his labour, was finally confronted by them at his home in Harare after leaving his farm.[94] These occurrences undermine the established notion of a healthy relationship between white farmers and black labourers. While white farmers tended to see their relationships with labour as static, there is evidence to suggest that the black labour was keenly aware of the changing situation in the countryside. They could see the writing on the wall before the white farmers, and realised that retrenchment was probably their last opportunity to benefit from their farming employment before it was lost. None of the farmers offered their workers any leeway in this regard. Very little thought was given to how they would survive after their livelihoods were taken away. Rather, they were often blamed for not doing more to protect the farmer (despite the evident dangers in doing so).[95] Farmer 4 said that after he was forced to pay out the SI6 package and shut down operations, one of his older farm labourers asked him:

> 'Ah boss, what are we going to do [now]?' and I said, 'Where were you, where were you guys when I needed you, remember the day in the workshop when we, by the tractors, and that mob was there shouting pamberi ne [up with the] package, you know and all that, all the youth' .... I said 'where were you? You buggers were all standing around the outside, you did nothing because you probably thought at the back of your mind you were also going to get package, and you've got your package now and your packages were spent.'[96]

The security of white farmers was totally undermined by the land occupations. They no longer owned the land (and all that was on it) and this fundamentally undermined their paternalistic relationship with their labour.[97] Some even blamed the farm labourers for the situation by voting for Mugabe as far back as 1980. Farmer 22 recalled:

> The election in 1980, which was quite interesting, they went round with a mobile on all the farms in our area and in our area, anybody who looked sixteen – male, female, whatever colour – was allowed to vote .... But, uh, in those days, you know, it was one man, one vote and I can remember, on [my farm], that kids that I knew weren't anywhere near sixteen, they all voted.

You know, 'Come in!' They didn't have to have papers or anything in those days, they just arrived, they just had to come. And, ya, they loved it then and I reminded one of the guys, because one of them was with us then. I told him at the time, I said, and he remembers it, because he had a badza [hoe] in his hand. He's now a driver. But, you know, they would rue the day that it happened. And I said, 'Do you remember?' He said, 'Yes,' he remembers. I said, 'You didn't listen, did you?' He said, 'No.'

Such assessments express similar ideas to the letters in *The Farmer* discussed in Chapter Three regarding what they (the blacks) 'asked for' when they voted for Mugabe.

Remaining Apolitical in a Political Crisis

A fundamental aspect of white farmers' lack of understanding was an inability to comprehend the political dimensions of the land occupations, the deepening crisis after 2000, and the hopes that independence represented for the vast majority of the population. They understood that the land movements were 'politically motivated', but only in a very utilitarian way. The land occupations, they understood, were initiated amongst black peasants to increase the popularity of Mugabe and ZANU-PF so as to win an election. However, there were other more direct motivations. ZANU-PF sought to disenfranchise the farm workers, who they feared would support opposition movements in parliamentary and presidential elections.[98] The narrow focus of the political motivations understood by white farmers prevented them from identifying with other victims of ZANU-PF's determination to hold onto power – the urban labour movements, civic bodies such as Women of Zimbabwe Arise (WOZA) and the National Constitutional Assembly (NCA), and even the MDC. The CFU refused to align itself to any of these.[99] Similarly, JAG, while seeking to champion the rights of and justice for white farmers, sought to remain 'apolitical' in its approach. Although it wanted the land issue to be resolved, this was pursued only to secure the existing properties and incomes of white farmers and not to challenge a system of political corruption and misrule. As such, it refused to align itself with the MDC or other opponents of ZANU-PF.

Many farmers expressed this continuing desire to be apolitical. For example, Farmer 29 said:

Never talked politics, that's one thing we had on the farm. I said to all my guys, you've got to understand three things in life when you work for me. First thing you don't talk about religion, you don't talk about politics and you don't talk about sex.[100]

However, some farmers did become involved with the MDC and campaigned for a 'No' vote in the constitutional referendum of 2000. Farmers 3, 6, 22 and 25 were all active in the MDC, printing MDC T-shirts and holding MDC rallies on their farms.[101] However, after the referendum defeat, ZANU-PF sought to neutralise the MDC threat by directly targeting many of those white farmers who were involved, including these four. The violence was highly effective. All of these farmers renounced their ties to the MDC, admitting they felt that supporting the party had been huge mistake, and that it was a key factor in the troubles they experienced after 2000. The backlash of this violence was extremely influential in separating the white farming community from the MDC. Although several farmers, such as Iain Kay and Roy Bennett, have persevered in supporting the MDC they remain a minority.[102]

This desire to remain apolitical in a political crisis of such epic proportions undermined the ability of white farmers to forge partnerships that would have brought their plight into the ambit of black-led organisations around them. They generally failed to comprehend that black Zimbabweans suffered in similar ways and because of the same political crisis. An obvious case in this regard was Operation Murambatsvina.[103] Instigated in May 2005, it sought to 'cleanse' the city of Harare by dismantling the 'informal' sector of the economy, evicting urban homeless people and forcing them to move 'back' to the rural areas.[104] According to a UN report, an estimated 650,000 to 700,000 people were directly affected by it, and a further 1.7 million adversely affected by its economic effects.[105] A distinguished academic related how an evicted white farmer told him in no uncertain terms that 'the blacks' had ruined this country and the farming sector and how disastrous the post-2000 land reforms had been. Yet he went on to say that 'they' knew how to look after a city and that, after Murambatsvina, the state of Harare was vastly improved. In fact, he said, Harare was looking like Salisbury again.[106] This despite the fact that some government officials linked Murambatsvina directly to the land reforms. Didymus Mutasa, the Minister of State for National Security, Lands, Land Reform and Resettlement said:

> Operation Murambatsvina should also be applied to the land reform programme to clean the commercial farms that are still in the hands of white

farmers. White farmers are dirty and should be cleared out. They are similar to the filth that was in the streets before Murambatsvina.[107]

Yet white farmers largely failed to understand the proximity of these two events. Their inability to see the link between their situation and that of others left them isolated and disconnected. Indeed, the white farmers' persistence in labelling the actions against them as 'ethnic cleansing', or 'genocide', has exacerbated this divide.[108] The actions against white farmers were extremely violent, but they never amounted to a form of ethnic cleansing.

Conclusion

These oral accounts confirm many of the findings of the previous chapters, but they also reveal other aspects of white farming voice, such as the troubling depth of unreconstructed prejudice. Crucially, the interviews reveal that there has been a disconcerting lack of 'redefinition' within the farming community. The Liberation War, those who fought in it, the aspirations of black peasants and farm workers, their economic position and their claims to land are all issues that have remained static in the minds of white farmers since independence. After the backlash to the February 2000 referendum defeat, which revived the discourse of apoliticism, the white farming community distanced itself from political struggles and focused single-mindedly on the resolution of the land question and compensation. White farmers have thus remained isolated, detached from others who have suffered at the hands of Mugabe and his violent and dogged resolve to remain in power. While many claimed to have changed their identity, to be Zimbabwean rather than Rhodesian, and to be 'white Africans', this is tempered by their use of the word 'African' to always and only refer to blacks. As such, white farmers in Zimbabwe are 'orphans of empire', unable to progress past this state of being and thus 'become' Zimbabwean.

Notes

1   I have adopted this term from Karin Alexander and her work on urban white voices in Zimbabwe. See K. Alexander, 2004.

2   Vaughan, 2001, p. 65.

3   Ibid., p. 66.

4 See JAG's mission statement online at Kubatana.net, 'Justice for Agriculture – JAG Zimbabwe'. http://www.kubatana.net/html/archive/agric/020803jag.asp?orgcode =jus002&year=2002&range_start=1 [accessed, 8 June, 2010].

5 The high turnover of staff, lack of skills and a lack of direction and stability had a severe impact upon the collection of data within JAG.

6 Zimbabwe Human Rights NGO Forum and the Justice for Agriculture (JAG) Trust, 2007.

7 Ibid., p. 2. Over 53,000 people were identified as having experienced at least one human rights violation, with many experiencing multiple abuses. This violence is discussed in Chapters Two, Three and Four.

8 The interviews were generally conducted with two interviewers employed by JAG, at the interviewee's home. The interviewees would normally consist of a male farmer, often accompanied by his wife. The interviews were all recorded on portable voice recorders and then transcribed verbatim and in their entirety.

9 See The JAG Trust and the General Agricultural and Plantation Workers Union of Zimbabwe (GAPWUZ), 2008; GAPWUZ, 2010.

10 JAG would, for example, close its offices on a Friday because a common tactic of the police and the CIO was to arrest people on Friday so that they would have to spend the weekend in jail.

11 Cohen, Miecher and White, 2001, p. 4.

12 I carried out most of my interviews with a woman evicted from her farm; my great-uncle was involved in large-scale cattle ranching in Matabeleland, so the Pilossof name was well known in farming circles.

13 The most notable examples of this were the interviews conducted with Farmer 14 and Farmer 32. Interview with Farmer 14, 21 March 2010, Harare; interview with Farmer 32, 31 July 2007, Harare. In addition, in many cases the farmers I interviewed used racist and bigoted language before and after the interview and not in the recorded session.

14 Farmer 29 said many times in his interview that he would prefer not to say things on tape. Interview with Farmer 29, 12 May 2007, Harare.

15 For example, see that represented by Lamb, 2006.

16 To maintain anonymity, I have changed every detail in the quotes selected. I have also randomly assigned every farmer a number, as I believe this is the easiest way to track multiple references to a particular interview or farmer throughout this chapter. In many of the interviews, another member of the family was present; if quoted, that person is referred to by their relationship to the farmer. I realise that this may be viewed as denying the farmer's wife her own identity. I recognise that women and farmers' wives were active agents on the farms in many ways, but this is the most concise and coherent way to reference the interviews and all those involved.

17 Such an attitude was clearly expressed in communications with JAG representatives. This situation was exacerbated by management crises that affected the organisation in 2010, which came to a head in the last 12 months and resulted in all of the board members resigning due to perceived mismanagement by the CEO. This has also

meant that the research projects, such as the one that collected the interviews used in this chapter, have been suspended and the partnership with RAU broken. This has resulted in confusion over ownership and control of the material collected.

18 Van Onselen, 1993, p. 513.

19 Portelli, 1997, p. 162.

20 See Chapter Two for an overview. Also, see Pilossof, 2008a.

21 As explained in the Introduction, the state of disarray of the National Archives of Zimbabwe (and the sensitive nature of this project) limited my ability to locate information in Zimbabwe. Furthermore, I was denied access to the archives and collections of the CFU.

22 White, 2000, p. 54. Also, see Portelli, 1991; Portelli, 1997.

23 Portelli, 1997, p. 21.

24 Ibid., p. 16.

25 White, 2000, p. 9.

26 Van Onselen, 1993, p. 502.

27 See de Swardt, 2009; Thompson and Bailey, 2009.

28 See Chapter Five for a more detailed discussion of the impact of trauma.

29 There were three main confrontations talked of in Farmer 3's interview. One particular event that deeply affected him and his wife was one of their horses being burnt alive in a portable stable during a confrontation with the land occupiers. See interview with Farmer 3, 2 March 2007, Harare. These confrontations were commonly referred to as a *jambanja*. As explained in Chapter Two, *jambanja* became synonymous with the land invasions. With no precise definition, the word was, and still is, used to encompass a range of violent and angry confrontations on the land, which varied in degree, severity and manner but generally involved the farmer being violently confronted by war veterans or land occupiers on the farm or at his homestead.

30 Interview with Farmer 3, 2 March 2007, Harare.

31 Ibid.

32 Interview with Farmer 10, 16 May 2007, Harare.

33 Interview with Farmer 13, 12 June 2007, Harare.

34 The deployment and tactical uses of violence by ZANU-PF, the war veterans, land occupiers and other forces needs further research, and is an area that could provide remarkable insights into how events in the countryside played out after 2000.

35 Many farmers talked of the strain the land occupations and evictions put on the personal and family lives of other farmers. Some talked of their own divorces and marital problems. See interview with Farmer 31, 27 June 2007, Harare; interview with Farmer 26, 19 June 2007, Harare.

36 Interview with Farmer 13, 12 June 2007, Harare.

37 Farmer 24 talked about his children having to go to school with 'black beneficiaries' [of the land reforms] kids', and how traumatic this was for them. Interview with Farmer 24, 29 May 2007, Harare. See the novel *Unfeeling*, which was inspired by the story of a farmer's son at school with black children of people who now lived on his farm. Holding, 2005.

38 Interview with Farmer 24, 29 May 2007, Harare.

39 Interview with Farmer 7, 2 July 2007, Harare; interview with Farmer 12, 13 June 2007, Harare; interview with Farmer 23, 4 June 2007, Harare.

40 Interview with Farmer 7, 2 July 2007, Harare.

41 See Selby, 2006, chapter six, and discussion of *The Farmer* in Chapter Three.

42 As explained in the previous chapters, it is suspected that these prejudiced terms of reference were part of white farming discourse in the 1980s and 1990s, but found few public avenues of expression. There are no published or written records in which to find such terms. However, the atrocities of the land occupations since 2000 have reopened the space for such language in the white farming community.

43 Interview with Farmer 3, 2 March 2007, Harare. Farmer 3 used the term 'gook' just about every time he mentioned the war veterans or land occupiers.

44 See interview with Farmer 17, 2 July 2007, Harare; interview with Farmer 1, 14 June 2007, Harare.

45 Interview with Farmer 14, 21 March 2007, Harare.

46 Interview with Farmer 20, 4 July 2007, Harare.

47 Interview with Farmer 32, 31 July 2007, Harare.

48 For the use of 'gook' during the Liberation War and after see Jim Barker's autobiography. Barker, 2007.

49 See Lyons, 2002, p. 305; Todd, 2007, p. 180. A young girl who undertook similar activities for the guerrillas was called a *chimbwido*.

50 Grundy and Miller, 1979, p. 63.

51 Interview with Farmer 2, 12 May 2007, Harare.

52 Interview with Farmer 15, 29 March 2007, Harare.

53 Interview with Farmer 17, 2 July 2007, Harare.

54 Of course the term 'war veteran' has been used by ZANU-PF. For ZANU-PF the term entitles legitimate veterans of the Liberation War to land and state support in the 'fight' against white farmers. As with the term 'settler', it has been employed deliberately to conflict with white farming perceptions of the term.

55 Interview with Farmer 14, 21 March 2007, Harare. He also commented that the resident 'gook' on his farm 'had set up residence in our compound and kicked our guys out. He brought his broken tractor and his stuffed plough and equally stuffed children.' Other terms of reference for settlers on his farm were, 'horrible shit', 'that ghastly peasant', 'pathetic creature', and generally 'very poor specimens of human beings'.

56 Interview with Farmer 5, 16 March 2007, Harare.

57 Interview with Farmer 4, 5 April 2007, Harare. He also said 'these nannies [women settlers] were urinating on the bloody walls [of his house]', and that all the settlers were only part of a 'rent-a-crowd'.

58 Interview with Farmer 21, 28 June 2007, Harare.

59 Fanon, 1967, p. 93.

60 Farmer 1 compared a group of 'squatters' who settled near a pump house as the 'pump house gang', explaining that 'the pump house gang is also referred to by these

people who did a study of the baboons in Kenya'. Calling black people baboons or monkeys has a troubled and racist past in Zimbabwe. See interview with Farmer 1, 14 June 2007, Harare. For more on the Pumphouse Gang, see the webpage for Shirley Strum, the main researcher on the project. http://www.anthro.ucsd.edu/Faculty_Profiles/strum.html [accessed, 8 June, 2010].

61 For example see the images presented in this small sample of British news sources: Peta Thornycroft, 'Mugabe's Workers Lament His Takeover', online edition of *The Telegraph*, 25 September, 2009. http://www.telegraph.co.uk/news/worldnews/africaandindianocean/zimbabwe/6231822/Mugabes-workers-lament-his-takeover.html [accessed, 12 July 2010]; Anon., '2000-2009: The World in Pictures', *The Independenedent*. http://www.independent.co.uk/news/world/20002009-the-world-in-pictures-1821685.html?action=Popup&ino=100 [accessed, 12 July 2010]; Anon., 'Veterans' Group Challenges Mugabe', *BBC News Online*, 20 February, 2001. http://news.bbc.co.uk/1/hi/world/africa/1180551.stm [accessed, 12 July 2010].

62 Kriger has written extensively on war veterans in Zimbabwe. For her books, see Kriger, 1992; 2003b. For articles, see Kriger, 2001; 2003a, 2003c. Also, see Desai 2002.

63 Italics in original. Fanon, 1967, p. 93.

64 Ngugi wa Thiong'o, in *Decolonising the Mind*, argued that African intellectuals and writers had to abandon the languages of their colonised past, and begin to write, think and talk in the languages of the African continent. By so doing, the mind of the African would be purged of the false inferiorities forced on it by colonialism. Ngugi, 2004.

65 Krog, 2002, p. 292.

66 For more on the TRC, see Gobodo-Madikizela, 1998; Orr, 2000; Wilson, 2001. For more of Krog's work on the TRC and post-TRC South Africa, see Krog, 2003; Krog, Mpolweni and Ratele, 2009.

67 Private conversation with a white farmer, 22 January 2008, Harare.

68 This failure of redefinition also meant many other aspects of the countryside were referred to in colonial terms. For instance the communal areas were called the TTLs, or Tribal Trust Lands, a pre-1980 designation. See interview with Farmer 20, 4 July 2007, Harare.

69 Interview with Farmer 32, 31 July 2007, Harare. 'Hout' means wood in Afrikaans and is used as derogatory term in southern Africa to refer to black people.

70 Chikanza, Paxton, Loewenson and Laing, 1981; Loewenson, 1986a; Loewenson, 1986b; Loewenson, 1992.

71 *The Farmer*, 17/24 April 2001, p. 9. Also, see Chinyangara, Chokuwenga, Dete, Dube, Kembo, Moyo and Nkomo, 1997, Chapter Six.

72 Barclay, 2010, p. 151.

73 For more discussion on farm workers see Chapters One and Two.

74 In an example of the possession of black workers Farmer 21's wife said, 'When I think back now, it was disgusting, but it was, I couldn't stand him and there was one [war veteran]. He was a tall, ugly, like almost an outcast of, you know, he was revolt-

ing. He had one eye and they wanted to beat up this driver and I kind of dragged him and I, you know, the funny thing, you don't think about it because your anger takes over and I stuck myself in between this man [and the driver] ... and I remember standing up to him saying, "Don't touch my driver, I'll ...." I don't know what I said to him. And he's going like this [pulls a face], and my driver behind is going like this [pulls a face] and it was funny then. They just, like suddenly stopped. I mean, I'm not saying it's because I said that, it was just like a frozen moment.' Interview with Farmer 21, 28 June, 2007, Harare.

75 Van Onselsen, 1996, p. 281.

76 *The Farmer*, 2 March 2000, p. 23.

77 Farmer 23 said, 'yeah, we had, we had good comms [communications] with labour up until then [the invasions]'. Interview with Farmer 23, 4 June 2007, Harare.

78 Interview with Farmer 32, 31 July 2007, Harare.

79 Farmer 29's wife also said of her workers, 'anybody who thinks they are brave, you go and see these poor uneducated illiterate people who just stand there and say "no it is enough", you know? They were wonderful.' Interview with Farmer 29, 12 May 2007, Harare.

80 In one example, Farmer 29's wife said, 'There was a big wedding and ... it was half past one and [my husband] was in the lands with his driver and this black van came ... I called on the radio and said ... [my husband] isn't here and I'm by myself and I'm worried ... my gardener dragged me under the garden table and there he and I were on our hands and knees under the table. [My labour] said "get out, get off the farm", I said "I can't, you know I can't get out" and they said "go and hide" and I couldn't get from where I was and my gardener ... bless his heart, dragged me under the garden table and the two of us hid ... I mean this was bravery, what stake did they have? They were brave, magnificent people.' Interview with Farmer 29, 12 May 2007, Harare.

81 Of course the evidence recorded in the interviews may not demonstrate the actual situation. The farmers may have been deliberately lying or misrepresenting the situation. However, the assessment made of Farmer 29 and his wife here is also based on my notes and memory of the interview.

82 Both Farmer 29 and his wife were beaten up on many occasions, threatened with beheading and had firearms trained on them. In addition several of their labour force were killed. Interview with Farmer 29, 12 May 2007, Harare.

83 Interview with Farmer 25, 28 June 2007, Harare. Farmer 25 also said, 'once or twice ... we had quite nasty incidents, but I had very good support from about a dozen of my farm labourers and in fact, I think on those two occasions, it was their intervention that prevented things from getting totally out of control. Ya, very gutsy youngsters who came in, just quietly infiltrated this mêlée of which I was in the middle um, and they were just, without being aggressive or saying anything, they would actually just place themselves between me and the antagonists ... and they would just quietly just come and stand in there, not say a word, not get involved and not say a word ... Listen, there were a couple of times our labour force turned out with *badzas* [hoes] and axes in my support and managed to tone down, without getting, you know,

violent. But, the simple fact that they were standing there with these weapons was not lost on these guys who were trying to antagonise us. That, you know, they were prepared to stand up and fight for me.'

84 See interview with Farmer 3, 2 March 2007, Harare; interview with Farmer 19, 28 March 2007, Harare.

85 Farmer 15 said his labour were 'fantastic', Farmer 28 that 'my labour treated me wonderfully. They were so loyal.' Interview with Farmer 15, 29 March 2007, Harare; interview with Farmer 28, 17 July 2007, Harare.

86 Interview with Farmer 21, 28 June 2007, Harare.

87 Interview with Farmer 4, 5 April 2007, Harare.

88 Interview with Farmer 5, 16 March 2007, Harare. Two common cautions about conducting oral history that I am mindful of are that researchers often hear what they want to hear, regardless of the answers given, and that interviewees often say what they want to say, regardless of the questions asked.

89 U.S. Department of State, 2004.

90 Selby, 2006, pp. 307-8.

91 Interview with Farmer 3, 2 March 2007, Harare.

92 Interview with Farmer 6, 5 June 2007, Harare; interview with Farmer 7, 2 July 2007, Harare; and interview with Farmer 9, 9 May 2007, Harare. Farmer 11 said, 'No, the problem started, you know right in the beginning we had absolute full cooperation from our staff and then when the SI6 packages story came into it, then it really became very, very ugly ... the war vets then got involved in trying to negotiate packages and that's when the wheels just fell off, hey? The staff just went completely, um, moggy.' Interview with Farmer 11, 22 March 2007, Harare. Farmer 11 had two farms. 'The SI6 became a big problem at [the other farm too]. Our staff voted to shut the farm down and receive their packages rather than to carry on farming. So I said fine, and that's why we stopped farming.'

93 Interview with Farmer 9, 9 May 2007, Harare. 'The only intimidation I really had was my own labour. They turned against me and I thought I'd treated them very well and then all of a sudden it was a total different attitude .... That was the beginning of the SI6.'

94 Interview with Farmer 29, 12 May 2007, Harare.

95 The following extract from Farmer 14 contains the elements of racism, paternalism and the effects of the SI6 package. He had been paying out SI6 packages, but ex-labourers who didn't qualify and other settlers started to threaten him and his family. Police arrived and they had a small window of time to flee the farm: 'And so ... it was more than ten minutes though we managed to get out. [My wife] drove out with the one vehicle, I took the Land Rover. My daughter was with me and I suppose because the maids, we had two maids there, because we felt they were part of us and didn't want to be victimised by the gang they were the first ones to tear branches off the trees as I drove out. It didn't last very long and my daughter's sitting with us and she saw her nannies as she knew them, tearing these branches and coming to hit the car which was, you know, I mean it was pathetic really, and it terrified, well it scared

[my daughter] ... Anyway so we drove out. Um, some of [the labour] gave us a very cheerful send-off, waving, ululating and thanking them for giving them their money ... we were waved down by this one guy and he said "I want to buy your Land Rover" and that's when I realised [my daughter] had been traumatised and she lay down in a ball at the bottom of the Land Rover and said "Please, daddy. I don't want to see any more munts". So I drove on.' Interview with Farmer 14, 21 March 2007, Harare.

96 Interview with Farmer 4, 5 April 2007, Harare.

97 These paternal/maternal relationships and structures of operation still exist in the white farming organisations of the CFU and JAG. The way the black staff were treated while I was carrying out research there confirmed this. Not only were the black staff poorly provided for, but I often overheard the use of racist language.

98 This argument has been made throughout this book. See Chapters Two and Three for more detailed assessments of this claim.

99 Interview with the director of a human rights organisation, 4 April 2009, Harare.

100 Interview with Farmer 29, 12 May 2007, Harare.

101 Interview with Farmer 3, 2 March 2007, Harare; interview with Farmer 6, 5 June 2007, Harare; interview with Farmer 22, 19 June 2007, Harare; interview with Farmer 25, 28 June 2007, Harare.

102 This is discussed in Chapter Two.

103 Murambatsvina is a Shona term which means 'clear out the filth'.

104 Estimates suggest that by 2005, half of this population were born in urban areas and had no rural area or homeland to return to. Raftopoulos, 2009, p. 220.

105 United Nations, 2005. Also, see Sachikonye, 2006; Potts, 2006.

106 Private conversation with academic who wished to remain anonymous, 22 August 2008, Sheffield.

107 The JAG Trust and GAPWUZ, 2008, p. 2.

108 See Chapter Three for discussion on the talk in the white farming community of genocide and ethnic cleansing.

Appendix 1

CFU structure & list of past presidents

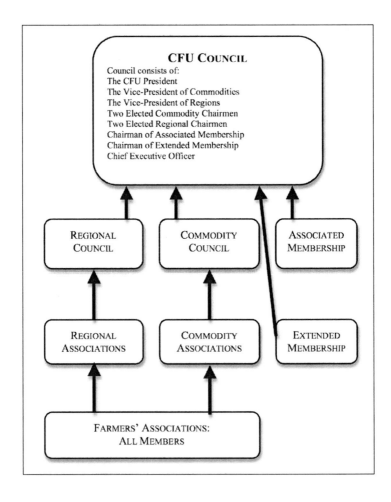

Source: http://www.cfuzim.org/index.php?option=com_content&view=article&id
=50:organisational-chart&catid=36:about-us&Itemid=75 [accessed, 22 July, 2010].

Past Presidents of the Rhodesian Agricultural Union, the Rhodesian National Farmers' Union (RNFU) & the CFU

The Rhodesian Agricultural Union
1910–1914	Hon. R.A. Fletcher
1914–1916	E. Wilson
1920–1923	C. S. Jobling
1923	S.M. Lanigan O'Keefe
1929–1931	H.B. Christian
1932–1935	G.N. Fleming

The RNFU
1942–1944	J. Dennis
1944–1946	Hon. H.V. Gibbs
1946–1948	J.M. Caldicott
1948–1951	E.D. Palmer
1951–1954	J. MacIntyre
1954–1956	M. Chennells
1956–1963	E.B. Evans
1963–1968	T. Mitchell
1968–1970	J.W. Field
1970–1972	R.G. Pascoe
1972–1974	M.E. Butler
1974–1976	C. Millar
1976–1978	C.J. Strong
1978–1979	D.R. Norman

The CFU
1979–1980	D.R. Norman
1980–1981	D.B. Spain
1981–1983	J.M. Sinclair
1983–1986	A.J. Laurie
1986–1988	J.R. Rutherford
1988–1990	J.H. Brown
1990–1992	A.D.P. Burl
1992–1994	A.J. Swire-Thompson
1994–1996	P. MacSporran
1996–1998	N. Swanepoel
1998–	R.D. Swift
1998–1999	N. Swanepoel
1999–2001	T. Henwood
2001–2003	C. Cloete
2003–2007	D.S. Taylor-Freeme
2007–2009	T.R. Gifford

Appendix 2

Land use on large-scale commercial farms & area under cultivation in hectares, 1970–1999[1]

Year	Grains	Industrial crops[2]	Fodder crops	Fruit	Other	Total
1970	277,847	148,581	30,706	5,626	87,153	**549,913**
1971	293,309	143,626	29,403	5,538	82,573	**554,449**
1972	333,029	149,642	24,581	5,841	82,207	**595,300**
1973	325,039	168,947	23,424	6,189	81,762	**605,361**
1974	313,626	199,997	16,877	5,983	77,592	**614,075**
1975	285,193	208,317	15,711	5,359	76,015	**590,595**
1976	271,085	191,531	18,756	5,228	79,835	**566,435**
1977	286,974	199,197	14,723	4,752	68,834	**574,480**
1978	263,074	215,769	12,919	4,275	67,463	**563,500**
1979	246,368	216,671	12,382	4,864	62,684	**542,969**
1980	271,969	226,583	11,189	3,663	61,428	**574,832**
1981	345,832	181,989	11,067	4,005	56,982	**599,875**
1982	320,447	197,888	11,440	3,679	51,556	**585,010**
1983	264,537	214,468	13,673	3,543	52,204	**548,425**
1984	232,946	225,796	13,673	4,062	51,383	**527,860**
1985	258,885	212,643	12,748	3,415	49,944	**537,635**
1986	–	–	–	–	–	–
1987	186,738	230,347	56,810	4,051	6,952	**484,898**
1988	202,776	228,409	54,279	5,710	9,380	**500,554**
1989	210,238	221,067	63,853	5,885	9,514	**510,557**
1990	208,426	206,716	63,852	6,426	9,561	**494,981**
1991	185,873	210,229	66,597	7,339	9,576	**479,614**
1992	154,391	201,619	60,462	7,270	8,989	**432,731**
1993	219,320	176,892	56,096	8,064	10,995	**471,367**
1994	233,724	192,514	51,501	8,321	12,452	**498,512**
1995	193,720	205,642	43,799	8,260	12,592	**464,013**
1996	207,868	221,235	43,361	8,039	14,040	**494,543**
1997	198,053	214,113	45,906	14,293	15,895	**488,260**
1998	175,514	210,713	51,515	14,318	17,593	**469,653**
1999	193,789	196,888	43,782	9,648	16,466	**460,573**

[1] Figures taken from Central Statistical Office (CSO), 2001:158. This was the last *Compendium* the CSO published. No similar publication has been produced since 2000, which is why this set of figures stops at 1999. No figures were avaialble for 1986.
[2] Includes tobacco, coffee, cotton, groundnuts, soya beans, sunflowers, sugarcane and tea.

Appendix 3

Summary of major crop[1] sales in $Z millions, 1970–1999

Year	Sales from Commercial Farms	Sales from Communal & Resettlement Farms	Total Z$ in millions	Commercial Crop Sales as Percentage of Total
1970	81	3	84 (126)	96.8
1971	106	6	112 (168)	94.6
1972	130	13	142 (213)	91.1
1973	125	8	133 (200)	93.8
1974	200	15	216 (278)	92.9
1975	224	14	238 (404)	94.0
1976	225	18	244 (366)	92.5
1977	229	16	244 (400)	93.6
1978	237	17	254 (423)	93.3
1979	249	12	261 (435)	95.3
1980	350	22	372 (620)	94.1
1981	518	64	582 (831)	89.1
1982	485	65	550 (687)	88.2
1983	451	46	497 (522)	90.8
1984	604	103	707 (707)	85.4
1985	857	225	1,082 (400)	79.2
1986	961	222	1,182 (236)	81.2
1987	765	124	889 (148)	86.0
1988	1,066	301	1,367 (227)	78.0
1989	1,229	295	1,523 (254)	80.7
1990	1,650	233	1,882 (313)	87.6
1991	2,825	287	3,112 (518)	90.8
1992	2,040	78	2,117 (352)	96.3
1993	3,075	1,055	4,130 (688)	74.5
1994	4,549	1,026	5,575 (696)	81.6
1995	5,071	282	5,353 (669)	94.7
1996	8,474	1,550	10,024 (100)	84.5
1997	7,544	1,463	9,007 (750)	83.8
1998	11,850	1,847	13,697 (805)	86.5
1999	–	–	24,496 (612)	–[2]

Source: CSO, 2001:177.

[1] Includes maize, groundnuts, sorghum, soyabeans, coffee, wheat, cotton, flue-cured tobacco, burley tobacco, sugar and sunflowers
[2] Figures not available.

Appendix 4

The number of large-scale commercial farms & the total area occupied in hectares, 1970–1999

Year	Number of Farms	Total Area (ha)
1970	7,116	14,801,369
1971	6,762	14,745,549
1972	7,048	14,884,658
1973	6,937	14,916,141
1974	6,938	14,839,754
1975	6,821	14,853,261
1976	6,682	14,440,218
1977	6,480	14,805,546
1978	6,337	14,820,341
1979	6,113	15,064,301
1980	6,034	14,798,302
1981	6,124	14,481,714
1982	5,915	13,516,357
1983	5,481	12,346,553
1984	5,171	12,539,970
1985	5,128	12,482,356
1986	5,129	12,145,668
1987	4,789	11,546,848
1988	5,015	11,707,233
1989	5,062	11,707,233
1990	4,992	11,433,986
1991	5,117	11,433,986
1992	5,131	11,375,215
1993	5,132	11,340,186
1994	5,164	11,321,617
1995	5,198	11,321,617
1996	5,185	11,187,348
1997	5,146	11,291,152
1998	4,694	11,286,140
1999	4,439	10,078,928

Source: CSO, 2001:157.

Appendix 5

White farmers killed between 1964–79, 1981–87 and 2000–04

RNFU members & relatives killed during the Liberation War (1964–1979), excluding those on active duty

1964
Mr P.A.J. Oberholtzer, Melsetter, 4/7/64

1966
Mr J.H. Viljoen, Gadzema, 16/5/66
Mrs Viljoen, Gadzema, 16/5/66

1973
Mr B. Couve, Shamva, 6/6/73
Mr T.V. Forbes, Mount Darwin, 23/4/73
Mr L.M. Jellicoe, Centenary, 4/2/73
Mr A. Joubert, Wedza, 30/3/73
Mrs I. Kleynhans, Centenary, 24/1/73
Mr D.M. Stacey, Karoi, 9/3/73
Mr D.J. Vincent, Centenary, 3/4/73

1974
Major E.C. Addams, Odzi, 14/8/74
Mr E. Fletcher, Centenary, 17/2/74
Mrs B. Fletcher, Centenary, 17/2/74
Mr P. Rouse, Centenary, 18/2/74
Mr V. Stockil-Gill, Marandellas, 27/10/74
Mr N. Willis, Shamva, 14/2/74

1975
Mr A.V. Howe, Umvukwes, 24/6/75
Mr P.J.O. Knight, Doma, 17/5/75
Mr P. Snyders, Vumba, 9/10/75
Mr C.A.S. Young, Melsetter, 29/4/75

1976
Mr L. Ashby, Mzingwane, 7/7/76
Mrs K. Backe-Hansen, Matetsi, 9/9/76
Mr D. Bashford, Karoi, 24/12/76
Mr A. Bathhurst, Karoi, 24/12/76

Mr N. Campbell, Marandellas, 23/5/76
Mr D. Carshalton, Gazaland, 27/8/76
Mr C.M. Cloete, Filabusi, 31/10/76
Mrs M. Cloete, Filabusi, 31/10/76
Mr A. Cumming, Matetsi, 5/11/76
Mr P. Crouch, Ayrshire, 17/12/76
Mr J.S. Donald, Umtali, 26/4/76
Mr S.L.J. Davies, Gwaai Valley, 26/7/76
Mr G. Farge, Gazaland 24/10/76
Mr T. Greyvenstein, Mayo, 16/9/76
Miss M. Habig, Gazaland, 6/6/76
Miss L. Habig, Gazaland, 6/6/76
Miss Y. Habig, Gazaland, 6/6/76
Mr J.E. Hudson-Beck, Melsetter, 12/8/76
Mr D.C. James, Gwelo, 27/4/76
Mrs L.M. McFedden, Plumtree, 7/9/76
Mr S.P. Naude, Somabula, 17/10/76
Mr A.C. Newman, Melsetter, 15/10/76
Mr P.S. Naude, Centenary, 21/10/76
Mr M. Nielsen, Karoi, 17/12/76
Mr F. Pitcher, Bindura, 14/6/76
Mrs W. Palmer, Mrewa/Mtoko, 19/10/76
Mr R. M. Smith, Insiza/Shangani, 28/7/76
Mr J.J.F. Van Vuuren, Matopos South, 22/5/76
Mr M.J. Van Vuuren, Matopos South, 22/5/76
Mr O.P. Valentine, Melsetter, 12/8/76
Mr G. West, Gazaland, 12/11/76

1977
Mr R.A. Barton, Melsetter, 6/4/77
Mr J. Blignaut, Ayrshire, 17/6/77
Mr A.P. Burger, Matetsi, 12/6/77
Mr A. Barclay, Gwanda/West Nicholson, 12/8/77
Mr D. Barclay, Ayrshire, 7/12/77
Mr W.P. Cremer, Bindura, 26/1/77
Mr D. Cookson, Centenary, Feb. 1977
Mr C.A. Capell, Shamva, 9/3/77
Mr C. Chapman, Melsetter, 22/5/77
Miss C. Chessworth, Figtree, 14/8/77
Mr E. Claasen, Odzi, 29/9/77
Mr J. F. Coomans, Cashel, 6/12/77
Mr D. Dodd, Ayrshire, 6/4/77
Mr D.W.S. Dunn, Shamva, 13/9/77
Mr C.A. Delaney, Melsetter, 3D/9/77
Mr B.J. Dean, Melsetter, 30/9/77
Mr D.R.C. Greef, Plumtree, 15/5/77

Mrs M.A. Greef, Plumtree, 15/5/77
Miss N. Glenny (Baby), Melsetter, 29/9/77
Mr H.T.J. Hastings, Shamva, 11/3/77
Mrs M.H. Hastings, Shamva, 11/3/77
Mr A. Hill, Wedza, 26/6/77
Mrs A.C. Horton, Nyamandhlovu, 29/8/77
Mr P.L. Hanson, Melsetter, 20/10/77
Mr H. Holstenberg, Melsetter, 20/10/77
Mr R.C. Hunt, Melsetter, 20/10/77
Mr H.J. Hurley, Centenary, 21/12/77
Mr J. Henry, Gazaland, 31/12/77
Master I. Johnson, Umvukwes, 26/12/77
Mr M. Langeman. Melsetter, 22/1/77
Mr W. P. Lilford, Karoi, 9/11/77
Mr D.H. MacKay, Melsetter, 1/1/77
Mr D.G. MacKenzie, Shamva, 1/2/77
Mr G.J. Myburgh, Mayo, 26/1/77
Miss S.G. McRoberts, Shamva, 11/3/77
Mr G.I. Murdoch, Selous, 18/6/77
Mr F.J. Nel, Tengwe, 23/11/77
Mr C.D. Northcroft, Shamva, 20/12/77
Mr C. Ogilvy, Shamva, 13/9/77
Mr N.G. Payne, Bindura, 26/1/77
Mr K. Prinsloo, Chiredzi, 16/4/77
Miss L.A. Philips, Insiza, 12/7/77
Mr E.A. Richardson, Belingwe, 24/3/77
Mr A.J. Ritson, Selukwe, 6/8/77
Mr A. Robertson, Gwelo East, 21/8/77
Mrs E.M. Rushmore, Myamandhlovu, 6/9/77
Mr L.R. Shakespeare, Karoi, 23/8/77
Mr J. Stopforth, Gwelo East, 23/9/77
Mr K.D. Viljoen, Melsetter, 1/10/77
Mrs E.A. Viljoen, Melsetter, 1/10/77
Mr J.J.F. Van Maarseveen, Cashel, 4/12/77
Mr J. Wright, Odzi, 10/9/77

1978
Mr J. Ashworth, Umtali, 18/1/78
Mr R. Abbot, Odzi, 10/4/78
Mr B. Brakenridge, Gadzema, 6/1/78
Mr B. Brakenridge [Son], Gadzema, 6/1/78
Mrs S. Brakenridge [Sen.], Gadzema, 6/1/78
Mr P. Bezuidenhout, Nuanetsi, 14/2/78
Mr D.C. Bagnall. Headlands, 14/3/78
Mr K.H. Bicknell, Selous, 10/4/78

Mr H. Blignaut, Doma, 20/4/78
Mr I.D. Black, Odzi, 17/5/78
Mr D. Burton, Lonely District, 25/5/78
Mrs E. Botha, Gazaland, 6/6/78
Mr P. Bouwer, Tengwe, 13/7/78
Mr O. Bordini, Shamva, 31/7/78
Mr C. Brent, Marula, 20/10/78
Mr A. Beamish, Horseshoe, 2/11 /78
Mr S.H. Barnard, Cashel, 6/12/78
Mr W. Bezuidenhout, Gazaland, 20/12/78
Mr J.A. Bennett, Shamva, 23/12/78
Mrs M. Bennett, Shamva, 23/12/78
Bennett [Minor], Shamva, 23/12/78
Bennett [Minor], Shamva, 23/12/78
Mrs S.A. Cumming, Norton, 7/1/78
Miss S.C. Cumming, Norton, 7/1/78
Mr D.L. Courtney, Mrewa, 6/4/78
Mr D.I. Crombie, Macheke, 8/8/78
Mr P.J. Cloete, Centenary, 8/8/78
Mr K. Cremer, Gazaland, 18/8/78
Mr D. de Coupelay, Macheke/Virginia, 4/6/78
Mr S. Donnelly, Karoi, 21/6/78
Mrs F.M. du Toit, Gutu, 23/7/78
Mr C.J.J. Davies, Umtali, 20/8/78
Miss J. Douglass, Melsetter, 22/8/78
Mr A. de Nadai, Mayo, 21/8/78
Mr T.H. Elton, Cashel, 19/5/78
Mr H. Fenzel, Melsetter, 16/4/78
Mr F. Falzoi, Karoi, 12/6/78
Mr H. Franken, Selukwe, 17/7/78
Mr F.N.J. Fourie, Tengwe, 14/8/78
Mr P.H. Fairbanks, Gazaland, 2/9/78
Mr F.A. Grobler, Matopos South, 17/6/78
Mrs A.E. Grobler, Matopos South, 17/6/78
Mr K. Gifford, Gazaland, 6/7/78
Mr P.J. Gunn, Middle Sabi, 5/10/78
Mr D.A. Galloway, Melsetter, 24/10/78
Mr E.J. Hards, Shamva, 10/4/78
Mr A.A. Hess, Karoi, 25/5/78
Mr J.R. Hill, Tokwe, 11/12/78
Mr D.B. Hutchinson, Lalapanzi, 29/12/78
Mrs D.I. Hutchinson, Lalapanzi, 29/12/78
Master B. Hutchinson (6 yrs), Lalapanzi, 29/12/78
Master V. Hutchinson (3 yrs), Lalapanzi, 29/12/78
Mr L.M. Jellicoe, Centenary, 9/7/78

Mr G.D. Joubert, Ayrshire, 22/12/78
Mr T.F. Koen, Centenary, 2/2/78
Mr S. Le Vieux, Chiredzi, 7/2/78
Mr R.J. Liebermann, Marandellas, 4/6/78
Mr J.H.C. Liddle, Bindura, 1/10/78
Mr K. Mrowic, Que Que, 25/5/78
Mr H.M. Meyer, Plumtree, 29/9/78
Mrs E.L. Meyer, Plumtree, 29/9/78
Mr F.J. Mee, Inyanga, 26/10/78
Mrs M.A. Mee, Inyanga, 26/10/78
Mr T. Margarson, Gwelo, 15/11/78
Mr D. Moorcroft, Bindura, 15/12/78
Mr G.J. Muller, Centenary, 25/12/78
Mr D.S. Muir, Mount Darwin, 13/5/78
Mrs Y. Nicol, Gazaland, 17/3/78
Mr J.D. Nicholson, Nyamandhlovu, 25/5/78
Mr C.H. Olivey, Melsetter, 15/5/78
Mr F.J. Oosthuizen, Gwelo, 26/9/78
Mr N.H.E. Prince, Tengwe, 23/3/78
Mr F. Pretorius, Nuanetsi, 18/4/78
Mr P. Potgieter, Doma, 9/7/78
Mr T.M.S. Peech, Macheke/Virginia, 13/7/78
Mr J.F.B. Payn, Matopos South, 21/9/78
Mr R.W.G. Puckrin, Insiza, 30/10/78
Mrs F.I. Pearson, Selukwe, 28/12/78
Mr W.E. Read, Gatooma, 15/1/78
Mr N.J. Royston, Karoi, 18/2/78
Mr J. Reyneke, Gazaland, 8/3/78
Mr I. Rosenfels, Marula, 29/3/78
Mr J. Roberts, Penhalonga, 22/4/78
Mr P.J. Richards, Gwanda, 27/11/78
Mr A. Stander, Nuanetsi, 22/2/78
Mr J.N. Strydom, Headlands, 9/3/78
Mr C.A. Steyn, Cashel, 4/4/78
Mr J.U. Stanley, Tengwe, 5/4/78
Mr G. Swartz, Gazaland, 12/4/78
Mr R. Swemmer, Macheke/Virginia, 3/6/78
Mr H. Stander, Nuanetsi, 5/8/78
Mr A. Stander, Beit Bridge, 15/8/78
Mr E. Swanepoel, Melsetter, 22/8/78
Mr J.K.G. Syme, Melsetter, 13/9/78
Mrs H.A. Syme, Melsetter, 13/9/78
Mr R.S. Smallman, Melsetter, 11/9/78
Mr F.C. Steyn, Cashel, 18/12/78
Master C.C. Tilley, Mashonaland South, 11/1/78

Mr C.C. Tompson, Nuanetsi, 14/2/78
Miss C.C. Tilley, Mashonaland South, 3/9/78
Mr B. Vermeulen, Headlands, 11/1/78
Mr J. l_. S. Vorster, Melsetter, 23/1/78
Mr M.A. van Aard, Macheke/Virginia, 30/1/78
Mr S.P. van Blerk, Headlands, 26/5/78
Mrs G. van Blerk, Headlands, 26/5/78
Miss L. van Blerk, Headlands, 26/5/78
Miss M.A. van Reenen, Macheke/Virginia, 15/9/78
Mr R.S. Williams, Inyanga, 17/1/78
Mr J.F. Wolfaard, Nuanetsi, 9/2/78
Mrs C. J. Willers, Gazaland, 10/6/78
Mr D. Ward, Mazoe, 23/6/78
Mr B.H. Williams, Inyati, 3/8/78
Master M. Wilger, Nyamandhlovu, 3/9/78
Miss L. Wilger, Nyamandhlovu, 3/9/78
Mr S. Ziegler, Marandellas, 16/1/78

1979
Mr L.L. Brooks, Darwin, 19/3/79
Mr I.R. Brown, Sipolilo, 28/3/79
Mr M. Brooke-Mee, Gwelo, 30/3/79
Mr V. Conlon, Mazoe, 11/1/79
Mr G. Crane, Goromonzi, 19/3/79
Mr M.D. Cleave, Juliasdale, 1/5/79
Mr M.J. Chance, Bindura, 15/5/79
Mr H. du Plessis, Gazaland, 28/1/79
Mr I.J. Eksteen, Inyazura, 11/1/79
Mrs J.M. Eksteen, Inyazura, 11/1/79
Mr B.T. Furber, Gwanda, 16/4/79
Mrs R. Hacking, Odzi, 8/1/79
Mr P. Hovell, Mazoe, 13/1/79
Mr T. Hulley, Tengwe, 23/2/79
Mr W. Houston, Inyanga, 14/3/79
Mr P. Kenchington, Mid-Sabi, 3/2/79
Mr B.J.S. Kearns, Bindura, 15/4/79
Mr P. Lentner, Shamva, 18/2/79
Mrs M.E.G. Liebenberg, Shangani, 11/4/79
Mr P. Purcell-Gilpin, Headlands, 4/3/79
Mr A. Purcell-Gilpin, Headlands, 4/3/79
Mr D.C. Rosenfels, Marula, 8/2/79
Mr C. Rosenfels, Kezi, 24/4/79
Mr J. Souter, Nuanetsi, 23/1/79
Mr J. Smit, Beatrice, 30/1/79
Mrs C. Smit, Beatrice, 30/1/79

Mr J. Strydom, Inyanga, 2/2/79
Mrs M.O.A. Scott, Gwelo, 7/2/79
Mr P. Steyn, Odzi, 13/2/79
Infant son G. P. Starling, Mtepatepa, 30/3/79
Mrs V.E. Trinder, Nyamandhlovu, 3/9/79
Mrs H. Turner, Gazaland, 9/1/79
Miss S. Turner, Gazaland, 9/1/79
Mr S. van der Merwe, Nuanetsi, 15/2/79
Mr R.C. Vassard, Chipinga, 12/5/79
Mrs S. Watkins, Nuanetsi, 29/12/79
Mr R.D. Kennedy, Mzingwani, 7/5/79
Mr K.F. Hogg, Fort Victoria, 19/6/79
Mr S.J. Stander, Beitbridge, 19/6/79
Mr P.J.D. Breytenbach, Headlands, 25/6/79
Mr C.P. Beale, Nyamandhlovu, 27/6/79
Mrs M. Hofmeyr, Fort Victoria, 6/7/79
Mr J.M. Jeffreys, Marandellas, 7/7/79
Mr T. Hartley, Headlands, 8/7/79
Mrs S. Bother, Somabula, 18/7/79
Master A. Smit, aged 2 years, Somabula, 18/7/79
Mr I.D.N. McGiles, Penhalonga, 21/7/79
Mr R. Beamish, Sipolilo, (1979)
Mr T. Speight, Umvukwes, (1979)
Mr E. Volker, Arcturus, 5/8/79
Mr W.A. Reinsford, Nyamandhlovu, 10/8/79
Mr B.L.T. Eastwick, Centenary, 17/8/79
Mr D.A. Baker, Macheke, 18/8/79
Mr B.S. Bassett, Rusape, 19/8/79
Mr J.E. Oostindien, Macheke, 15/8/79
Mr S. Edridge, Wedza, 11 /9/79
Mr F. Forward, Sinoia, 16/9/79
Mr J.D. Jordaan, Odzi, 17/9/79

White farmers whose deaths were recorded in *The Farmer*, 1981–1987

1981
Abraham Barend Roux and wife Margaret, Victoria East, no date given.
Helen van As and grandson Philip, Victoria East, no date given.
John Patrick Franklin, Umtali, no date given.

1982
Brian Dawe, Chinhoyi, 26/4/1982.
Hilton-Barber, Filabusi, no date given.

1983
Gerrit Malan, Rusape, no date given.
Senator Paul Savage, his daughter, Colleen and her British friend, Gwanda, no

date given.

Barry Brooke and wife Diana, Glendale, 28/5/1983.

Ian Brebner, Figtree, no date given. (This report claimed Brebner was the 39th member of either the Union, or of members' families to have been murdered since independence.)

Joe van Vuuren, Matabeleland, no date given.

Trevor Smith, Matabeleland, no date given.

Four members of the Loxton family, Matabeleland, 23/12/1983.

Three people, names not supplied, Kezi, 28/12/1983.

1985
Jack and Joy Ehlers, Nyamandhlovu, 23/10/1985. (The foreman was also killed.)

1986
It was reported that from October 1985 to March 1986, three white farmers, a foreman and one farmer's wife were killed by dissidents.

1987
Andy MacDonald and wife Nettie, Figtree/Marula, 18/8/1987. (The article claimed that these murders brought to over 40 the number of Matabeleland and Midlands commercial farmers and family members who had lost their lives since independence 'at the hands of murderous dissidents'.)

John Norvall, Nyamandholovu, 26/8/1987 (Eighth farmer murdered since May 1987, and 50th since 1980.)

Brian Hubard, Gwanda, no date given.

White farmers killed between 2000 and 2004

David Stevens, Murehwa, 15/04/2000

Martin Olds, Nyamandhlovu, 18/04/2000

Allan Dunn, Seke, 13/05/2000

John Weeks, Seke, 14/05/2000

Tony Oats, Zvimba North, 31/05/2000

Willem Botha, Seke, 23/05/2000

Henry Elsworth, Kwekwe, 12/12/2000

Gloria Olds, Nyamandhlovu, 04/03/2001

Robert Cobett, Kwekwe, 06/08/2001

Terry Ford, Norton, 18/03/2002

Charles Anderson, Glendale, 02/06/2002

Appendix 6

Date of purchase on the title deeds of farming properties listed in the 1997 acquisition list

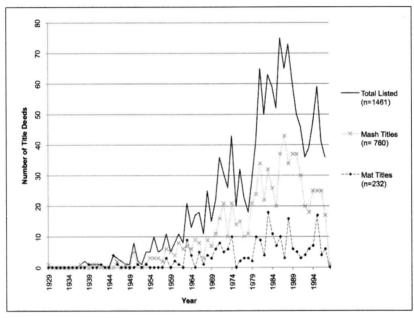

'Mash Titles' refers to Mashonaland.

'Mat Titles' refers to Matabeleland.

34.5 per cent of these title deeds were registered before 1980.

Source: The data for this graph was collected from the full reproduction of the 1997 gazetted acquisition list in *The Farmer*, 4 December 1997, pp. 23-75.

Appendix 7

Biographical data on white farmers interviewed

Farmer 1 – Zimbabwean passport holder, born 1933, farmed in Goromonzi, Mashonaland East. Farmer 1 bought his farms from his mother in 1969. He had leased them from her since 1961. He had two title deeds for neighbouring properties, which he ran as one unit, totalling over 1,000 hectares. He mainly farmed maize, groundnuts and cattle. Had done tobacco in the past. Squatters first occupied his farm in 1998. After 2000, more occupiers moved on. The occupation of the farm was not particularly violent, but he and his wife were both physically assaulted at various stages. He was forced off the farm in 2002.

Farmer 2 – British passport holder, born 1957, farmed in Goromonzi, Mashonaland East. Farmer 2's Grandfather bought the original farm in 1911. His father took over in 1939 and he joined his father in 1980. One of the neighbouring farms had been purchased and added to the original in the mid-1950s. His father had also purchased two farms in the Shamva area, which were run as one unit. Farmer 2's brother and sister lived on these farms. Mixed farming took place, including potatoes, wheat, seed maize, commercial maize, soya beans and cattle. Occupations started in April 2000, but were largely very peaceful. Farmer 2 did not experience any major violence. However, since his farm was so close to Harare, it was often visited by senior ZANU-PF members interested in the property. He moved off in August 2002.

Farmer 3 – South African passport holder, born 1963, farmed in Hurungwe, Mashonaland West. The farm had been bought in 1976 by his parents in a company name. Farmer 3 moved onto the farm in 1990 and was in the process of buying out his mother's shares when the land invasions started in 2000. Tobacco was the main activity, but maize and cattle were also undertaken. The occupation of Farmer 3's farm was extremely violent. He and his family experienced numerous death threats, and were involved in a number of violent confrontations that involved firearms and direct shootings. It was obvious that the taking of their farm was hugely traumatic. Farmer 3's family moved off the farm in early 2002, followed by Farmer 3 later that year. Farmer 3 then let a black farm manager manage his farm in his absence. This worked for a little while, but Farmer 3 said that by 2005 the manager had formed an alliance with a local ZANU-PF councillor, which resulted in the looting of the last of his equipment.

Farmer 4 – Zimbabwean passport holder, born in 1944, farmed in Chegutu, Mashonaland West. Farmer 4's father bought the farm in 1944. He purchased a neighbouring farm in the 1950s. Farmer 4's father then died in 1963, which resulted in Farmer 4 leaving school to manage the farms. After that he added another three neighbouring properties to the farm. The total area was over 5,000 hectares. He grew tobacco, cotton, maize and pastures. Farmer 4 also had over 1,200 head of cattle and won Cattleman of the Year. As a large land-owner, he attracted a lot of attention and had a large number of settlers on his farm. The occupation was not very violent, but conformed to Operation 'Give-Up-And-Leave' (referred to in Chapter Two). Farmer 4 moved off his farm in 2003. Since then some of his land has been used for cropping by a white farmer in league with some of the settlers on his farm.

Farmer 5 – Zimbabwean passport holder, born in 1958, farmed in Hurungwe Mashonaland West. Farmer 5 did not state when or how he acquired his farm, but it was before independence. He mainly grew tobacco and maize, but also had over 300 head of cattle. Occupations started in 2000, but were very limited. Over the course of the next two years Farmer 4 was arrested several times, and his family were barricaded in their household more than once. There were also numerous rape and death threats. The actual eviction was fairly swift and the family moved off the farm by 2002

Farmer 6 – Zimbabwean passport holder, born in 1956, farmed in Zvimba, Mashonaland West. Farmer 6 bought his farm in 1983, with a Certificate of No Present. Farmer 6 bought a neighbouring farm in 1999, making the total land about 1,500 hectares. He mainly grew tobacco, maize, Rhodes grass and cattle. Farmer 6's farm was heavily affected by the food riots of 1997, which caused massive damage to his farm. After 2000, numerous settlers moved onto his farm, reaching over 60 at the height of the violence. He and his family never experienced any direct violence, but witnessed a lot of intimidation and threats. He finally moved off in 2003.

Farmer 7 – Zimbabwean passport holder, born in 1956, farmed in Nyabira, Mashonaland West. Farmer 7's husband bought the farm, of about 2,000 hectares, in 1965. When he passed away in 1981, she transferred the farm into her name. She needed no Certificate of No Present Interest to do this. She farmed tobacco mainly, with maize, groundnuts, crocodiles and pigs on the side. Numerous settlers moved onto her farm after the referendum in 2000. She never experienced any violence, but made sure she did as the settlers and political connected individuals interested in her farm told her to do. She received her eviction order in August 2003 and decided to vacate the farm then.

Farmer 8 – Zimbabwean passport holder, born in 1931, farmed in Zvimba, Mashonaland West. Farmer 8 bought his first farm in 1966. In the 1970s he acquired a neighbouring farm and ran the two as one unit. It totalled over 1,800 hectares and wheat was the principal crop. He also farmed maize, soya and cattle. The occupation of his farm was largely very peaceful. A number of settlers moved on but Farmer 8 maintained that he had very good relations with them. He was forced out by an elected official who personally delivered his eviction order and saw that Farmer 8 left the farm in 2002.

Farmer 9 – Zimbabwean passport holder, born in 1938, farmed in Hurungwe, Mashonaland West. Farmer 9 bought his farm in 1976. He principally grew tobacco, along with maize, cotton, coffee and cattle. His farm was only first occupied in 2002. He thought that he may have been safe from acquisition, but settlers moved on in late 2002 and he was off by September 2003. After the initial few settlers moved on, his labourers demanded the SI6 package, because neighbouring farmers had left and paid the severance package. This was the most intimidation Farmer 9 received and after that he knew his time on the farm was over and left.

Farmer 10 – Zimbabwean passport holder, born in 1932, farmed in Centenary, Mashonaland Central. Farmer 10 bought the farm in 1982. The main activities were tobacco, maize, mangoes, sunflower seed and tomatoes. Their eviction was late and extremely swift. In September 2002, Farmer 10 was taken down to the compound by war veterans. He was assaulted and forced to chant ZANU-PF slogans. Over the next 26 days, Farmer 10 and his wife were physically assaulted a number of times, before being told to vacate the farm by the person promised the homestead.

Farmer 11 – Zimbabwean passport holder, born in 1957, farmed in Chegutu and Harare South, Mashonaland East and West. Farmer 11's father bought the first farm in Mashonaland West in 1977. His father passed away in 1978, and he inherited the farm, owing a lot of money. He took over managing the farm and later bought another one about 20 kilometres away in 1983, with a Certificate of No Present Interest. His first farm was a huge operation, encompassing tobacco, maize, cattle, game, ostriches, Rhodes grass, an abattoir and a tannery. His other farm also grew tobacco, as well as paprika, seed maize, wheat, Rhodes grass and crocodiles. From 2000, Farmer 11 had a great deal of interference and intimation on his second farm. However, his first farm was left alone because it was a big exporter and earner of foreign currency. Plus he was told that if he gave up half of his second farm, his first would be left alone. He did so, but because of continuing intimidation, violence and interference he soon gave up the second farm entirely. Soon after that he started to have trouble on his first farm. There were large numbers of occupiers and settlers, and despite his good reputation in the area, he faced numerous threats to his personal safety. He was arrested dozens of times and eventually left his first farm in 2005.

Farmer 12 – Zimbabwean passport holder, born in 1929, farmed in Goromonzi, Mashonaland East. Farmer 12 bought his farm in 1980. He had been farming in Centenary prior to that, but felt that was going to be one of the first areas to be resettled after independence, and so moved to Goromonzi. The new farm was 1,097 hectares and the principal crop was tobacco. Farmer 11 had no settlers or occupiers move onto his farm. He got his first notice of the government's intent to take his farm in 2000. Then he received an eviction order in 2002 and decided that he and his wife would prefer to leave the farm than face the prospect of time in jail. They left at the end of September 2002. An army general then took over the farm.

Farmer 13 – Zimbabwean passport holder, born in 1946, farmed in Norton, Mashonaland West. Farmer 13 had a very small farm in Norton, only 126 hectares, which he bought in 1989 with a Certificate of No Present Interest. He started growing vegetables, but later added tobacco and seed maize. Farmer 13's farm was in a very violent area and situated close to one of the most brutal white farmer murders in 2002. Because of its small size, his farm was technically exempt from acquisition, and from 2000 to 2002 he had no problems. Then in 2002, a woman appeared claiming the farm was hers and for the next year, Farmer 13 had a terrible time with intimidation, threats and interference. In 2003 he moved off the farm. During the affair, his wife died of a heart attack, which Farmer 13 maintains was due to the stress of the situation.

Farmer 14 – Zimbabwean passport holder, born in 1959, farmed in Bindura, Mashonaland Central. Farmer 14 did not own his farm. He was leasing a portion of his father-in-law's farm, having moved there in 1994. Prior to that he had been leasing land from the government in Ruwa since 1989, when in 1993 a well-known army general arrived on the farm and told them their lease was cancelled with immediate effect and that he was taking over. After moving onto the father-in-law's farm, they managed the tobacco and set about creating a game park. From early 2000 they began to have troubles on the farm. A number of settlers moved in and the farm was also visited by a number of politicians and army personnel. They faced daily disruption to work and farm activity, as well as the constant threat of violence and intimidation. Farmer 14 and his family also experienced a number of *jambanjas* and they eventually left the farm in October 2002.

Farmer 15 – Zimbabwean passport holder, born in 1945, farmed in Marodizi, Mashonaland Central. Farmer 15 bought his farm, measuring 650 hectares, in 1973 and wheat and tobacco were his main crops. In April 2000, settlers and youth militia started to move in, and the farm was then occupied consistently until Farmer 15 left at the end of 2003. While Farmer 15 and his family experienced no direct violence, there were often violent confrontations between the labour force and the settlers. Many political rallies were held on the farm, with frequent visits by individuals connected to ZANU-PF.

Farmer 16 – British passport holder, born in 1948, farmed in Concession, Mashonaland Central. Farmer 16 had bought the farm he owned in 2000 in 1979 and was primarily a tobacco farmer. He and his family were farming in the Mutoko region before 1980, but Farmer 16 feared that many of the farms in Mutoko would be taken for resettlement after independence. His assessment proved true when most of the area was claimed for resettlement in 1982 and he vacated his Mutoko farm and moved to Concession. As part of that relocation

Farmer 16 claimed that the government assured him that he would not be asked to offer land in future relocation and reform exercises. When Farmer 16's farm was listed for acquisition in 2001, he appealed and had his farm officially removed, but was relisted again in 2002 and 2003. Eventually he was told by government officials that the earlier resettlement schemes had nothing to do with the fast-track land reform programme. Throughout this, Farmer 16's farm was never settled or occupied. Finally in 2003, the son of an extremely high-ranking ZANU-PF party member arrived on the farm with a group of armed personnel and announced that the farm was his and the farmer had to vacate. Farmer 16 took this threat seriously and moved off the farm within 24 hours

Farmer 17 – Zimbabwean passport holder, born in 1946, farmed in Karoi, Mashonaland West. Farmer 17 bought shares in a company that owned two farms run as one unit in Karoi in 1981. The farms were originally purchased by the company in 1978, but the farms were managed remotely by the initial investors. The farms were not profitable and Farmer 17 was brought in to run them. He bought out the other investors during the 1980s. Farmer 17 mainly grew tobacco, with maize and cattle on the side. Both farms were gazetted for acquisition in 2001. There had been several small groups of people move on and off the farms between 2001 and 2002. In 2002 one of the farms was occupied by about 70 settler families. As a result, Farmer 17 shut down operations on that farm to focus his efforts on the remaining farm. The labourers on the occupied farm, antagonised by the settlers, barricaded Farmer 17 and his family into the homestead on several occasions, demanding retrenchment packages (SI6). He eventually paid the SI6 and tried to concentrate on farming the remaining title. But by this stage the farm had attracted the interest of high-ranking ZANU-PF members and Farmer 17 was arrested, intimidated and threatened on several occasions, including numerous *jambanjas*. Farmer 17 and his family left the second farm at the beginning of 2005.

Farmer 19 – Zimbabwean passport holder, born in 1953, farmed in Makondi, Mashonaland West. Farmer 19 bought his farm in 1986 with a Certificate of No Present Interest, and focused on coffee, horticulture and flower production. Farmer 19 received a number of notifications for acquisition after 2000, but experienced no real intimidation or invasion of his farm. In 2002 he was informed that he had 48 hours to vacate his farm, or face arrest. He and his wife decided to leave at that point and try to run the farm remotely. This failed to work because from that point onwards there was a great deal of interference on the farm and a number of settlers moved on to it. Farmer 19 was married to a foreign national and they approached her national embassy asking for protection and representation, but little was forthcoming and this did nothing to stop the invasion and acquisition of Farmer 19's farm.

Farmer 20 – Zimbabwean passport holder, born in 1930, farmed in Murehwa, Mashonaland East. Farmer 20 owned two adjoining farms which he ran as one unit. The first, measuring 1,100 hectares, he acquired in 1983, and he obtained a Certificate of No Present Interest. The second, of 1,300 hectares, he bought in 1995 after leasing it for five years. He did not need a Certificate of No Present Interest for this farm because he bought it via a share transfer. It had been bought in a company name by the previous owner, and to purchase the farm, Farmer 20 bought the company that owned the farm. This tactic circumnavigated the Certificate issue, as well as that of transfer duties. Farmer 20 farmed with his son, and their main activities were tobacco, maize and cattle. His farms were initially listed in 1997 and he had letters from the Chiefs of the neighbouring communal areas saying they wanted him to stay on his farm and remain in the area. In 2000 Farmer 20 received more notices of acquisition and started to get visited by groups of people on the weekends. Many of these visitors were then allocated plots on the farm and they moved in and settled permanently. There were several violent confrontations over the next couple of years, many involving firearms. In August 2002 Farmer 20 was given 48 hours to leave the farm; he decided there was no point in trying to carry on farming and he moved to Harare.

Farmer 21 – South African passport holder, born in 1948, farmed in Trelawney, Mashonaland West. Farmer 21 bought his farm from his father in 1978. It was a small farm of only 560 hectares and he focused on tobacco. His farm was listed in 1997, but was later removed from that list. The farm was pegged for A1 plots and about 10 settlers moved onto the farm in 2000. These settlers severely disrupted the running of the farm, continually stopping labourers working, blocking tractors and holding political rallies in the workers compound. Over the next couple of years the interference became so bad that as soon as Farmer 21 got his last crop of tobacco off the farm in 2002, he and his family moved of the farm.

Farmer 22 – Zimbabwean passport holder, born in 1938, farmed in Mazowe, Mashonaland Central, and Nyabira, Mashonaland West. Farmer 22 owned two farms. The one in Mazowe (1,700 hectares), his grandfather had taken over from his brother in 1920. His father then took control of the farm in 1935 and Farmer 22 started there in the 1950s. This farm was first occupied in early November 2000 by a dozen settlers. There were also constant visits by politicians and government officials on the weekends because the farm was so close to Harare. Farmer 22 tried to co-exist with the settlers and war veterans, but the interference and intimidation gradually got worse until he moved off the farm in October 2003. The pattern of his invasion conforms to Operation 'Give-Up-And-Leave'. The other farm was a large tract of land in Nyabira, measuring over 6,500 hectares. There was no homestead on that farm and Farmer 22 only ran cattle there. This piece of land was largely overlooked and only received its first acquisition letter in 2004. In 2003 it was occupied by a large number of villagers from a nearby communal area. At the same time large numbers of Farmer 22's cattle were stolen and destroyed so he decided to abandon that piece of land too.

Farmer 23 – British passport holder, born in 1957, farmed in Glendale, Mashonaland Central. Farmer 23's parents farmed in Glendale and he took over operations in the 1980s. The farm consisted of 5 titles, which had been bought in the 1960s, 1970s and 1980s. They grew maize, tobacco, wheat, barley and cotton, and kept cattle and pigs. After the referendum in 2000, settlers were constantly moving on and off the farm and disrupting activities. In 2001 over half the farm was permanently settled and Farmer 23 had to focus his attentions on the remaining land. He managed to plant two more tobacco crops, but because of the hassles on the farm, had moved his family to Harare and he had moved out of the main homestead, which was now occupied by a senior government official. Farmer 23 ceased all operations and left the farm in 2003.

Farmer 24 – Zimbabwean passport holder, born in 1955, farmed in Makoni, Manicaland. Farmer 24 came from an established and well-known farming family. He moved onto his own farm in 1983, originally leased with an option to purchase, which he exercised in 1987. It was a mixed farm but the main activities were cattle, sheep, tobacco, maize and paprika. Farmer 24 was one of the last in his district to be targeted by settlers. In 2002, he received numerous death threats for his role in local politics and it became apparent his farm was being monitored by a number of high-ranking politicians. Farmer 24 took these threats seriously and he and his family left the farm. He tried to lease it out to interested farmers, but failed for a number of reasons, including political interference and settler issues. Finally, in 2004, he gave up all operations and his homestead and farm were occupied by settlers.

Farmer 25 – Zimbabwean passport holder, born in 1956, farmed in Makondi, Mashonaland West. Farmer 25 bought his farm in 1996, via a share transfer. As a result he needed no Certificate of No Present Interest. The farm was made up of three separate titles, which were run as one unit and focused on tobacco, cattle and maize. Farmer 25 had been leasing land before that and had worked on other tobacco farms. In 1997, his farm was listed for acquisition, but he challenged the order, with a letter of support signed by his entire labour force, and continued farming. Just after the referendum in 2000, settlers moved on to the farm, but none stayed for long. There was then a steady build-up of people settling on the farm. In 2001, Farmer 25 was told by police and army personnel that he had to vacate his farm immediately. As a result he deliberately destroyed his own tobacco seedlings, only to be told a week later he could remain on the farm. He planted one more tobacco crop, but as he was being continually harassed by settlers and youth militia during that final season he decided to leave the farm once that crop was out.

Farmer 26 – Zimbabwean passport holder, born in 1959, farmed in Mount Darwin, Mashonaland Central. Farmer 26's farm consisted of two title deeds, run as one unit. The first was acquired by his farther to grow tobacco in the 1960s, and the second in the 1970s, and both remained in his father's name until his parents left the farm. Farm 26's farm was one of the first to be occupied in his area, and was subsequently used by the war veterans and others in charge of the land movements as a base of operations. Those original settlers stayed on the farm for the next three years and constantly interfered with farming operations. Farmer 26 was forced to downsize his operations, until there was no longer enough space to farm effectively. Initially he was told to hand over half his land in 2000, then over the next couple of years more and more land was annexed by the settlers for themselves. Farmer 26 and his family were never the victims of any violence, but farming became a constant battle (typical of Operation Get Up and Leave). Because of other commitments, he found himself spending more and more time in Harare, and eventually decided in 2003 to move his family there and let go of the farm.

Farmer 29 – Zimbabwean passport holder, born in 1946, farmed in Chegutu, Mashonaland West. Farmer 29 had been farming in Rhodesia/Zimbabwe before he bought his own farm in 1982, with a Certificate of No Present Interest. His principal activities were tobacco, cattle and maize. In 1997 his farm was designated for acquisition, which he successfully contested. His farm was one of the first to be occupied after the referendum in 2000. On 26 February, a local ZANU-PF councillor arrived on the farm with over 1,000 people. Farmer 29 insisted this was to make an impression on the district. The farm was then vacated and things quietened down for a while. However, soon a handful of settlers occupied the farm and began interfering with operations. Farmer 29's farm was very close to Harare and, as with many farms in this situation, on the weekends the farm was usually overrun with occupiers who would then hold political rallies, intimidate the labour, abuse the farmers and disrupt farming. Large quantities of alcohol were supplied to those bussed in and the weekends became very trying times for the farmers and labourers. Over the next two years Farmer 29 and his wife had an extremely traumatic time. On several occasions they were threatened with firearms and machetes, beaten up, and at one stage barricaded in their house for seven weeks. Their labour tried to help as much as they could, but eventually the intimidation and violence quelled their resistance. Farmer 29 and his wife moved to Harare in 2002.

Farmer 31 – Zimbabwean passport holder, born in 1957, farmed in Bindura, Mashonaland Central. Farmer 31's father bought the farm in the 1950s; Farmer 31 bought it from him and added another title in 1988, with a Certificate of No Present Interest. Each title was only 300 hectares and the farm focused on citrus, cotton and wheat. In 2001, after receiving a notice of intent to acquire by the government, Farmer 31 decided to offer one of the titles for resettlement, for full compensation, as long as he could retain the other. This was agreed to in court, but two weeks later he received a notice for the other title. Farmer 31 managed to remain on this farm for another three years, though, despite constant interruption. He was one of the last farmers in his area to move off, which he attributed to the farm's small size. He moved off in 2004, along with all the remaining white farmers in his area, and his farm was taken over by high-ranking ZANU-PF member.

Bibliography

Achebe, Chinua. 1989. *Hope and Impediments: Selected Essays* (New York, Doubleday).

Alexander, Jocelyn. 1993. 'The State, Agrarian Policy and Rural Politics in Zimbabwe: Case Studies from Insiza and Chimanimani Districts 1940–1990 (D.Phil. thesis, University of Oxford).

— 1994. 'State, Peasantry and Resettlement in Zimbabwe', *Review of African Political Economy*, 21, 61, 325-45.

— 1998. 'Dissident Perspectives on Zimbabwe's Post-independence War', *Africa: Journal of the International African Institute*, 68, 2, 151-82.

— 2003. '"Squatters", Veterans and the State in Zimbabwe', in Amanda Hammar, Brian Raftopoulos, and Stig Jensen (eds), *Zimbabwe's Unfinished Business: Rethinking Land, State and Nation in the Context of Crisis* (Harare, Weaver Press).

— 2006. *The Unsettled Land: State-Making and the Politics of Land in Zimbabwe 1893-2003* (Oxford, James Currey).

— 2007. 'The Historiography of Land in Zimbabwe: Strengths, Silences, and Questions', *Safundi*, 8, 2, 183-98.

Alexander, Jocelyn and JoAnn McGregor. 2001. 'Elections, Land and the Politics of Opposition in Matabeleland', *Journal of Agrarian Change*, 1, 4, 510-33.

Alexander, Jocelyn, JoAnn McGregor, and Terence Ranger. 2000. *Violence and Memory: One Hundred Years in the 'Dark Forests' of Matabeleland* (Oxford, James Currey).

Anderson, Benedict. 1991. *Imagined Communities: Reflections on the Origin and Spread of Nationalism* (London, Verso).

Arnolds, W.E. 1980. *The Goldbergs of Leigh Ranch* (Bulawayo, Books of Zimbabwe).

Arrighi, G. 1967. *The Political Economy of Rhodesia* (The Hague, Mouton).

— 1970. 'Labour Supplies in Historical Perspective: A Study of the Proletarianization of the African Peasantry in Rhodesia', *Journal of Development Studies*, 6, 197-234.

Auret, Michael. 2009. *From Liberator to Dictator: An Insider's Account of Robert Mugabe's Decent into Tyranny* (Claremont, David Philip).

Barclay, Philip. 2010. *Zimbabwe: Years of Hope and Despair* (London, Bloomsbury).

Barthes, Roland. 1972. *Mythologies* (New York, Hill and Wang).

Beinhart, William. 1984. 'Soil Erosion, Conservationism and Ideas about Development: A Southern African Exploration, 1900–1960', *Journal of Southern African Studies* 1, 52-83.

Bell, Alice Elsie. 2005. *A Decade in Rhodesia* (London, Athena).

Bhebe, Ngwabi and Terence Ranger (eds). 1996. *Society in Zimbabwe's Liberation War* (Oxford, James Currey).

Blair, David. 2002. *Degrees in Violence: Robert Mugabe and the Struggle for Power in Zimbabwe* (London, Continuum).

Boggie, Jeannie Marr. 1938. *Experience of Rhodesia's Pioneer Women* (Bulawayo, Philpott and Collins).

— 1959. *A Husband and a Farm in Rhodesia* (Gwelo, Catholic Mission Press).

— 1966. *First Steps in Civilising Rhodesia* (Edinburgh: Philpott and Collins).

Bond, Patrick and Masimba Manyanya. 2002. *Zimbabwe's Plunge: Exhausted Nationalism, Neoliberalism and the Search for Social Justice* (Pietermaritzburg, University of Natal Press).

Bratton, Michael. 1986. 'Farmer Organizations and Food Production in Zimbabwe', *World Development*, 14, 3, 367-84.

— 1994. 'Micro-democracy? The Merger of Farmer Unions in Zimbabwe', *African Studies Review*, 37, 1, 9-37.

— 1987. 'The Comrades and the Countryside: The politics of Agricultural Policy in Zimbabwe', *World Politics*, 39, 2, 174-202.

Bulman, Mary. 1975. *The Native Land Husbandry Act of Southern Rhodesia: A Failure in Land Reform* (Salisbury, Tribal Areas of Rhodesia Research Foundation).

Burton, Orville Vernon. 2000. 'Three Articles of a Century of Excellence: The Best of "The South Carolina Historical Magazine"', *The South Carolina Historical Magazine*, 101, 3, 182-9.

Catholic Commission for Justice and Peace in Zimbabwe. 1997. *Breaking the Silence, Building True Peace: A Report on the Disturbances in*

Matabeleland and the Midlands 1980 to 1988 (Harare, Legal Resources Foundation).

— 2007. *Gukurahundi in Zimbabwe: A report on the disturbances in Matabeleland and the Midlands 1980–1988* (London, Amnesty International).

Caute, David. 1983. *Under the Skin: The Death of White Rhodesia* (Harmondsworth, Penguin).

Central Statistics Office. 2001. *Compendium of Statistics 2000* (Harare, Government of Zimbabwe).

Centre on Housing Rights and Evictions Africa Programme. 2001. *Land, Housing and Property Rights in Zimbabwe* (Amsterdam, Centre on Housing Rights and Evictions).

Chabal, Patrick. 2002. *A History of Postcolonial Lusophone Africa* (London, Hurst).

Chaumba, Joseph, Ian Scoones, and William Wolmer. 2003a. 'From Jambanja to Planning: The Reassertion for Technocracy in Land Reform in South-eastern Zimbabwe', *Journal of Modern African Studies*, 41, 4, 533-54.

Chennells, Anthony. 1977. 'The Treatment of the Rhodesian War in Recent Rhodesian Novels', *Zambezia*, 5, 2, 177-202.

— 1982. 'Settler Myths and the Southern Rhodesian Novel' (PhD thesis, University of Zimbabwe).

— 1996. 'Rhodesian Discourse, Rhodesian Novels and the Zimbabwe Liberation War', in Ngwabi Bhebe and Terence Ranger (eds), *Society in Zimbabwe's Liberation War* (Oxford, James Currey).

— 2005. 'Self-representation and National Memory: White Autobiographies in Zimbabwe', in Robert Muponde and Ranka Primorac (eds), *Versions of Zimbabwe: New Approaches to Literature and Culture* (Harare, Weaver Press).

Chikanza, I., D. Paxton, R. Loewenson and R. Laing. 1981. 'The Health Status of Farm Worker Communities in Zimbabwe', *Central African Journal of Medicine*, 27, 5, 172-5.

Chinyangara, I., I. Chokuwenga, R.G. Dete, L. Dube, J. Kembo, P. Moyo, and R.S. Nkomo. 1997. *Indicators for Children's Rights: Zimbabwe Country Case Study* (Oslo, Childwatch International).

Chuma, Wallace. 2004. 'Liberating or Limiting the Public Sphere? Media Policy and the Zimbabwean Transition, 1980-2004', in Brian Raftopoulos and Tyrone Savage (eds). *Zimbabwe: Injustice and Politi-*

cal Reconciliation (Harare, Weaver Press).

Clark, Duncan. 1977. *Agricultural and Plantation Workers in Rhodesia* (Gwelo, Mambo Press).

Cleary, Frederick E. 1998. *Kamoto: The Life of Winston Joseph Field 1904–1969* (Victoria, St Arnaud).

Clements, Frank and Eric Harben. 1962. *Leaf of Gold: The Story of Rhodesian Tobacco* (London, Methuen).

Clingman, Stephen. 2004. 'Bram Fischer and the Question of Identity', *Current Writing*, 16, 1, pp. 61-79.

Coetzee, J.M. 1988. *White Writing: On the Culture of Letters in South Africa* (New Haven, Yale University Press).

— 1992. *Doubling the Point: Essays and Interviews* (Cambridge, Harvard University Press).

Cohen, David William, Stephan F. Miecher and Luise White. 2001. 'Introduction', in Luise White, Stephan F. Miescher and David William Cohen (eds), *African Words, African Voices: Critical Practices in Oral History* (Bloomington, Indiana University Press).

Cohen, Paul. 1997. *History in Three Keys: The Boxers as Event, Experience, and Myth* (New York, Columbia University Press).

Coldham, Simon. 1993. 'The Land Acquisition Act, 1992, of Zimbabwe', *Journal of African Law*, 37, 1, 82-8.

Commercial Farmers' Union of Zimbabwe. 1991. *Proposals for Land Reform for Zimbabwe, 1991* (Harare, Commercial Farmers' Union of Zimbabwe).

— *Situation Reports 2000–2002* (Harare, Commercial Farmers' Union of Zimbabwe).

Commercial Farmers' Union of Zimbabwe and Affiliated Organizations, *Financial Statements, 1992–2000* (Harare).

Compagnon, David. 2011. *A Predictable Tragedy: Robert Mugabe and the Collapse of Zimbabwe* (Philadelphia, University of Pennsylvania).

Cooper, Frederick. 2005. *Colonialism in Question: Theory, Knowledge, History* (Berkeley, University of California).

— 2008. 'Possibility and Constraint: African Independence in Historical Perspective', *Journal of African History*, 49, 167-96.

Cooper, Frederick and Roger Brubaker. 2005. 'Identity', in Frederick Cooper, *Colonialism in Question* (Berkeley, University of California Press).

Crisis in Zimbabwe Coalition. 2002. *Zimbabwe Report* (Harare, Crisis in

Zimbabwe Coalition).

Davies, W.T. 1958. *Fifty Years of Progress: An Account of the African Organisation of the Imperial Tobacco Company, 1907–1957* (Bristol, Marden, Son and Hall).

Dirks, Nicholas. 1996. 'Is Vice Versa? Historical Anthropologies or Anthropological Histories,' in T.J. McDonald (ed.), *The Historical Turn in the Human Sciences* (Ann Arbor, University of Michigan Press).

Dorman, Sara, Daniel Hammett and Paul Nugent (eds). 2007. *Making Nations, Creating Strangers: States and Citizenship in Africa* (Leiden, Brill).

Drinkwater, Michael. 1989. 'Technical Development and Peasant Impoverishment: Land Use Policy in Zimbabwe's Midlands Province', *Journal of Southern African Studies*, 15, 2, 287-305.

Duggan, William. 1980. 'The Native Land Husbandry Act of 1951 and the Rural African Middle Class of Southern Rhodesia', *African Affairs*, 79, 227-39.

Dzimba, John. 1998. *South Africa's Destabilization of Zimbabwe, 1980–1989* (Basingstoke, Macmillan).

Eppel, Shari. 2009. 'A Tale of Three Dinner Plates: Truth and the Challenges of Human Rights Research in Zimbabwe', *Journal of Southern African Studies*, 35, 4, 967-76.

Fanon, Franz. 1967. *White Skins, Black Masks* (New York, Grove).

Flower, Ken. 1987. *Serving Secretly: An Intelligence Chief on Record* (London, John Murray).

Frederikse, Julie. 1982. *None But Ourselves: Masses vs. Media in the Making of Zimbabwe* (Harare, Zimbabwe Publishing House).

Freeman, Linda. 2005. 'South Africa's Zimbabwe Policy: Unraveling the Contradictions', *Journal of Contemporary African Studies*, 32, 147-72.

Fuller, Alexandra. 2003. *Don't Let's go to the Dogs Tonight: An African Childhood* (London, Random House).

General Agricultural and Plantation Workers' Union of Zimbabwe. 2010. *If Something is Wrong: The Invisible Suffering of Farm Workers due to 'Land Reform'* (Harare, GAPWUZ and Weaver Press).

Gewald, Jan-Bart, Marja Hinfelaar and Giacomo Macola (eds). 2008. *One Zambia, Many Histories: Towards A History of Post-Colonial Zambia* (Lieden, Brill).

Gobodo-Madikizela, Pumla. 1998. 'Healing the Racial Divide? Personal Reflections on the Truth and Reconciliation Commission', *South African Journal of Psychology*, 27, 271-2.

Godwin, Peter. 2006. *When a Crocodile Eats the Sun: A Memoir of Africa* (New York, Little, Brown).

Godwin, Peter and Ian Hancock. 1993. *'Rhodesians Never Die': The Impact of War and Political Change on White Rhodesia, c. 1970–1980* (Oxford, Oxford University Press).

Graham, James. 2009. *Land and Nationalisms in Fictions from Southern Africa* (New York, Routledge).

Haarhoff, Dorian. 1991. *The Wild South West: Frontier Myths and Metaphors in Literature set in Namibia, 1760–1988* (Johannesburg, Witwatersrand University Press).

Hall, Stuart. 1997. 'The Work of Representation', in Stuart Hall (ed.), *Representation: Cultural Representations and Signifying Practices* (London, Sage).

Hammar, Amanda. 2001. '"The Day of Burning": Eviction and Reinvention in the Margins of Northwest Zimbabwe', *Journal of Agrarian Change*, 1, 4, 550-74.

Hammar, Amanda and Brian Raftopoulos. 2003. 'Zimbabwe's Unfinished Business: Rethinking Land, State and Nation', in Amanda Hammar, Brian Raftopoulos and Stig Jensen (eds), *Zimbabwe's Unfinished Business: Rethinking Land, State and Nation in the Context of Crisis* (Harare, Weaver Press).

Hammar, Amanda, Brian Raftopoulos and Stig Jensen (eds). 2003. *Zimbabwe's Unfinished Business: Rethinking Land, State and Nation in the Context of Crisis* (Harare, Weaver Press).

Hanlon, Joseph. 1986. *Beggar Your Neighbour: Apartheid Power in Southern Africa* (London, James Currey).

Harold-Barry, David (ed.). 2004. *Zimbabwe: The Past is the Future* (Harare, Weaver Press).

Harris, Ashleigh. 2005. 'Writing Home: Inscriptions of Whiteness/ Descriptions of Belonging in White Zimbabwean Memoir-Autobiography', in Robert Muponde and Ranka Primorac (eds), *Versions of Zimbabwe: New Approaches to Literature and Culture* (Harare, Weaver Press).

Harvey, Karen. 'Introduction', in Karen Harvey (ed.), *The Kiss in History* (Manchester, Manchester University Press).

Hill, Geoff. 2003. *Battle for Zimbabwe: The Final Countdown* (Cape Town, Zebra).

Hills, Dennis. 1981. *The Last Days of White Rhodesia* (London, Chatto and Windus).

Hodder-Williams, Richard. 1983. *White Farmers in Rhodesia 1980–1965: A History of the Marandellas District* (London, Macmillan).

Holding, Ian. 2005. *Unfeeling* (London, Scribner).

Hughes, David M. 2006a. 'The Art of Belonging: Whites Writing Landscape in Savannah Africa', paper presented to Program in Agrarian Studies, Yale University, New Haven, 6 October.

— 2006b. 'Whites and Water: How Euro-Africans Made Nature at Kariba Dam', *Journal of Southern African Studies*, 32, 4, 823-38.

Human Rights NGO Forum. 2006. *An Analysis of the Zimbabwe Human Rights NGO Forum Legal Cases, 1998-2006* (Harare, Human Rights NGO Forum).

Hyden, G., M. Leslie and F.F. Ogundimu (eds). 2003. *Media and Democracy in Africa* (New Brunswick, Transaction).

International Crisis Group. 2004. *Blood and Soil: Land, Politics and Conflict Prevention in Zimbabwe and South Africa* (New York, International Crisis Group).

Isin, Engin. 2002. *Being Political: Genealogies of Citizenship* (Minneapolis, University of Minnesota Press).

Jones, Neville. *Rhodesian Genesis* (Bulawayo, Rhodesia Pioneers and Early Settlers' Society).

Justice for Agriculture Trust and the General Agricultural and Plantation Workers' Union of Zimbabwe. 2008. *Destruction of Zimbabwe's Backbone Industry in Pursuit of Political Power: A Qualitative Report on Events in Zimbabwe's Commercial Farming Sector Since the Year 2000* (Harare, Zimbabwe Human Rights NGO Forum).

Justice for Agriculture Trust and the General Agricultural and Plantation Workers Union of Zimbabwe. n.d. *Reckless Tragedy: Irreversible? A Survey of Human Rights Violations and Losses Suffered by Commercial Farmers and Farm Workers in Zimbabwe from 2000 to 2008* (Harare, Justice for Agriculture Trust).

Kennedy, Dane. 1987. *Islands of White: Settler Society and Culture in Kenya and Southern Rhodesia, 1890–1939* (Durham, Duke University Press).

Keyter, Carl K. 1978. 'Maize Control in Southern Rhodesia 1931–1941:

The African Contribution to White Survival', *Central African Historical Association Local Series*, 34 (Salisbury, Central African Historical Society).

Kriger, Norma. 1992 *Zimbabwe's Guerrilla War: Peasant Voices* (Cambridge, Cambridge University Press).

— 2001. 'Zimbabwe's War Veterans and the Ruling Party: Continuities in Political Dynamics', *Politique Africaine*, 81.

— 2003a. 'Zimbabwe: Political Constructions of War Veterans', *Review of African Political Economy*, 30, 96, 323-8.

— 2003b. *Guerrilla Veterans in Post-war Zimbabwe: Symbolic and Violent Politics* (Cambridge, Cambridge University Press).

— 2003c. 'Zimbabwe's War Veterans and the Ruling Party: Continuities in Political Dynamics', in Staffan Darnolf and Liisa Laakso (eds), *Twenty Years of Independence in Zimbabwe: From Liberation to Authoritarianism* (Basingstoke, Palgrave Macmillan), pp. 104-21.

— 2003d. 'War Veterans: Continuities Between the Past and the Present', *African Studies Quarterly*, 7, 2 and 3, available at www.africa. ufl.edu/asq/v7/v7i2a7.htm (viewed, 26 February, 2008).

Krog, Antjie. 2002. *Country of my Skull* (Johannesburg, Random House).

— 2003. *A Change of Tongue* (Johannesburg, Random House).

Krog, Antjie, Nosisi Mpolweni and Kopano Ratele. *There Was This Goat: Investigating the Truth Commission Testimony of Notrose Nobomvu Konile* (Pietermaritzburg, University of KwaZulu-Natal Press).

Kundera, Milan. 1984. *The Unbearable Lightness of Being* (London, Faber and Faber).

Lamb, Christina. 2006. *House of Stone: The True Story of a Family Divided in War-torn Zimbabwe* (London, HarperCollins).

Legal Resources Foundation. 2002. *Justice in Zimbabwe* (Harare, Legal Resources Foundation).

Loewenson, Rene. 1986a. *Farm Labour in Zimbabwe: Modern Plantation Agriculture* (London, Zed Books).

— 1986b. 'Farm Labour in Zimbabwe: A Comparative Study in Health Status', Health Policy and Planning, 1, 1, 48-57.

— 1992. 'Health in Large-scale Farming Areas of Zimbabwe: A Response', Health and Policy Planning, 7, 186-90.

Logan, B. Ikubolajeh. 2007. 'Land Reform, Ideology and Urban Food Security: Zimbabwe's Third Chimurenga', *Journal of Economic and Social Geography*, 98, 2, 202-24.

Lyons, Tanya. 2002. 'Guerrilla Girls and Women in the Zimbabwean National Liberation Struggle', in Susan Geiger, Jean Marie Allman and Nakanyike Musisi (eds), *Women in African Colonial Histories* (Bloomington, Indiana University Press).

Macola, Giacomo. 2010. *Liberal Nationalism in Central Africa: A Biography of Harry Mwaanga Nkumbula* (New York, Palgrave Macmillan).

Manby, Bronwen. 2009. *Struggles of Citizenship in Africa* (London, Zed Books).

Mandaza, Ibbo. 1986. 'Introduction: The Political Economy of Transition', in Ibbo Mandaza (ed.), *Zimbabwe: The Political Economy of Transition, 1980-86* (Dakar, Codesria).

Maroleng, Chris. 2004. *Situation Report: Zimbabwe, Reaping the Harvest?* (Pretoria, ISS).

Marongwe, Nelson. 2003. 'Farm Occupations and Occupiers in the New Politics of Land in Zimbabwe', in Amanda Hammar, Brian Raftopoulos and Stig Jensen (eds), *Zimbabwe's Unfinished Business: Rethinking Land, State and Nation in the Context of Crisis* (Harare, Weaver Press).

Martin, David and Phyllis Johnson. 1981. *The Struggle for Zimbabwe: The Chimurenga War* (Harare, Faber and Faber).

— (eds) 1986. *Destructive Engagement: Southern Africa at War* (Harare, Zimbabwe Publishing House).

Mattes, Robert, Micheal Bratton, Yul Davids and Cherrel Africa. 2000. *Afrobarometer Paper No. 7: Public Opinion and the Consolidation of Democracy in Southern Africa* (Cape Town, IDASA).

Mbanga, Trish. 1991. *Tobacco: A Century of Gold* (Harare, ZIL Publications).

Mbembe, Achille. 2001. *On the Postcolony* (Berkeley, University of California Press).

McCallum, Wayne. 2006. 'Land, Property and Power: The Land Issue in Zimbabwe' (PhD thesis, University of Adelaide).

McCarthy, Cormac. 2007. *No Country for Old Men* (London, Picador).

McKenzie, John Alistair, 'Commercial Farmers in the Governmental System of Colonial Zimbabwe, 1963–1980' (PhD thesis, University of Zimbabwe).

Melber, Henning (ed.). 2004. *Media, Public Discourse and Political Contestation in Zimbabwe* (Göteborg, Elanders Infologistics Väst).

Meldrum, Andrew. 2005. *Where We Have Hope: A Memoir of Zimbabwe* (New York, Atlantic Monthly Press).

Meredith, Martin. 2003. *Our Votes, Our Guns: Robert Mugabe and the Tragedy of Zimbabwe* (New York, PubicAffairs).

— 2007. *Mugabe: Power, Plunder and the Struggle for Zimbabwe* (London, Simon and Schuster).

Metcalf, C.B. 1971. *A Guide to Farming in Rhodesia* (Salisbury, Rhodesian Farmer).

Ministry of Information, Immigration and Tourism [Rhodesia], *The Murder of Missionaries in Rhodesia* (Salisbury, Government of Rhodesia).

Mlambo, Alois. 2002. *White Immigration into Rhodesia: From Occupation to Federation* (Harare, University of Zimbabwe Publications).

Moore, David. 1988. 'Review Article: The Zimbabwean "Organic Intellectuals" in Transition', *Journal of Southern African Studies*, 15, 1, 96-105.

Moyana, Henry. 1984. *The Political Economy of Land in Zimbabwe* (Gweru, Mambo Press).

Moyo, Sam. 1994. 'Economic Nationalism and Land Reform in Zimbabwe', *Southern African Political Economy Series*, Occasional Paper, No. 7.

— 1995. *The Land Question in Zimbabwe* (Harare, SAPES).

— 2000a. 'The Political Economy of Land Acquisition and Redistribution in Zimbabwe, 1990–1999', *Journal of Southern African Studies*, 26, 1, 5-28.

— 2000b. *Land Reform under Structural Adjustment in Zimbabwe* (Uppsala, Nordic Africa Institute).

— 2001. 'The Land Occupation Movement in Zimbabwe: Contradictions of Neoliberalism', *Millennium: Journal of International Studies*, 30, 311-30.

— 2004. 'The Land and Agrarian Question in Zimbabwe', paper presented to The Agrarian Constraint and Poverty Reduction: Macroeconomic Lessons for Africa Conference, Addis Ababa, 17-8 December.

Moyo, Sam and Paris Yeros. 2005. 'Land Occupations and Land Reform in Zimbabwe: Towards the National Democratic Revolution', in Sam Moyo and Paris Yeros (eds), *Reclaiming the Land: The Resurgence of Rural Movements in Africa, Asia and Latin America* (Claremont, David Philip).

Mtisi, Joseph, Munyaradzi Nyakudya, and Teresa Barnes. 2009a. 'Social and Economic Developments During the UDI Period', in Brian

Raftopoulos and Alois Mlambo (eds), *Becoming Zimbabwe* (Harare, Weaver Press).

— 2009b. 'War in Rhodesia, 1965–1980', in Brian Raftopoulos and Alois Mlambo (eds), *Becoming Zimbabwe* (Harare, Weaver Press).

Mudimbe, V.Y. 1988. *The Invention of Africa: Gnosis, Philosophy, and the Order of Knowledge* (Bloomington, Indiana University Press).

Mugabe, Robert. 1982. 'Foreword', in Bernard Miller (ed.), *Zimbabwe Agricultural and Economic Review* (Harare, Modern Farming Publications).

— 1983. *Our War of Liberation: Speeches, Articles, Interviews, 1976–1979* (Gwelo, Mambo Press).

— 1984. 'Independence Message', in Anon., *The Struggle for Independence: Documents on the Recent Developments on Zimbabwe 1975-80*, Vol. 7 (Hamburg, Institute for African Affairs).

— 2001. *Inside the Third Chimurenga* (Harare, Government of Zimbabwe).

Mungazi, Dickson. 1998. *The Last Defenders of the Laager: Ian D. Smith and F.W de Klerk* (Connecticut, Praeger).

Muzondidya, James. 2009. 'From Buoyancy to Crisis, 1980–1997', in Brian Raftopoulos and Alois Mlambo (eds), *Becoming Zimbabwe* (Harare, Weaver Press).

Ngugi wa Thiong'o. 1986. *Decolonising the Mind: The Politics of Language in African Literature* (London, Heinemann).

— 1997. *Writers in Politics: A Re-engagement With Issues of Literature and Society* (Oxford, James Currey).

Njogu, Kimani and John Middleton (eds). 2009. *Media and Identity in Africa* (Edinburgh, Edinburgh University Press).

Nordstrom, Carolyn. 1997. *A Different Kind of War Story* (Philadelphia, University of Philadelphia Press).

Norman, Andrew. 2004. *Robert Mugabe and the Betrayal of Zimbabwe* (Jefferson, McFarland and Company).

Norman, Dennis. 1986. *The Success of Peasant Agriculture in Zimbabwe 1980–1985* (Lancing, Food and Agricultural Mission).

Nyambara, Pius. 2001. 'The Closing Frontier: Agrarian Change, Immigration and the "Squatter Menace" in Gokwe, 1980–1990s', *Journal of Agrarian Change*, 1, 4, 534-49.

Nyamnjoh, Francis. 2005. *Africa's Media, Democracy and the Politics of Belonging* (Pretoria, UNISA).

— 2006. *Insiders and Outsiders, Citizenship and Xenophobia in Contemporary Southern Africa* (London, Zed Books).

Nyarota, Geoffrey. 2006. *Against the Grain: Memoirs of a Zimbabwean Newsman* (Cape Town, Zebra).

Okada, H. Richard. 1991. *Figures of Resistance: Language, Poetry, and the Narrating in The Tale of Genji and Other Mid-Heian Texts* (Durham, Duke University Press).

Olick, Jeffrey. 2007. *The Politics of Regret: On Collective Memory and Historical Responsibility* (New York, Routledge).

Orr, Wendy. 2000. *From Biko to Basson; Wendy Orr's Search for the Soul of South Africa as a Commissioner of the TRC* (Johannesburg, Contra).

Palmer, Robin. 1977. *Land and Racial Domination in Rhodesia* (London, Heinemann).

— 1990. 'Land Reform in Zimbabwe, 1980–1990', *African Affairs*, 89, 163-81.

Palmer, Robin and Neil Parsons (eds). 1977. *The Roots of Rural Poverty in Central and Southern Africa* (Berkeley, University of California Press).

Parker, John and Richard Rathbone, R. 2007. *African History: A Very Short Introduction* (Oxford, Oxford University Press).

Phimister, Ian. 1986. 'Discourse and the Discipline of Historical Context: Conservationism and Ideas About Development in Southern Rhodesia 1930–1950', *Journal of Southern African Studies*, 12, 263-75.

— 1987. 'The Combined and Contradictory Inheritance of the Struggle Against Colonialism', *Transformations*, 5, 51-9.

— 1988. *An Economic and Social History of Zimbabwe, 1890–1948* (London, Longman).

— 1993. 'Rethinking the Reserves: Southern Rhodesia's Land Husbandry Act Reviewed', *Journal of Southern African Studies*, 19, 226-7.

— 2005a. '"*Rambai Makashinga* (Continue to Endure)": Zimbabwe's Unending Crisis', *South African Historical Journal*, 54, 112-26.

— 2005b. 'South African Diplomacy and the Crisis in Zimbabwe: Liberation Solidarity in the 21st Century', in Brian Raftopoulos and Tyrone Savage (eds), *Zimbabwe: Injustice and Political Reconciliation* (Harare, Weaver Press).

— 2008. 'The Making and Meaning of the Massacres in Matabeleland', *Development Dialogue*, 50, 199-218.

— 2009. '"Zimbabwe is mine": Mugabe, Murder and Matabeleland',

Safundi, 10, 4, 471-8.

Pilossof, Rory. 2008a. 'The Land Question (Un)Resolved: An Essay Review', *Historia*, 53, 2, 270-9.

— 2008b. 'The Unbearable Whiteness of Being: Land, Race and Belonging in the Memoirs of White Zimbabweans', *South African Historical Journal*, 61, 3, 621-38.

Pollack, Oliver. 1975. 'Black Farmers and White Politics in Rhodesia', *African Affairs*, 74, 263-77.

Portelli, Alessandro. 1991. *The Death of Luigi Trastulli and Other Stories: Form and Meaning in Oral History* (Albany, University of New York Press).

— 1997. *The Battle of Valle Giulia: Oral History and the Art of Dialogue* (Madison, University of Wisconsin Press).

Potts, Deborah. 2006. '"Restoring Order"? Operation Murambatsvina and the Urban Crisis in Zimbabwe', *Journal of Southern African Studies*, 32, 2, pp. 153-71.

Primorac, Ranka. 2003. 'The Novel in a House of Stone: Re-categorising Zimbabwean Fiction', *Journal of Southern African Studies*, 29, 1, 49-62.

Raby, Hamish. 2000. 'Ethnicity and Identity in a Commercial Farming Ward, Zimbabwe' (M.Phil. thesis, University of Sussex).

Raftopoulos, Brian. 2003. 'The State in Crisis: Authoritarian Nationalism, Selective Citizenship and Distortion of Democracy in Zimbabwe', in Amanda Hammar, Brain Raftopoulos and Stig Jensen (eds), *Zimbabwe's Unfinished Business: Rethinking Land, State and Nation in the Context of Crisis* (Harare, Weaver Press).

— 2004a. 'Current Politics in Zimbabwe: Confronting the Crisis', in David Harold-Barry (ed.), *The Past is the Future*. (Harare, Weaver Press).

— 2004b. 'Unreconciled Differences: The Limits of Reconciliation Politics in Zimbabwe', in Brain Raftopoulos and Tyrone Savage (eds), *Zimbabwe: Injustice and Political Reconciliation* (Harare, Weaver Press).

— 2007. 'Nation, Race and History in Zimbabwean Politics', in Sara Dorman, Daniel Hammett and Paul Nugent (eds), *Making Nations, Creating Strangers: States and Citizenship in Africa* (Leiden, Brill).

— 2009. 'The Crisis in Zimbabwe', in Brian Raftopoulos and Alois Mlambo (eds), *Becoming Zimbabwe* (Harare, Weaver Press).

Raftopoulos, Brian and Alois Mlambo (eds). 2009. *Becoming Zimbabwe*

(Harare, Weaver Press).

Raftopoulos, Brian and Ian Phimister. 2004. 'Zimbabwe Now: The Political Economy of Crisis and Coercion', *Historical Materialism*, 12, 4, 355-82.

Raftopoulos, Brian and Tyrone Savage (eds). 2004. Zimbabwe: Injustice and Political Reconciliation (Harare, Weaver Press).

Ranger, Terence. 1978. 'Growing From the Roots: Reflections on Peasant Research in Central and Southern Africa', *Journal of Southern African Studies*, 5, 119-20.

— 1985. *Peasant Consciousness and Guerrilla War in Zimbabwe* (London, James Currey).

— 1989. 'Matabeleland Since the Amnesty', *African Affairs*, 88, 351, 161-73.

— 1997. 'Violence Variously Remembered: The Killing of Pieter Oberholzer in July 1964', *History in Africa*, 24, 273-86.

— 1999. *Voices from the Rocks: Nature, Culture and History in the Matopos Hills of Zimbabwe* (Oxford, James Currey).

Ransome, Paul. 1992. *Antonio Gramsci: A New Introduction* (London, Harvester Wheatsheaf).

Rhodesian National Farmers' Union. 1977. *A Guide to the RNFU* (Salisbury, Rhodesian National Farmers' Union).

Richards, Hylda. 1975. *Next Year Will be Better* (Bulawayo, Books of Rhodesia).

Riddell, Roger. 1978. *The Land Problem in Rhodesia* (Gwelo, Mambo Press).

Robertson, Wilfred. 1935. *Rhodesian Rancher* (Glasgow, Blackie and Son).

Roos, Neil. 2009. 'The Springbok and the Skunk, War Veterans and the Politics of Whiteness in South Africa During the 1940s and 1950s', *Journal of Southern African Studies*, 35, 3, 643-61.

Rubert, Steven. 1998. *A Most Promising Weed: A History of Tobacco Farming and Labor in Colonial Zimbabwe, 1890–1945* (Athens, Ohio University Press).

Rukuni, Mandivamba. 1994. *Report of the Commission of Enquiry into Appropriate Agricultural Land Tenure Systems, Volume One, Main Report* (Harare, Government of Zimbabwe).

Rutherford, Blair. 2001a. 'Commercial Farm Workers and the Politics of (Dis)Placement in Zimbabwe: Colonialism, Liberation and Democracy', *Journal of Agrarian Change*, 1, 4, 626-51.

— 2001b. *Working on the Margins: Black Workers, White Farmers in Post-colonial Zimbabwe* (Harare, Weaver Press).

— 2007. 'Shifting Grounds in Zimbabwe: Citizenship and Farm Workers in the New Politics of Land', in Sara Dorman, Daniel Hammett and Paul Nugent (eds), *Making Nations, Creating Strangers: States and Citizenship in Africa* (Leiden, Brill).

Rutherford, Blair and Eric Worby. 1998. 'Zimbabwe's Agrarian Answer: The Rhetoric of Land Redistribution', *Cultural Survival*, 22, 4 (1998), available at www.culturalsurvival.org/ourpublications/csq/article/zimbabwes-agrarian-answer-the-rhetoric-redistribution (viewed 18 June 2010).

Sachikonye, Lloyd. 2003. *The Situation of Farm Workers After Land Reform in Zimbabwe* (Harare, Farm Community Trust of Zimbabwe).

— 2005. 'The Promised Land: From Expropriation to Reconciliation and *Jambanja*', in Brian Raftopoulos and Tyrone Savage (eds), *Zimbabwe: Injustice and Political Reconciliation* (Harare, Weaver Press).

— 2006. *The Impact of Operation Murambatsvina/Clean Up on the Working People in Zimbabwe* (Harare, LEDRIZ).

Said, Edward. 1994. *Culture and Imperialism* (London, Vintage).

— 2003. *Orientalism* (London, Penguin).

Schaffer, Kay and Sidonie Smith. 2004. 'Conjunctions: Life Narratives in the Field of Human Rights', *Biography*, 27, 1, 1-24.

Scoones, Ian, Nelson Marongwe, Blasion Mavedzenge, Jacob Mahenehene, Felix Murimbarimba, and Chrispen Sukume. 2010. *Zimbabwe's Land Reform: Myths and Realities* (Oxford, James Currey).

Selby, Angus. 2006. 'Commercial Farmers and the State: Interest Group Politics and Land Reform in Zimbabwe', (D.Phil. thesis, University of Oxford).

Sibanda, Eliakim. 2005. *The Zimbabwe African People's Union, 1961–87: A Political History of Insurgency in Southern Rhodesia* (Trenton, Africa World Press)

Smith, Ian. 2001. *Bitter Harvest: The Great Betrayal and the Dreadful Aftermath* (London, Blake).

— 2008. *Bitter Harvest: Zimbabwe and the Aftermath of its Independence* (London, Blake).

Solidarity Peace Trust. 2003. *National Youth Service Training – "Shaping Youths in a Truly Zimbabwean Manner": An Overview of Youth*

Militia Training and Activities in Zimbabwe, October 2000–August 2003 (n.p., Solidarity Peace Trust).

Somerville, D.M. 1976. *My Life was a Ranch* (Salisbury, Kailani).

Stoler, Ann and Frederick Cooper. 1997. 'Between Metropole and Colony: Rethinking a Research Agenda', in Frederick Cooper and Ann Stoler (eds), *Tensions of Empire: Colonial Cultures in a Bourgeois World* (Berkeley, University of California Press).

Stoneman, Colin. 1981. 'Agriculture', in Colin Stoneman (ed.), *Zimbabwe's Inheritance* (Hong Kong, Macmillan).

Stoneman, Colin, and Lionel Cliffe. 1989. *Zimbabwe: Politics, Economics and Society* (London, Pinter).

Suzuki, Yuka. 2005. 'Black Baboons and White Rubbish Trees: The Cultural Politics of Race and Nature in Zimbabwe' (PhD thesis, Yale University).

Tettey, Wisdom J. 2001. 'The Media and Democratization in Africa: Contributions, Constraints and Concerns of the Private Press', *Media, Culture and Society*, 32, 5, 5-31.

Thomas, Anthony. 1997. *Rhodes: The Race for Africa* (London, London Bridge).

Thomas, Keith. 1988. *History and Literature* (Swansea, University College of Swansea).

Todd, Judith. 2007. *Through the Darkness: A Life in Zimbabwe* (Cape Town, Zebra).

Townsend, Hazel. n.d. *The History of the Umvukwes* (Salisbury, A.W. Bardwell and Co.).

Tracey, C.G. 2009. *All for Nothing? My Life Remembered* (Harare, Weaver Press).

Tracey, L.T. 1953. *Approach to Farming in Southern Rhodesia* (London, University of London Press).

Truepeney, C. 1965. *Our African Farm* (London, Victor Gollancz).

U.S. Department of State, 'Zimbabwe: Country Reports on Human Rights Practices' February 25, 2004, available at www.state.gov/g/drl/rls/hrrpt/2003/27760.htm (viewed 31 May 2010).

United Nations. 2005. *Report of the Fact-finding Mission to Zimbabwe to Assess the Scope and Impact of Operation Murambatsvina by the UN Special Envoy on Human Settlements Issues in Zimbabwe Mrs Anna Kajumulo Tibaijuka* (n.p., United Nations).

Utete, Charles. 2003. *Report to the Presidential Land Review Commit-*

tee into the Implementation of the Fast-track Land Reform Program, 2000–2002 [The Utete Report] (Harare, Government of Zimbabwe).

Uusihakala, Katja. 2008. 'Memory Meanders: Place, Home and Commemorations in an Ex-Rhodesian Diaspora Community' (PhD thesis, University of Helsinki).

Vambe, Maurice T. 2004. 'Versions and Sub-versions: Trends in Chimurenga Musical Discourses of Post Independence Zimbabwe', *African Studies Monographs*, 25, 4, 167-93.

Van der Vlies, Andrew. 2007. *South African Textual Cultures: White, Black, Read All Over* (Manchester, Manchester University Press).

Van Onselen, Charles. 1993. 'The Reconstruction of a Rural Life From Oral Testimony: Critical Notes of the Methodology Employed in the Study of a Black South African Sharecropper', *Journal of Peasant Studies*, 20, 3, 494-514.

— 1996. *The Seed is Mine: The Life of Kas Maine, a South African Sharecropper 1894–1985* (New York, Hill and Wang).

VanBuskirk, Bruce. 2006. *The Last Safari: A Season of Discovery in Zimbabwe* (Bloomington, Authorhouse).

Vaughan, Megan. 2001. 'Reported Speech and Other Kinds of Testimony', in Luise White, Stephan F. Miescher and David William Cohen (eds), *African Words, African Voices: Critical Practices in Oral History* (Bloomington, Indiana University Press).

Wainaina, Binyavanga. 2005. 'How to Write About Africa', *Granta*, 92, available at www.granta.com/Magazine/92/How-to-Write-About-Africa?view=articleAllPages (viewed 28 October 2008).

Wasserman, Herman. 2009. 'Learning a New Language: Culture, Ideology and Economics in Afrikaans Media After Apartheid', *International Journal of Cultural Studies*, 12, 1, 61-80.

Wasserman, Herman and Gabriël Botma. 2008, 'Having it Both Ways: Balancing Market and Political Interests at a South African Daily Newspaper', *Critical Arts*, 22, 1, 137-58.

Weinrich, A.K.H. 1975. *African Farmers in Rhodesia* (London, Oxford University Press).

Werbner, Richard. 1991. *Tears of the Dead: The Social Biography of an African Family* (Edinburgh, Edinburgh University Press).

— 1996. 'In Memory: A Heritage of War in Southwestern Zimbabwe', in Ngwabi Bhebe and Terence Ranger (eds), *Society in Zimbabwe's Liberation War* (Oxford, James Currey).

— 1998. 'Smoke From the Barrel of a Gun: Memory, Postwars of the Dead, and Reinscription in Zimbabwe', in Richard Werbner (ed.), *Memory and the Postcolony: African Anthropology and the Critique of Power* (London, Zed).

White, Luise. 2000. *Speaking With Vampires: Rumor and History in Colonial Africa* (Berkeley, University of California Press).

— 2003. *The Assassination of Herbert Chitepo* (Bloomington, Indian University Press).

White, Luise, Stephan F. Miescher, and David William Cohen (eds). 2001. *African Words, African Voices: Critical Practices in Oral History* (Bloomington, Indiana University Press).

Whitlock, Gillian. 2000. *The Intimate Empire: Reading Women's Autobiography* (London, Cassell).

Willems, Wendy. 2004. 'Peaceful Demonstrators, Violent Invaders: Representations of Land in the Zimbabwean Press', *World Development*, 32, 10, 1767-83.

— 2005. 'Remnants of Empire? British Media Reporting on Zimbabwe', *Westminster Papers in Communication and Culture*, 91-108.

Wilson, Richard. 2001. *The Politics of Truth and Reconciliation in South Africa: Legitimizing the Post-Apartheid State* (Cambridge, Cambridge University Press).

Windrich, Elaine. 1981. *The Mass Media in the Struggle for Zimbabwe: Censorship and Propaganda Under Rhodesian Front Rule* (Gwelo, Mambo Press).

Wolmer, William. 2007. *From Wilderness Vision to Farm Invasions: Conservation and Development in Zimbabwe's South-east Lowveld* (Harare, Weaver Press).

Worby, Eric. 2001. 'A Redivided Land? New Agrarian Conflicts and Questions in Zimbabwe', *Journal of Agrarian Change*, 1, 4, 475-509.

Yeros, Paris. 2002. 'Zimbabwe and the Dilemmas of the Left', *Historical Materialism*, 10, 2 (2002).

Yudelman, M., 1964. *Africans on the Land* (London, Oxford University Press).

Zaffiro, James. 2002. *Media and Democracy in Zimbabwe, 1931–2001* (Colorado Springs, International Academic Publishers).

Zhira, Maxwell. 2004. 'Uncovering the Reality of State Violence in Western Zimbabwe, 1982–1987', *Past Imperfect*, 10, 61-77.

Zimbabwe Human Rights NGO Forum. 2000. 'A Report on Post-election Violence', (2000), available at www.hrforumzim.com/frames/ inside_frame_reps.htm (viewed 18 February 2010).

— 2001a. *Complying with the Abuja Agreement: Two Months Report* (Harare, Zimbabwe Human Rights NGO Forum).

— 2001b. *Politically Motivated Violence in Zimbabwe 2000–2001: A Report on the Campaign of Political Repression Conducted by the Zimbabwean Government Under the Guise of Carrying out Land Reform* (Harare, Zimbabwe Human Rights NGO Forum).

— 2003. *Zimbabwe, the Abuja Agreement and Commonwealth Principals: Compliance or Disregard* (Harare, Zimbabwe Human Rights NGO Forum).

— 2007. *Their Words Condemn Them: The Language of Violence, Intolerance and Despotism in Zimbabwe* (Harare, Zimbabwe Human Rights NGO Forum).

Zimbabwe Human Rights NGO Forum and The Justice for Agriculture Trust. 2007. *Adding Insult to Injury: A Preliminary Report on Human Rights Violations on Commercial Farms, 2000–2005* (Harare, Zimbabwe Human Rights NGO Forum).

Zimbabwe Liberators' Platform, The. 2004. 'What Happened to Our Dream?', in David Harold-Barry (ed.), *Zimbabwe: The Past is the Future* (Harare, Weaver Press).

Films & Documentaries

De Swardt, Simon (dir.). 2009. *House of Justice* (Harare).

Desai, Rehad (dir.). 2002. *My Land My Life: A Journey Into the Heart of Zimbabwe* (Johannesburg).

Dimbleby, David (dir.). 2000. *Mugabe, Smith and the Union Jack*, (Great Britain).

Thompson, Andrew and Lucy Bailey (dirs). 2009. *Mugabe and the White African* (Stoud).

Magazines & Newspapers

Cattle World (Zimbabwe)
Countdown (Zimbabwe)
Daily News, The (Zimbabwe)
Daily Telegraph, The (UK)
Farmers Weekly (South Africa)

Herald, The (Zimbabwe)
Independent, The (Zimbabwe)
Property and Finance (Zimbabwe/Rhodesia)
Scotsman, The (UK)
Star, The (South Africa)
Sunday Times, The (UK)
Tobacco News (Zimbabwe)
Rhodesian Farmer (Zimbabwe)
Farmer, The (Zimbabwe)
The Independent Online (UK)
BBC News Online (UK)
Mail & Guardian Online (South Africa)
Telegraph.co.uk (UK)

Internet Sources

Books of Zimbabwe Online, available at www.booksofzimbabwe.com (viewed 22 July 2010).

Catherine Buckle, 'Letters Written By Cathy Buckle', available at www.cathybuckle.com (viewed 24 June 2010).

Commercial Farmers Union of Zimbabwe, available at www.cfuzim.org/ (viewed 22 July 2010).

Justice for Agriculture (JAG) Trust, 'Confirmed VIP's allocations- The landless poor?', available at www.zimbabwesituation.com/VIP_farm_allocations.pdf (viewed 8 June 2010).

Kubatab.net, 'Justice for Agriculture – JAG Zimbabwe', available at, www.kubatana.net/html/archive/agric/020803jag.asp?orgcode=jus002&year=2002&range_start=1 (viewed 8 June 2010).

Lekkerwear, available at rhodesiawassuper.com (viewed 22 July 2010).

Livelihoods After Land Reform, available at www.lalr.org.za (viewed 20 June 2010).

Mugabe and the White African, available at www.mugabeandthewhiteafrican.com (viewed 12 August 2010).

Rhodesians Worldwide, available at www.rhodesia.com (viewed 22 July 2010).

SW Radio Africa, available at www.swradioafrica.com/Documents/addendum.htm (viewed 18 June 2010).

Index

wildlife farming 30-2, 88
Wildlife Producers Association 31
Wiles, Richard 152, 154, 159, 161-2, 164, 166-70, 174, 176, 178
'willing buyer, willing seller' clause to land reform 25, 29-30
Winkfield, Richard 73, 99, 106, 137
Wolhuter, Cecil 81
Wolmer, William 164
Women of Zimbabwe Arise (WOZA) 204
Wood, Felicity 73, 90-8, 106
Wood, Mike 130
Worby, Eric 45
workers on farms *see* farm labourers
work ethic *see* hard work of white farmers
World Bank (WB) 35
World War Two 15-16, 174
WOZA *see* Women of Zimbabwe Arise (WOZA)

Zambia 24-5
ZANLA *see* Zimbabwe National Liberation Army (ZANLA)
ZANU *see* Zimbabwe African National Union (ZANU)
ZANU-PF, ; 1980 election 27, 30, 33; constitutional referendum of 2000 35-6, 43, 99-100; *Farmer, The* 89; farm labourers 204-5; *jambanja* 47-56, 58-9; violence in 1980s 126-9, 133; violence in 2000 and after 137, 141
ZAPU *see* Zimbabwe African People's Union (ZAPU)

ZCTU *see* Zimbabwe Congress of Trade Unions (ZCTU)
Zimbabwe African National Union (ZANU) 21, 24-5, 79-80
Zimbabwe African People's Union (ZAPU) 21, 24-5, 79-80, 88, 126-8, 134
Zimbabwe Congress of Trade Unions (ZCTU) 35
Zimbabwe Human Rights NGO Forum 56, 57, 141, 188
Zimbabwe Independent 175
Zimbabwe Joint Resettlement Initiative (ZJRI) 52
Zimbabwe Liberators' Platform 50
Zimbabwe National Liberation Army (ZANLA) 21
Zimbabwe National Liberation War Collaborators' Association 50
Zimbabwe National Liberation War Veterans' Association (ZNLWVA) 44, 137
Zimbabwe People's Revolutionary Army (ZIPRA) 21, 128
Zimbabwe Tobacco Association (ZTA) 51
ZIPRA *see* Zimbabwe People's Revolutionary Army (ZIPRA)
ZJRI *see* Zimbabwe Joint Resettlement Initiative (ZJRI)
ZNLWVA *see* Zimbabwe National Liberation War Veterans' Association (ZNLWVA)
ZTA *see* Zimbabwe Tobacco Association (ZTA)

Epigraph

This really happened when I was back visiting the old man who lived across the road from my mother in my home town of Ninety Six, South Carolina. J. Hilton Lewis was his name. While I was there two other men, who I also knew well, drove up. As they approached us, they asked Hilton if he had heard about the murder. Hilton said he hadn't heard of it, and one of the visitors explained that it happened 'on Saturday, or maybe Friday, or sometime at the weekend, maybe even late Thursday evening, but at any rate it happened in Saluda or Modoc, or maybe in Aiken or near Edgefield.' It happened down the road, he was pretty sure. Hilton asked what happened, and the other visitor said that a man 'was shot, or maybe stabbed to death'. The other visitor disagreed: 'he was clubbed to death, or maybe hit with a tire iron, it could have been a golf club ...' Hilton interrupted: 'Oh yes, I'd heard about it, I just didn't have any of the details till now.'

– Story told by Vernon Burton

(Quoted in White, 2000, p. 2. For a slightly longer version of this story as written by Burton himself, see Burton, 2000: 182).

Lightning Source UK Ltd.
Milton Keynes UK
UKOW02f0824170415

249828UK00002B/73/P